Landmark

D0774610

Upper Intermediate Teacher's Book

Simon Haines & Barbara Stewart

OXFORD
UNIVERSITY PRESS

OXFORD
UNIVERSITY PRESS

Great Clarendon Street, Oxford OX2 6DP

Oxford University Press is a department of the University
of Oxford.
It furthers the University's objective of excellence in
research, scholarship, and education by publishing
worldwide in

Oxford New York

Athens Auckland Bangkok Bogotá Buenos Aires Calcutta
Cape Town Chennai Dar es Salaam Delhi Florence Hong Kong Istanbul
Karachi Kuala Lumpur Madrid Melbourne Mexico City Mumbai
Nairobi Paris São Paulo Shanghai Singapore Taipei Tokyo Toronto
Warsaw

with associated companies in
Berlin Ibadan

Oxford and Oxford English are registered trade marks of
Oxford University Press in the UK and in certain other
countries

Photocopying

The Publisher grants permission for the photocopying of
those pages marked 'photocopiable' according to the
following conditions. Individual purchasers may make
copies for their own use or for use by classes that they
teach. School purchasers may make copies for use by staff
and students, but this permission does not extend to
additional schools or branches

Under no circumstances may any part of this book be
photocopied for resale

ISBN 0 19 433086 9

Second Impression 2000

Printed in Hong Kong

Acknowledgements

Text and photocopiables by Richard Rogers

The authors and publisher are grateful to © Grolier
Incorporated for giving permission to reproduce the
following extracts and adaptations of copyright material:
The Kennedy family p.83; Bedouins and Gypsies p.93;
Mikhail Gorbachev and Ronald Reagan p.128.

Contents

Introduction

Landmark is a two-level general English course, which recognizes that learners at intermediate levels already have a strong background in the language. The course builds on their existing knowledge and at the same time systematically helps them to develop their understanding and range of language abilities.

What's in the book?

Twelve 10-page units each with five clear lesson sequences. There are thematic and language links between the lessons, but they can be taught separately. The first three sequences and *Language in action* can each be taught 'in one go' or may be divided into their parts.

The five sequences are:
- **Preview** (Grammar 1 Review): An introduction to the unit theme and revision of an area of grammar.
- **Reading or Listening** (Grammar 2): Skills development followed by the exploration and exploitation of grammar related to the Review grammar.
- **Listening or Reading** (Grammar 3): Skills development followed by the exploration and exploitation of a further area of grammar.
- **Vocabulary**: A focus on vocabulary systems.
- **Language in action** (**Writing**): Listening and focus on functional language, followed by speaking and writing practice.

Approach to Grammar

We recognize that much grammar at this level is not new to students, so the course clearly distinguishes between review grammar and the exploration and practice of what is new or less familiar. All grammar, whether known or new, is contextualized in reading or listening texts, so its presentation is integrated with the development of these skills. The course takes a guided discovery approach, based on concept checking and on making use of learners' existing knowledge.

The *Language commentary*, a separate grammar reference section, complements the guided discovery approach by allowing students to check their answers and consolidate their understanding.

Functional language and Conversation strategies

These are the main focus in the first part of the Language in action section of each unit. Students listen for, list, and then use a range of functional language, as well as looking at how speakers interact in conversation.

Vocabulary

Vocabulary development features prominently in *Landmark*. Each unit has a full page devoted to vocabulary systems, for example, collocations, connotations, etc. In addition, there are vocabulary sections related to some reading and listening texts.

Approach to Skills

There is a systematic development of the four skills. An important feature of receptive skills work is that students are expected to be able to interpret the underlying meaning and implications of what they hear or read.

Speaking
Landmark provides frequent speaking activities in each lesson sequence to discuss topics, to practise the grammar points, and to express personal opinions.

Listening
Listening material ranges from authentic to semi-scripted or scripted. Authentic recordings focus learners' attention on functional language, conversational strategies, features of natural speech and pronunciation. The tapescripts of selected extracts of authentic language are included on the page as support for learners faced with natural rapid native speech. These also provide an opportunity for the analysis of spoken language.

Reading
The reading material in the book comes from authentic sources suitable for adult learners. Pre-, while-, and post-reading tasks help students get the most out of the texts.

Writing
The course adopts a process-oriented approach to writing. A range of writing tasks forms the last section of each unit. Students develop their awareness of register through contrasting spoken and written language, before they produce a range of different types of writing, from notes and personal letters to instructions and radio scripts. The **Writing guidelines** provide examples and writing tips for the various text types students are expected to produce.

Themes

Each unit of *Landmark* is based on a general theme; the different sections develop aspects of this theme. In Unit 7 for example, the overall theme is Survival. The Preview topic is the *Aborigines of Australia*; Listening features stories of *individual survival*; in Reading the article is about *Curitiba*, a Brazilian city managing its problems. Where appropriate, topics are personalized: students are expected to contribute their knowledge, experience, and opinions to the learning process.

How to use the book

Preview — First sequence

The overall theme of the unit is introduced with photographs or illustrations.

Your thoughts

Questions and discussion points elicit students' initial thoughts and responses to the theme and to the photographs or illustrations.

Can be done as whole-class activities or by pairs or groups.

Reading or listening

A short reading text or listening expands on the theme and offers opportunities for discussion and comprehension work.

Students work individually to read or listen and then work in pairs to answer the related questions.

Person to person

Pairs or groups give personal reactions to the theme.

Here it is important to stress interest and involvement, rather than formal language content.

Grammar review

The review uses concept questions to check students' understanding of what is assumed to be familiar grammar. This approach also gives the teacher a chance to see how much students already know and prepares them for the grammar in the next sections.

If you are confident of students' knowledge, let them work independently through this section. They should use the Language commentary at the back of their book to check their answers and consolidate their understanding.

There is extra controlled practice of the review grammar point in the Workbook.

Pronunciation

To remind students of, and practise pronunciation points related to, the review grammar.

Work through this briskly, concentrating on getting students to hear and accurately reproduce sounds.

Check

Brief controlled practice of the review language.

Students work individually through this accuracy practice exercise. Check answers and clarify any points of difficulty.

Reading / Listening — Second and third sequences

Reading or listening introduces the new topic and contextualizes the 'new' grammar point. Pre-listening and pre-reading tasks prepare students for the text or recording that follows. They may be asked to:

- give a personal opinion
- make predictions
- think about words from the text.

This leads students into the topic. Do not pre-teach all the difficult words which will come up; restrict yourself to items which are essential to students' understanding. The teacher's notes sometimes suggest a few items to pre-teach.

As you listen / read

This provides students with a purpose for reading or listening. They may be asked to:

- check their predictions
- read or listen for ideas or opinions they expressed.

Draw attention to these activities before students start to read or listen. Set realistic time limits for the first reading of a text, based on the type of text and task. At this level students should be able extract information quickly from texts.

For Listenings, decide how many times to play the recordings, but encourage students to try and make sense of what they hear on first listening.

Close up

In reading sections, this feature focuses on interesting or unusual points of grammar or vocabulary in the text.

There is no single 'correct' time to do *Close up*. It may be done immediately after the first reading, or can be left until later if you don't want to interrupt the flow of the skills development work.

Interpretation / Comprehension

As well as understanding the literal meaning of texts, students are asked to interpret what they read or hear – to read or listen between the lines. This means that a variety of interpretations may be equally valid.

Encourage students to suggest a range of interpretations. Where possible, students should give reasons or evidence for their ideas. Possible answers are suggested in the teacher's notes.

Speaking personally

This rounding-off activity gives students a chance to react personally to the theme of the reading or listening.

This is a fluency activity, so monitor, but allow students to discuss the subject without interruption.

■ 'New' grammar 1 (Part of the second sequence)

The language here is a development of the Review grammar in *Preview*.

■ 'New' grammar 2 (Part of the third sequence)

The third language point introduced here is either a further development of the previous grammar area or a new point. Follow the same procedure as with the previous grammar section.

■ Exploring Concepts

Concept questions and other tasks get students to analyse examples of the target language and help them to understand the key features of form and use.

Get students to work individually or in pairs through the tasks.

Students should work out their own ideas before checking them in the **Language commentary**. You may prefer to check students' answers yourself after each question.

■ Exploitation

Each Grammar section is followed by tasks which practise the form and use of the target language. Some activities develop accuracy, while others develop fluency. Many are personalized pair or group activities.

Where accuracy is the aim, start by giving an example, then correct errors as you monitor. Where fluency is the prime aim, as in *Free speech*, *Role play*, let students work uninterrupted. If necessary, return to problem areas after the completion of the task.

■ Pronunciation

For students to practise pronunciation points related to the grammar.

Concentrate on getting students to hear and accurately reproduce sounds.

Vocabulary – Fourth sequence

This focuses on key vocabulary systems: *Collocations*, *Connotations*, *Suffixes* etc. Two units focus on learner training – Unit 3 *Using a dictionary* and Unit 5 *Learning new vocabulary*.

The tasks are designed to:
*   expose students to more examples and/or check existing knowledge
*   provide practice in using the vocabulary.

Work through the introductions to make sure everyone understands the key concepts.

Students can work individually, in pairs, or in groups. Monitor, helping where necessary. Check concepts and answers with the whole class if there are common problems.

Monitor speaking tasks, listening for appropriate use of vocabulary. Don't interrupt the flow of discussions. Save any feedback until after the exercise is over.

Language in action – Fifth sequence

The focus here is on:
*   Functional language – e.g. *opinions*
*   Conversation strategies – e.g. *interrupting*
*   Features of natural speech – e.g. *repetition*
*   Pronunciation
*   Writing

■ Eavesdrop!

Students predict the content of the first listening from a cryptic picture.

Encourage students to guess what is happening in the picture. Elicit ideas, but do not confirm answers. Students will be able to check their guesses in *Listening 1*.

■ Listening 1

Students listen to a conversation related to the *Eavesdrop!* picture and check their guesses. This conversation is scripted and contains examples of the target language.

Play the recording so that students can check their guesses. Play a second time for students to identify and list target language. Students then share information in pairs or groups.

■ Listening 2

Students listen to one or two authentic conversations which contain further examples of the target language. Extracts from these conversations are printed in the Student's Book.

As they listen for the first time, students answer questions about the subject matter and the relationship between the speakers.

As students listen again, they follow the extracts in their books and mark the functional language. Check through their lists, referring to the complete list in the teacher's notes. You could photocopy this list for students.

■ Features of natural conversation

This helps raise students' awareness of aspects of natural speech which occur in the authentic conversations. Encourage students to identify these features and understand their meaning, but don't expect them, at this level, to incorporate these features into their own use of language.

After discussing and explaining the particular feature, get students to find examples in the printed extracts. You may wish to play the recording again.

Work briskly through these tasks, checking answers and providing clarification where needed.

Practice

This combines practice of the target functional language with pronunciation practice.

Work briskly through this section. Get every student to use the target language. Correct errors of form and pronunciation.

Exploitation (role play / discussion / situation)

This provides more open-ended practice of the functional language.

Usually activities involve pairs or groups of students interacting to reach an outcome. The situations all allow for the natural use of the functional language.

Check through the instructions with the class and, if appropriate, allocate roles. Once students are talking, monitor conversations, listening for the correct and appropriate use of the target language. Don't interrupt the flow of conversations but make a note of any points that need reviewing at a later stage.

Writing

This starts with a comparison between an extract from an earlier conversation and a piece of writing expressing the same function. This draws attention to register and degrees of formality.

Introduce the task.

Elicit differences between the spoken and the written language. Then, ask students to work through the related questions.

The practical task gives students the opportunity to incorporate the target language into a piece of writing.

Students work through a series of stages:
* thinking and planning
* writing a first draft
* exchanging work with a partner
* reading and thinking of improvements to each other's writing
* discussing suggested improvements in pairs
* writing a final draft.

Set time limits and monitor stages carefully.

Longer pieces of writing could be done for homework.

If students are not used to working co-operatively, explain the advantage of a 'new pair of eyes' looking at their work.

Reassure students that you – the teacher – will mark and assess their final draft.

Unit summary

A checklist for students to focus on the areas they have covered in the unit.

Getting feedback from students on areas they have ticked and crossed should give an indication of any class revision necessary.

Writing guidelines

Notes with examples on the different text types students are asked to write.

Refer students to the guidelines at any stage during the writing process.

Language commentary

The *Language commentary* provides unit-by-unit information on the grammar. Detailed notes on meaning and form as well as numerous examples help students to answer the Exploring concepts tasks.

Teacher's Book

Unit-by-unit notes consist of:
* step-by-step suggestions for exploiting the Student's Book
* an answer key, including suggested or possible answers for exercises which do not have specific right or wrong answers, for example Interpretation exercises in reading or listening sections
* tapescripts
* additional activities which extend or develop Student's Book material
* extra notes on grammar and vocabulary as well as some background notes on certain topics.

Photocopiable material: a range of interactive activities for further practice.

Six tests – one after every two units.

Workbook

The 12 units of the Workbook will help students to develop their reading skills, increase their vocabulary, consolidate their grammar and improve their writing.

1 Why do they do it?

Theme

Activities which are nerve-racking, risky, or dangerous.

Preview Dangerous activities
Reading Dangerous activities
Listening Dangerous jobs

Grammar

- Present simple, Present continuous (LC p.124)
- Aspect (progressive and perfect aspects) (LC p.124)
- Action verbs and state verbs (LC p.124)

Vocabulary

- Overview: *Collocation, Connotation, Word-building Formality, Homonyms, Metaphorical language*
- Collocations with *keep, play, run, waste*

Functional language

- Agreeing and disagreeing

Conversation strategies

- Getting into a conversation
- Preventing someone from getting into a conversation

Pronunciation

- Third person singular endings
- Sounding interested
- Showing strong disagreement

Features of natural conversation

- Exclamations

Writing

- A formal letter (WG p.155)

Workbook

- A newspaper article about white-water rafting
- *turn up*, *set off*, *break up*; Word groups; Topic vocabulary: smoking
- Present tenses review; Aspect; Action verbs and state verbs
- Adjectives and adverbs; Describing an incident

Preview

■ **Your thoughts** ━━━━━━━━━━━━━━━ p. 4 ■

These questions introduce the theme of the unit by getting students to react personally to the photographs.

1 • Before asking students for personal reactions, the whole class could spend a few minutes talking about the content of the photographs.
  • Check that students understand the meaning of the four reactions. (*You wouldn't catch me doing that!* – Under no circumstances would I do that!)
  • Students compare reactions to the four activities in pairs or groups.

2 • This could be a class discussion, or pairwork.
  • You could spend a minute or two on why people do these things. Do they have to or do they choose to?
  • Elicit students' ideas. Is there a class consensus on this subject?

■ **Listening** ━━━━━━━━━━

1 • **1.1** Explain the task and play the recording. This is a global understanding task, so it should not be necessary to play the recording again at this stage.
  • Check answers.

Answers
Speaker 1 – fire-walking
Speaker 2 – standing up in front of a large audience
Speaker 3 – snakes kept as pets

Note Spacewalking is not referred to on the tape.

1.1

Speaker 1
I've done over twenty walks now and have never been hurt. The reason for this has nothing to do with the old idea of 'mind over matter'. It can all be explained by the laws of physics. A normal fire-walk is made of red-hot wood or charcoal and it's a well-known fact that wood does not conduct heat well. Because of this, your feet are safe.
More and more people are taking it up as a regular activity. It's exciting and it makes them feel good. It's certainly made me more confident.

Speaker 2
I attend two or three conferences a year in different parts of the world. It's the preparation and the waiting that really get to me, I always feel nervous for several days in advance, but once I'm up there with the lights on me, I forget my nerves and concentrate on what I've got to say to my audience.

Speaker 3
Whenever you're near the creatures, it's extremely important to watch their body language carefully for danger signs. For example, at the moment he's coming slowly towards me. He's staring at me and his tongue is going in and out. He may be hungry and looking for food, so I have to watch out. Sometimes he moves backwards, his neck becomes s-shaped and he breathes heavily, or hisses. In this case, he's probably frightened and so may attack in self-defence.

2 • Ask students to read questions **a–b** and play the recording again.
  • Allow students to discuss in pairs for a few minutes, then check answers.

Answers
a Speaker 1 has a matter-of-fact, rational attitude to fire-walking. She finds it exciting and something which boosts her self-confidence.
  Speaker 2 is nervous before having to stand in front of a large audience but is able to concentrate when she has to.
  Speaker 3 has a serious, matter-of-fact approach to his subject. \ enthusiastic
b Speaker 3 gives advice (being careful with snakes).
  Speaker 1 is explaining a process (how fire-walkers manage to avoid burning their feet). This speaker also describes personal reactions.
  Speaker 2 is describing personal reactions (to standing in front of an audience).

Reading — p. 5

This text relates to the photograph not mentioned by any of the speakers in the previous listening.

1 • Elicit a few ideas for questions **a** and **b** before students read. You could write them on the board.

Possible answers
a It's exciting, challenging, difficult, out-of-the-ordinary. It's an opportunity available to only a few people.
b Running out of oxygen, unknown viruses, becoming detached from the spacecraft, being unable to get back down to earth.

  • Allow two or three minutes for students to read the text. Did the text provide any other answers to **a** and **b**?
  • If necessary, students read the text again. Deal with any vocabulary queries at this stage.

Answers (from text)
b The *leaking fuel tank* suggests the possibility of an explosion or of the spacecraft being stranded in space with insufficient fuel to get back. *Running out of air* is also mentioned.

2 • On the basis of what they have already discussed and read, students now think about, discuss, and compile lists of the abilities, skills, and qualities needed by astronauts.
  • Ask for students' ideas.

Possible answers
Abilities knowledge and understanding of scientific and
and skills technological background to space travel, engineering ability to fix faults, knowledge of languages (to

communicate with fellow astronauts), ability to amuse oneself, be able to cope with stress, isolation, and confined spaces
Qualities intelligence, strength, stamina, stable personality, sociability, bravery, patience, physical fitness

Person to person

This is a chance for students to relate the unit theme to their own experience.

1–2 Monitor discussions but do not interrupt or correct errors at this stage.
  • Elicit some of the more interesting or exciting experiences described by students.

Grammar – Present tenses review

This first 'review' grammar section checks students' awareness of the basic uses of the Present simple and the Present continuous. Most of the examples used are from the recordings and the text already studied.

In grammar sections like these, students should work individually or in pairs through the concept questions, though you may prefer to discuss the questions and check answers from the whole class.

Students can do all of the questions at one time, or you could do each question and then check answers before doing the next question.

Tell students that the **Language Commentary** at the back of the Student's Book on p.124 provides all the information they need to answer concept questions but they should try and answer the questions first if they can.

1 • Allow students a minute or two to match the extracts **a–d** with the uses **1–4** and then check answers.

2 • Students work out the other uses of present tenses in **a–c**.

Answers
1 a 2, **b** 4, **c** 3, **d** 1
2 a *I fly ... future.* Present simple is used when a timetable is involved.
  b *We're meeting our friends ...* Present continuous is used to describe a future arrangement already made.
  c *He's always losing his keys.* Present continuous to refer to annoying habits.

Pronunciation

3 a Check that students are aware of the different sounds of third person singular endings of Present simple verbs. Give a few examples before setting the task.
  likes /s/ hides /z/ dances /ɪz/

Note You may need to check that students understand the difference between terms *voiced* and *voiceless*. Demonstrate the difference if necessary: ask students to put their fingers in their ears or their hand over their larynx and say the sounds /s/ and /z/. They should notice a 'buzzing sound' when they say the voiced consonant /z/ and no buzzing when they say the voiceless consonant /s/.

- Students put the 11 words into the correct lists.
b **1.2** Students listen to check their lists and work out rules of pronunciation and spelling.
- Check answers and write them on the board.

1.2
/s/ types, writes, asks
/z/ buys, rides, runs
/ɪz/ rises, catches, washes, damages, kisses

Answers
3 a See tapescript **1.2** .
  b **Rules of pronunciation**
  The third person singular ending is pronounced:
  - /s/ after most voiceless consonants /f/ /p/ /k/ /t/
  - /z/ after most voiced consonants and all vowels
  - /ɪz/ after the following sounds /s/ /z/ /ʃ/ /tʃ/ /dʒ/

  Rules of spelling
  Most verbs add -s to the infinitive: *likes, dances, hides*.
  1 You add -es when the infinitive ends in -o (*go/goes*); -x (*fix/fixes*); -ch (*catch/catches*); -sh (*wash/washes*)
  2 For verbs ending in consonant + *y* add -s (*play/plays*): For verbs ending in vowel + *y*, change the *y* to *i* and add -es (*cry/cries*).

Check

This is a final controlled exercise to check the correct use of the two Present verbs.

4 • Check answers and elicit reasons for students' choices.

Answers
a *dive* (Present simple – regular action)
b *speeds up* (Present simple – always true)
c *is climbing, he's jumping, he's wearing* (Present continuous – actions happening now)
d *are taking up* (Present continuous – present trend)
e *I'm doing* (Present continuous – arrangement)
f *takes off* (Present simple – timetabled future)

▶ **Photocopiable activity 1 p.157**

— p. 6 —

Reading

The articles focus on three different risky activities.

1 a Students could work in pairs to discuss their ideas. Make sure they do not look at the articles at this stage.
  • Elicit their ideas.
  b The words in the list may help students to make more predictions about the articles. This is a type of word–association exercise.
  • Elicit ideas, but do not confirm answers yet. Allow students to check for themselves as they read.

Answers
The dangerous games … *fell off   injuries   lift   speed   train*
An easy, risky way … *motorist   road   thumb*
A restaurant dish … *chef   meal   poisonous   taste*

2a–b Students work in threes, each reading a different article. As they read they match their article with a title and check their predictions for 1a–b.
  c Explain to students that, at a later stage, they are going to write a sentence summarizing what their articles are about. They should underline four or five of the most important words to help them remember the main points.

Background information
Article 1
The Republic of Ireland (also known as Southern Ireland, or Eire) has a reputation for being a quiet, peaceful country with friendly people. This article, about hitch-hiking, suggests that Ireland, and especially the big cities, is becoming as dangerous as other modern countries.

Article 3
Despite the impression given in this text, *train surfing*, *lift surfing*, *bonnet surfing* and *tombstoning* are not common activities among British teenagers.

Close up

Close up sections focus on points of grammar or vocabulary in reading texts. Normally they should be done as post-reading interpretation activities, but they may be referred to while reading, if a detailed understanding is important.

Initially, students work on the *Close up* points related to the articles they read. At the checking stage, elicit answers from the students who worked on the particular items, but make sure the whole class is involved in the process.

Answers
Article 1
• l.8 *get around* is a phrasal verb meaning to travel (from one place to another)
• l.21 *pick up* means to stop a car or vehicle to let someone else get in
  Some of the other meanings of *pick up*:
  – to get something which has fallen on to the floor
    *I saw a £10 note on the floor, so I **picked** it **up** and put it in my pocket.*
  – to catch an illness
    *I don't feel well. I may have **picked up** a virus while I was abroad.*
  – to learn by doing or without making an effort
    *Nobody taught me Spanish. I just **picked** it **up** from my friends.*
  – to increase
    *I put my foot down and the car **picked up** speed.*
Article 2
• l.6 *Apparently* tells us that the writer has not eaten Fugu fish. He is relying on what other people have said.
• l.10 *numbness* means the condition of having no power to feel or move. Your fingers can be *numb* with cold; your arm can be *numb* after you have been lying on it.
  The related adjective is *numb*.
  The letter **b** is not pronounced.
Article 3
• l.4 *pick up speed* – to increase speed, to go faster. For other meanings, see *Close up* for Article 1 above.

- l.4 *to rock* is intransitive and means to shake violently. It can also be transitive: *The earthquake rocked the town.*
  As a plural noun *the rocks* (l.19) means large pieces of stone which form part of the earth's surface.

Interpretation p. 7

1 • Students should only answer the questions related to their article. Explain to students that the answers to the questions are not in the articles, and that they should use their general knowledge and common sense to think of possible answers.
   • Go through the possible answers quickly.

Possible answers

Article 1
a Transport systems in rural areas are probably not very good. / People know and do favours for each other. / People without cars, especially young people, need cheap travel.
b People work in the towns during the week, then go back to their (parents') homes at the weekends. / Some may be university students. / People who work in the cities like to spend their weekends in the countryside.

Article 2
c The Fugu fish may be rare or difficult to catch. / The preparation of the fish probably takes a long time and needs a highly skilled chef.
d Some people like the excitement of dangerous activities. / People want to impress friends or colleagues. / Fugu eaters may enjoy the effect in the same way as others enjoy drugs.

Article 3
e Boys may be more likely to do dangerous things because of pressure from their friends. / Taking part in life-threatening activities may be seen by boys as a way of proving their masculinity. It's possible that this is only done by boys.
f Children may have used the tops of the lifts for other games. / Maybe they sit and drink while the lift goes up and down.

2 **a** Each student completes the sentence summarizing their text in a maximum of ten extra words.

Possible answers

1 ... *the increasing dangers of hitch-hiking in Ireland.*
2 ... *the poisonous Fugu fish served in some expensive Japanese restaurants.*
3 ... *train surfing and other dangerous games played by British teenagers.*

b–c Students give their sentences to the rest of their group to read, then the group discusses what the three texts have in common.

Possible answers

All the articles, especially **2** and **3**, are about dangerous activities, which could end fatally for those involved.
In all three stories people *choose* to do the dangerous activity, so *calculated risks* are involved.

Speaking personally

1–2 Students could discuss these two questions in pairs, groups, or as a whole class. Encourage students to share personal experiences.

Class survey

3 • Allow about five minutes for the preparation of questions and 10–15 minutes for conducting the survey.
   • Students work in groups of four or five. They think up as many questions as there are students in the group.
   • Each student in the group asks everyone else in the class **one** of their group's questions, then reports the answers back to the group.
   • Finally, the group compiles a summary of its findings.

Example

	Yes	No	Maybe
Q1 *Would you eat something you knew might be dangerous?*	3	6	2
Q2 ... ?			

   • Finish the activity with a brief reporting-back session on the most interesting findings, or by getting the groups to display their results in the classroom.

Grammar – Aspect

Exploring concepts

   • Read through the opening rubric with students to check that they understand the term *aspect*, before getting them to work through the concept questions. Point out that people choose a particular *aspect* in order to convey a specific meaning in addition to the time reference (past, present, future).
   • Remind students that they can refer to the **Language Commentary** on p.124.

1 • Students sort the verbs into three groups.

Answers

Continuous	Perfect	Other
d *are recommending*	**b** *has not been seen*	**a** *accepted*
g *was shouting*	**e** *have had*	**c** *advise*
	i *have been*	**f** *die*
	h *lost / fell off*	

2 • Allow students time to discuss their ideas, then elicit answers.

Answers

a The *perfect aspect* describes actions which are finished but are still relevant.
b The *continuous aspect* describes actions which are / were temporary or in progress.

3 • Elicit ideas for describing the verbs in the 'other' group.

Answer

The verbs in the 'other' list are all Present or Past simple. They simply report facts.

Pronunciation

4 a This exercise makes students aware of the importance of showing interest when asking personal questions. In English this is largely achieved with use of pitch.

- **1.3** Pause the recording after the first two questions and check answers.

1.3

1 What are you studying?
2 What are you studying?
3 Where are you studying?
  Where are you working at the moment?
4 Where have you been recently?
  What have you done this week?

5 Where do you live?
  Where do you work?
  Where do you study?
  When did you start there?

Answer

The second speaker sounds more interested because he starts HIGH on *What*.
The first speaker sounds less interested because he starts LOW on *What*.

- Ask students to repeat sentence 2 (interested), doing choral and individual repetition as necessary.

b Play the remaining questions 3–5 and get students to practise saying them with a partner.

Note Make sure students use the weak forms of the auxiliary verbs, start HIGH on the question word, and use falling intonation.

Exploitation

1 • Go through the examples given and elicit others. Then allow time for individuals to make up their own sentences.

Possible answers

holidays	I'm enjoying my holiday in Spain.
	I've been on holiday for two weeks.
	Last year I went to Turkey for my holiday.
television	I'm watching a series about the Romans.
	I've never spent much time watching TV.
	I always watch the news on TV.
sports and other interests	My hockey team is playing well at the moment.
	I've played football since I was six years old.
	Rugby football is a dangerous game.

- Monitor, giving help where necessary.
- Finally, students could compare sentences in pairs and discuss whether appropriate verb forms have been used.

2 • In this practice activity students interview each other asking questions in *continuous*, *perfect*, and *simple* forms.
- Work through the examples given and elicit a few more from the class.
- As students talk in pairs, monitor, giving help and correcting where necessary.

Free speech

3 • This group activity allows students to use a full range of verb forms (*continuous*, *perfect*, and *simple*) to discuss the subjects listed.

- Set up the activity and monitor, but, as this is a free practice, do not interrupt or correct language errors.
- You could finish with a reporting-back session getting students to report any interesting points they discussed.

— p. 8 —

Listening

The theme now moves on to *dangerous jobs*.

1 a Students make a list of jobs and the dangers involved.
  b They compare their lists with a partner.
  c Allow time for students to check meanings in their dictionaries. Elicit ideas about the jobs, but do not confirm or deny their suggestions yet.

2 • **1.4** Students listen and check their predictions.

1.4

Speaker 1
Of course there's no doubt about it – it is a risky business, but I try not to think about the risks – I mean they're always there at the back of my mind, but you've just got to get on with it, haven't you? Most of the work is pretty routine – not specially exciting or dangerous. When you are faced with a life-and-death situation, you haven't got time to think – you just get in there. If there are people inside the building, your job is to get them out safely – the smoke and flames are obstacles to overcome. Afterwards it hits you – when you get home and relax when everything's peaceful – that's when I think about what might have happened.

Speaker 2
For as long as I can remember I've been obsessed with kicking a ball about – it's all I ever really wanted to do. When I signed up at sixteen, I thought the worst that could happen would be that I'd waste a couple of years of my life. No one ever tells you about the risks you run – mental and physical – when you play the game at international level, though I don't suppose it would have made any difference if I had known. This is the third time I've been into hospital for operations on my legs – and it probably won't be the last.

Speaker 3
I started off in Cambodia and I've recently finished a spell in the Middle East. Of course it's dangerous work and we're all well aware of the physical risks involved. I've been arrested more times than I can remember. Usually they ask you a few questions, chuck you in a cell overnight, then the next morning you get your camera back with the lens missing – without the film of course – and then they let you go. If you take on a job like this, you've just got to accept that certain risks are involved, but they're calculated risks. As far as I'm concerned, what I do is worth taking risks for. The world needs to know what's going on in these places.

Speaker 4
The most important thing is to keep a cool head – I'd say the risks are fairly low – of course it can be nerve-racking and you worry about the car, but the vast majority of learners are ultra cautious and they hardly ever go over the speed limit. I've had a few minor accidents over the years, but that's all. And of course these days you've got dual control cars – so that means there's even less to worry about.

- Check answers.

Answers

Speaker 1 *fire-fighter* (a term which applies to both *firemen*
and *firewomen*)

Speaker 2 *professional footballer*

Speaker 3 *international news (war) photographer*

Speaker 4 *driving instructor*
dual control cars are for learner drivers – they can be
controlled by the driver and the instructor

- Draw students' attention to the collocations with *risk*. You
could ask them to find them in the tapescript on p.140.
it is a risky business (1), *the risks you run* (2), *certain risks
are involved* (3), *they're calculated risks* (3), *what I do is
worth taking risks for* (3), *the risks are fairly low* (4)

3 Students can now react personally to what the four speakers
have said.
- Students work in pairs. Some more dangerous jobs: *bomb
disposal expert, soldier, policeman, diver, racing driver.*
- Monitor conversations, but do not interrupt.
- You could get feedback from the whole class. Which jobs
are most or least popular?

▮ Interpretation ▮

1–4 Remind students that they have to use their own ideas to
answer these questions. They could discuss in pairs or
groups before you elicit possible answers.

Possible answers

1 probably feelings of retrospective panic, the sudden
realization that what she has done was very dangerous

2 *mental* risks might involve stress brought about by big
occasions, performing in front of TV cameras and live
audiences, lack of privacy, attention of the media, dealing
with losing important matches, insecurity, losing one's place
in a team
physical risks might involve broken bones, pain, permanent
injuries

3 *calculated risks* are risks someone is aware of. They know
what may happen if they do something, they weigh the pros
and cons and take the risk. The speaker takes risks because he
thinks people need to know what is going on in the world.

4 *to keep a cool head* means to avoid panicking. If a driving
instructor panics there could be serious consequences.

▮ Vocabulary ▮

This collocation exercise uses verbs from **1.4**.

1 - You could start by explaining how important it is for
words to be learnt in groups or as phrases.
- Go through one or two examples with the whole class. Ask
which verb or verbs collocate with (*a*) *cassette* or which
nouns collocate with *keep*.
- Check answers.

Answers

keep	*control, your head, your job, your temper, a secret*
play	*a cassette, football, the guitar, a trick on someone*
run	*a business, ten kilometres, a race, a risk*
waste	*time, energy, money*

Note

1 *to keep time* describes what a watch or clock does if it is always
right and is neither slow nor fast.

2 The opposite of *keep* is *lose* in all cases except *a secret*, where the
opposite is *give away*.

2 - Elicit a few examples to check that students understand.
- Monitor, giving help and correcting where necessary.

3 - Students discuss the differences between the words from
the recording.
- Check answers.

Answers

a *job* is a countable noun which means occupation, paid
position of regular employment.
*What's your **job**? I've got a new **job**. I love my **job**.*
It is also a particular piece of work.
*I've done lots of **jobs** around the house today.*
work is an uncountable noun which means physical or
mental activity.
*Teaching is hard **work**. There's lots of **work** to do.*

b *smoke* is an uncountable noun which means the white, grey,
or black gas produced when something burns.
*I hate the smell of cigarette **smoke**.*
flame(s) is a countable noun which means a pointed stream of
burning gas that comes from something which is burning.
*The **flames** from the burning house lit up the night sky.*

c *mental* is to do with the mind or the brain.
*Depression is a **mental** illness.*
physical is to do with the body.
*Sport is an enjoyable form of **physical** exercise.*

d *obsessed with* means unable to stop thinking about
something. It is much stronger than *interested in*.
*I'm quite **interested in** football, but my brother's completely
obsessed with it.*

4 These questions give students a chance to use the pairs of
words actively.
- Set a time limit for this activity (about five minutes).
- Monitor conversations.
- Finish by eliciting a few of the ideas students discussed.

— Grammar – Action verbs and state verbs —

▮ Exploring concepts ▮ p. 9 ▮

- You could let students work through concept questions
1–2 by themselves, or read through the introduction with
them first to check their understanding of *action verbs* and
state verbs. Do not tell them yet that state verbs are rarely
used in the continuous form as this is covered in **1b**.
- Remind students that they can refer to the **Language
Commentary** on p.124.

1 • Sorting the verbs from the text into two lists will demonstrate to students that only *action* verbs (not *state* verbs) are used in the continuous form.
  • Check answers.

Answers

a **Action**
I'm working, left, walked, was approaching, broke out, attacked, was getting on, dragged, kicked, punched, radioed, said, going on, was waiting, threw, hit, woke up, will catch

State
belong, love, wish, thought, ⁓ op'⁓⁵ *knew, need, hope, believe, involves, doubt*

b While action verbs can be used in simple and continuous forms, state verbs cannot be used in the continuous form.

2 • Elicit students' ideas. From the list of state verbs in the text, students may suggest categories such as *knowledge* or *opinions*. Accept these, then refer students to the **Language Commentary** where five meaning groups are listed.
  • Work together as a whole class to categorize the verbs.

Answers
The groups of state verbs:
feelings and emotions	*love, hope, wish, need*
being	*involves*
having	*belong*
opinions	*think, believe, doubt*
senses	none in the text. *feel, smell.*

■ **Exploitation** ■■■■■■■■■■■■■■■■

This structured interview task should enable students to use a mixture of action and state verbs.

1 • Elicit a few sample questions that the interviewer might ask to check that students understand. Make sure they take notes on the answers as they will need them for exercise 2.
    Where do you work? Do you like your job?
    Is there anything you dislike? What does your daily routine involve?
  • Monitor, listening out for the correct verb forms.
  • The two students swap roles and do the interview again.
  • Finish the activity by drawing students' attention to any errors you heard while monitoring.

2 • If this writing task is set for homework, use class time for preparation, planning, and writing a first draft. Suggest a maximum length of 100 words.
  • Explain that students should use their notes to form the basis of an article. The focus of the writing should be their partner's feelings about their job.
  • Students exchange pieces of writing and discuss any factual inaccuracies and language errors.
  • You may then ask students to write a final, corrected version of the article.

Vocabulary development

This first Vocabulary section previews some of the important areas of vocabulary to be covered in subsequent units of the book. Explain this to the class.
  • You could start by writing the headings on the board: *collocations, connotation, prefixes and suffixes, formality, homonyms, metaphorical language.*
  • Ask students how many of these terms they know.

■ **Collocations** ■■■■■■■■■■■■■■■■ p. 10 ■
  • Read the two examples and check that students understand the idea of *collocation*. If necessary, remind them of the exercise on p.8 of the book (Listening, Vocabulary, question 1).

1 • Allow students time to think of and list verbs that collocate with *money*, then elicit examples and list them on the board.

Answers
change, invest, make, pay, save, spend, waste

2 • Each student in the pair talks for one minute, using as many of the verbs listed as possible. Their partner could then ask follow-up questions.

■ **Connotations** ■■■■■■■■■■■■■■■■
  • Read the two examples and check that students understand the idea of *connotation*.
  • Students discuss which of the two candidates, Sue or Dave, would make the better employee. This could be done as a class activity.
  • Elicit meanings of adjectives from students, and ask which have positive, neutral, or negative connotations.
  • Ask students who they would employ and why.

Answers
– a *serious* person does things properly. (neutral);
  a *humourless* person takes things too seriously, cannot see the funny side of anything, cannot take a joke. (negative)
– *inexperienced* means simply having no experience. (neutral);
  immature suggests a childish attitude. (negative)
– *ambitious* means wanting to progress or being determined to succeed. (it does not suggest an unpleasant or negative attitude);
  pushy, on the other hand, means over-ambitious to the extent of being unpleasant to other people. (negative)
Sue is probably the better employee, because the words used to describe her have positive or neutral connotations, whereas those used about Dave are negative.

■ **Word-building** ■■■■■■■■■■■■■■■■
  • Read the examples checking that students know the terms *suffix* and *prefix*.
  • Allow pairs a few minutes to write lists of words related to *use, believe,* and *advise.*
  • Elicit words and write on the board. Do not be tempted to spend too long at this stage on a detailed study of

these words. What is important here is the use of suffixes and prefixes.

Possible answers

use *useful, usefulness, useless, uselessness, unusable, abuse (n and v), misuse (n and v), disused, used, unused, usefully, uselessly, user*

believe *disbelieve, believer, non-believer, belief, disbelief, believable, unbelievable, unbelievably*

advise *advice (noun), advisory, adviser (or advisor), advisable, inadvisable, advisability, (advisedly)*

Formality

- Check that students understand the concept of *formal* and *informal* language.
- Elicit a few ideas about situations in which these registers are appropriate.
- Students could rewrite the sentences in pairs or individually.
- Check answers.

Possible answers

a *This is my Mum and Dad. I'd like you to meet my Mum and Dad.*

b *(I'm) sorry I'm late.*

c *Can I open the window? / Do you mind if I open the window? / Is it OK if I open the window?*

Homonyms

- Read through the examples and check that students understand the concept of *homophones* (words which sound the same, but have a different meaning), and *homographs* (which are spelt the same, but are pronounced differently).

Note This exercise only practises homophones.

1 • Elicit students' suggestions for homophones and list them on the board.

two to, too   *wait* weight
right write, rite   *wear* where, ware

2 • This could be done as a homework task, as it will probably take students different lengths of time to complete.

Possible answers

Two hours? That's far *too* long for me *to* wait.
I'm sorry but this is not *right*, you'll have to *write* it again.
I can't *wait* to lose *weight*.
Where I work we all *wear* jeans.

Metaphorical language

- Read the example and check that students understand the difference between *literal* and *metaphorical* (or non-literal).

1–2 Elicit ideas about the metaphorical meanings of these words and phrases.

Answers

1 *mousy* shy, quiet
a dinosaur someone who is old-fashioned and can't adapt to change

a rat an unpleasant person, someone who deceives or is disloyal
catty deliberately unkind in what one says

2 Someone who *buries their head in the sand* pretends that an unpleasant reality does not exist.

Language in action

The **Language in action** sections in *Landmark Upper Intermediate* provide a framework for the introduction and practice of functional language, conversational strategies, and related pronunciation and writing.

Eavesdrop!   p. 11

- The questions could be done as a class activity or as pairwork.
- Direct attention to the picture and elicit students' answers to the questions. They should be encouraged to speculate about what is going on from visual clues.

Note It is important to point out that there are no right or wrong answers to the *Eavesdrop!* questions. Students are practising interpreting what they see.

- Elicit a few ideas before playing the recording but don't confirm or deny suggestions at this stage as students will check their guesses in *Listening 1*.

Listening 1

This first conversation contains functional and conversational language and involves the people in the picture.

1 • **1.5** Students listen to check their *Eavesdrop!* ideas, and think about the answers to questions **a–b**.

1.5

J   OK, Liz, so what are we going to do? We've got less than a day left.
P   Er …
L   I've told you what I think, John. We can get Paul to do it. That way there's less chance of serious problems later.
P   Can I just say …
J   Hold on, Paul, what sort of problems are you thinking of, Liz?
L   Well, mainly another injury to Rob, of course.
R   I'd go along with that. The last thing I want is three more weeks in hospital.
P   Excuse me, could I …
L   Yes, that would delay the rest of the shoot by goodness knows how long. And that all adds to the expense.
R   I have to agree, John, – we're already over budget.
J   I'm not so sure, people really believe it's you, you know. If they found out it wasn't, …
P   I'd just like to say …
J   I haven't finished yet. Look Rob, people really believe you take the risks, you know.
R   I suppose so. Liz?
L   In the end it's up to you, Rob. I can only give you advice. The film industry can't afford to lose you just yet, you know.
P   Can I just get a word in, please? It's me you're talking about, you know – I may not be a well-known star like Rob but I am a human being …

- Check answers.

Possible answers
Eavesdrop!
It is a warm country (blue skies), possibly Southern Europe. The building is probably a hotel and they are talking around a table in a conference room or restaurant.

Listening 1
a They are all people who are taking part in a film. The older man is the director. The handsome younger man is a famous actor or film star. The other younger man is a stunt man who will stand in for the star.
The woman is the actor's agent.
b They are talking about a film. (*shoot / over budget / the film industry / a well-known star*)
They are discussing whether the star (Rob) should risk doing dangerous things in the film or whether the stunt man (Paul) should replace him. The speakers disagree; public trust and money (budget) are mentioned. No one takes any notice of Paul or seems to care if he injures himself or not.

2 The purpose of listening again is for students to identify the functional and conversational language used in the first conversation.
- To make the task possible, students work in groups of four: each individual in the group listens for and notes down different language items.
- Check students know what to do by eliciting a few examples of each type of language they are listening for.
- Allocate tasks and then play the recording for a second and, if necessary, a third time.
- Students note down the expressions and then compile lists. They help and correct each other at this stage.

Note Students add to these lists during the next listening task.

Answers
See full list of expressions after *Listening 2*, question 2.

■ Listening 2

This section contains extracts taken from authentic conversations using similar functional language as in *Listening 1*.

Note The first time the students hear the conversations they should just listen to get a general idea, and answer the questions. In **1.6** students hear the whole of each tapescript. In **1.7** they hear an extract of conversation 1 and the whole of conversation 2 and they can follow them in their books.

1 · **1.6** Play the first conversation and check answers before listening to the second conversation.

1.6 including **1.7**
Conversation 1
K Couldn't I have just one str ... one colour in the room, if I was going to say go for a ... for a strong colour on the curtains? Wouldn't that be enough? Wouldn't ...
R I think, I think that would be better.
J **1.7** It might look a bit strange if you've just ... got one sort of colour, don't you think?
R Not necessarily.
J I think it could be like a little rich gem in here with all sorts of deep vibrant colours, like a fruit cake.

K Oh, I don't know about that. I don't know that I could live in it.
J Don't you like that?
K Ooh ...
R Well, as you say, a room this size.
J Right. What would you do?
R Well, ... I'd ...
S I'd ... Sorry.
R I tend to go along with the neutrals, but with a splash of ... strong, strong ...
J Something bright ...
R ... strong ... but not make that the overall theme ... you know ...
J Mmm – I see your point. Mmm ...
R ... you know.
S Yeah, I agree with you, I think, I think. The other thing I think about is, strong colours is they're likely to date.
J Mmm ...
S I mean I wouldn't ...
R Yeah, that's a good point ...
S I mean, I wouldn't want to redecorate in less than about ten years.
J A Victorian house would have had very deep and rich colours for – years and years and years. It's a very classic look for that period.
K But it's very difficult to get anything to match though, isn't it?...
R Absolutely. Absolutely.
K ... if I go for very strong colours.
J No, not strong primary colours, but deep colours, deep rich colours, you see.
K Mmm. I don't know.
J Don't you think?
K No, I don't think so.
R Don't know.

Conversation 2
T **1.7** Yes, I know, but the point the point is we work our guts out for this place and they're just constantly leaning on us all the time. It's more work, it's more money, it's more hours, it's more admin.
J Oh Tony, Tony, be reasonable.
T This is getting ridiculous.
R Wait a minute, wait a minute. You know, I mean if everyone could bring their car in, nobody could park in there anyway because ...
J Exactly!
R ... there'd be too, too many cars.
J Absolutely. Absolutely right! Absolutely! So that's going to give you a great opportunity of a guaranteed place to park.
T Where's the money going to go to? What's it going to be used for?
J Well, I suppose they're going to have a security man there so that your car at least it'll be safe – it's not on the road, Tony.
T Oh come on, I mean, ... it's, the, there're gates, the gates are normally closed – that's no particular problem anyway, is it?
R But that can be decided later.
T This is just one way of ripping off the staff.
J Oh no, that's not true.
T It is!
J No, I don't agree. Oh come on, Roger, you know you're nearly there. It is ...
T Twenty quid a year, well all right, but a hundred, a hundred is absurd.
J Oh twenty's nothing. What's that going to do?
T Yes, but think how many people there are. If everybody's chipping in twenty quid, that's plenty of money to pay a security man or one or two people to run round with walky-talkies and this sort of silly equipment.
J A hundred is nothing if you work out how much that is a quarter. What do you pay in the multi-storey?
R It's really nothing for over a year, I mean what is it? Two pounds a week?

J   Exactly! How much do the meters cost?
R   Yeah, what is it? Two pounds an hour or something in a meter?
J   You're right, you're right.
T   Well that's, all right, yes …
R   I understand why they're charging …

- Check answers.

Possible answers

	Conversation 1	Conversation 2
a	Decorating a room or apartment	Employees having to pay to park cars at work
b	Friends	Colleagues

2 • ▊ ▊ Students listen to the extracts and follow the extracts, and mark the expressions on p.12 of their books.
- Students add the expressions to their lists.
- Play the recording again if necessary.
- Check students' lists. To save time you could photocopy the list below for all students. (It is important for students to have a list to refer to when doing the Exploitation tasks later.)
- Draw attention to any expressions you think need explanation.

Answers

(This includes expressions from **Listening 1** and **2**.)

Agreeing

▊

I'd go along with that.   I have to agree,   I suppose so.
(reluctant agreement)

▊ **Extract 1**

I tend to go along with …   I see your point.   (Yeah) I agree with you, …   (Yeah) that's a good point …

▊ **Extract 2**

Exactly!   Absolutely (right)!   You're right.

Disagreeing

▊

I'm not so sure, … (a polite, indirect form of disagreement)

▊ **Extract 1**

Not necessarily. (The speaker thinks that what another speaker has said may not be true.)   *Oh, I don't know about that.*
(From full conversation
No, I don't think so …)

▊ **Extract 2**

Oh come on … (This means *You can't be serious!*)
Oh no, that's not true.   No, I don't agree.

Getting into a conversation

▊

Er …   (a weak attempt to get attention)
Can I just say …   (The use of *just* in this and other
Excuse me, could I …   expressions makes the speaker sound
                               less aggressive and so more polite)
I'd just like to say …
Can I just get a word in …   (The full expression is *to get a word
                               in edgeways*. It refers to situations in
                               which other speakers talk without
                               pausing.)

▊ **Extract 2**

Wait a minute …

Preventing someone from getting into a conversation

▊

Hold on … (*Hold on* means *wait*)   *I haven't finished yet.*

Features of natural conversation ▬▬▬▬ p. 12 ▬

The main purpose of these sections is to make students aware of words and other conversational devices which occur mainly in natural speech and to help them interpret their meanings or implications. It is not anticipated that students will incorporate them all into their own speech.

1 • Students mark the exclamations in the extracts.
- Elicit students' ideas about their meanings.

Suggested answers
a *Mmm* suggests that the speaker does not agree with what has been said but wants to think before expressing direct disagreement.
b *Ooh* similar to *Mmm*, but there is an element of surprise here. Again, the speaker is showing that she does not immediately agree with what has been said.
c *Oh* is being used here to attract the listener's attention and to express the strength of the speaker's opinions. In other situations it can also express surprise or fear.

2 • Play the conversations again.

Practice

1 a ▐ **1.8** ▐ Play the recording, stopping after each expression and do choral and individual repetition as appropriate.
  b Continue playing the recording for 1–7 said with strong agreement.
  • Students repeat the expressions showing strong agreement.

▐ **1.8** ▐

Agreement	Stronger agreement
1 I agree with you.	1 I agree with you.
2 You're right.	2 You're right.
3 I'd go along with that.	3 I'd go along with that.
4 That's a good point.	4 That's a good point.
5 Absolutely!	5 Absolutely!
6 Exactly!	6 Exactly!
7 Absolutely right!	7 Absolutely right!

2 a ▐ **1.9** ▐ Play the recording and get students to repeat 1–4.
  b Continue playing the recording and get students to repeat 1–4 showing stronger disagreement.

▐ **1.9** ▐

Disagreement	Stronger disagreement
1 That's not true.	1 That's not true.
2 I don't agree.	2 I don't agree.
3 I'm not so sure.	3 I'm not so sure.
4 I don't know about that.	4 I don't know about that.

3 • Working in pairs, students take turns saying the statements while the other agrees or disagrees using the expressions from ▐ **1.8** ▐ and ▐ **1.9** ▐.
- Monitor, listening for correct intonation and stress.

4 • ▐ **1.10** ▐ Play the recording and ask students to repeat a–d.
- Check answers.

▐ **1.10** ▐

a Excuse me, could I just say what I think?
b Can I just say what my opinion is?

c I'd just like to say I'm not happy about this.
d Can I just get a word in, please?

Answer
They are all spoken in loud voices and start HIGH. (They also all contain the word *just*!)

Exploitation

This section gives students a chance to use the functional language introduced in the recordings and the pronunciation points they have just practised.

- Divide the class into groups and make sure students understand the task. They should choose one of the situations described: there is a business situation (1), and a more personal situation (2).
- Point out that members of the group should have different viewpoints and be prepared to agree and disagree with each other. If they do this, it is probable that at various times individuals will want to get into the conversation and that others may want to prevent them from doing so.
- Give students time to think of ideas before they begin their discussions.
- Monitor conversations, listening for use of the functional language and correct pronunciation. Encourage groups to agree and disagree, but otherwise allow the discussions to follow their natural course.
- You could finish this activity with a brief reporting-back session in which a spokesperson for each group, tells the class what their group decided.

Writing   p. 13

The focus is on how the functional language of speech differs from that used in writing. The first section makes a comparison between an extract from one of the earlier conversations and writing which expresses the same function.

1 a Elicit from the class some of the differences between spoken language and formal writing before they look at the examples in their books.
b–e When they have suggested a few general differences, ask them to look at the examples and answer b–e.
- Check answers.

Answers
b **Formal language**
   I completely agree ... /On the other hand ... /I do not accept ... /I have nothing against ... /However, I entirely disagree ... /This is unacceptable in any situation ...
c **Agreement**
   I completely agree with ... /(I have nothing against the activities)
   Disagreement
   I do not accept that ... /I entirely disagree with ... /(This is unacceptable)
d The words *completely* and *entirely* show the writer's strength of feeling.
e *On the other hand ...* and *However ...* are used to link the writer's opinions. They signal to the reader that what follows is going to be in contrast with what has just been said.

Note Make the general point that some people are more tentative and less direct in their spoken agreements and disagreements. Their opinions may be usually more clearly stated when they write. (Point out these very indirect expressions in the spoken extract: *I tend to go along with, I see your point.*)

- Before setting the writing task, direct students' attention to the **Writing guidelines** on letters at the back of their books p.155.

2 - In preparation for the writing task, discuss the problem described, relating it to a town or city the students know.
- If students are not used to planning what they write, work through the suggested paragraph plan, eliciting ideas and possible phrases or sentences, and write them on the board. Remind students to incorporate some of the expressions from the sample letter in their books.
- The first draft of the letter could be set for homework.

Sample letter

I am writing to express my opinions about plans for improving the traffic problems of our town. I have to drive to work in town every day. The journey is taking longer and longer and I am getting more and more unhappy about the situation.
I completely agree with the suggestion that there should be new bus or rail links into the town and that the centre of the town should be for pedestrians only. However, I do not accept that there should be an increased tax on local roads. Also, I entirely disagree with the idea of building a new ring road as I think this would make more traffic.
I would like to end by suggesting that more people should cycle to work. This is cheaper and healthier than going by car.

3 - If students are not used to working co-operatively as suggested, they could check through their own writing. Make it clear that the final version of their letter will be checked and marked by you, the teacher.
- Explain the task and why it is important. Set a time limit, 5–10 minutes for students to read each other's writing and think of improvements, then allow a further five minutes for pairs to discuss each other's suggestions.
- Monitor these stages carefully, especially if students have not worked in this way before. Be prepared to arbitrate in cases of disagreement.
- Set the writing of the final version of the letter as classwork or homework.

Summary

- Encourage students to use the tick boxes to help them keep a record of their learning.

2 First person singular

Theme

Personal narratives – accounts and stories in the 'first person singular' – *I*.

Preview Childhood confessions and early memories
Listening Hidden talents – confessions of an untidy person
Reading A young woman leaves home

Grammar

- Past simple and Past continuous (LC p.125)
- Past perfect (LC p.125)
- *used to, would* (LC p.125)

Vocabulary

- Collocations: Verbs and nouns; Adjectives and nouns; Verbs and adverbs

Functional language

- Expressing and asking about opinions
- Avoiding expressing an opinion

Conversation strategies

- Involving someone in a conversation

Pronunciation

- Past tense regular verb endings
- *had / used to*
- Identifying main stressed syllables

Features of natural conversation

- Vague language

Writing

- Notes for a semi-formal speech (WG p.155)

Workbook

- An extract from a short story
- Topic vocabulary: eating, drinking, talking; *get away, come off, take over*; Collocations: verb + noun
- Past simple and Past continuous review; Past perfect; *used to, would*
- Using correct punctuation; Describing a personal experience

Preview

Your thoughts   p. 14

These opening questions introduce the first topic of the unit: childhood memories. The competition advertised on the magazine cover is for readers' confessions: stories of 'naughty' things readers of the magazine did as children.

- Establish this idea, then give students time to think before they tell each other about naughty things they did as children.
- When students have exchanged stories in pairs, get a few volunteers to retell their stories to the whole class.

Reading

In addition to introducing the theme of the unit, these texts illustrate uses of the various past tenses.

1.
   - Explain the task, then check that students understand the words related to each title.
   - Elicit meanings or get students to use dictionaries.
   - You could check ideas at this stage, but do not confirm or deny answers.

2.
   - Students read quickly through the three stories to check their ideas.
   - You could set a time limit of four to five minutes for this.
   - You could elicit the basic plot of each story very briefly from the class before getting them to read again and note down how each of the writers felt after their actions.

   Answers
   - **Sorry grandad**   The storyteller felt guilty and burst into tears.
   - **Ten-year-old hoaxer**   The storyteller felt terrified and puzzled (she didn't know why she had phoned the fire brigade).
   - **My first lie**   The storyteller felt pleased with themself.

3.
   - Students think about and then discuss which of the three stories they have read should win the competition.
   - Allow thinking time before students discuss in pairs, and then elicit a few ideas, or take a class poll to find out which is the most popular story.

4. a
   Direct students back to the two stories listed on the magazine cover and check they understand them.
   to let down a tyre means to release the air from a car tyre, *to lock someone out* means to lock a door so that people cannot get in. (This may be deliberate or accidental.)

b In pairs, students make up a full version of one of the stories, answering the questions listed. Suggest they make up the story orally and write a few notes. Discourage them from writing the full version in class. This could be a homework task.

c When students tell their versions of the stories to another pair, they can refer to any notes they have made.

■ **Person to person** ▬▬▬▬▬▬▬▬▬▬▬▬▬ p. 15 ■

1–2 These discussion questions could be done in pairs, or as a whole class. Encourage students to give examples from their own experience.

—Grammar – Past simple and Past continuous review

Remind students that they can refer to the **Language Commentary** on p.125 but stress they should use this to check the answers they have already thought out for themselves.

1–2 Allow students time to work through the grammar concept questions individually or in pairs, but monitor their discussions carefully and give help where needed.

• When they have worked through 1 and 2, spend a few minutes with the whole class checking understanding and dealing with any general problem areas.

Answers

1 a Past continuous   **b** Past simple   **c** Past continuous

2 a 5 two actions in progress over the same period of time
b 4 a repeated action that took place at certain specified times
c 1 a specific action which took place while a longer action was in progress
d 6 a completed action which took place over a specified period of time
e 3 a number of completed actions which took place one after the other
f 2 an action in progress which forms the background to a story
You could also say that the actions in sentence **a** form the background to the story.

■ Check ▬▬▬▬▬▬▬▬▬▬▬▬▬▬▬▬▬▬▬▬▬

3 • Students work through this controlled practice exercise individually.
• Check answers.
• You could also ask them to say which descriptions 1–6 in question 2 explain their choice of answer.

Answers

a *was having*	1	**d** *was shining / were singing*	2
b *often phoned*	4	**e** *left / got / drove off*	3
c *was burning*	5	**f** *played*	6

■ Pronunciation ▬▬▬▬▬▬▬▬▬▬▬▬▬▬▬▬▬

This is a revision exercise.

4 • Set students a time limit to say the past tense and to put the words into three groups.

• **2.1** Students listen and check.
• Check answers and elicit rules for pronunciation and spelling.

2.1

/d/		/t/		/ɪd/	
longed	judged	laughed	watched	needed	added
loved	tried	knocked	stopped	wanted	waited
gazed		kissed	washed		

Answers

a See tapescript **2.1**.

b Pronunciation
The *-ed* ending of past tense regular verbs is pronounced:
• /d/ after a final voiced consonant or a vowel /b/ /g/ /dʒ/ /v/ /ð/ /z/ /m/ /n/ /ŋ/ /l/
• /t/ after a final voiceless consonant /p/ /k/ /tʃ/ /f/ /θ/ /s/ /ʃ/
• /ɪd/ after a final /t/ or /d/

Spelling
• Only *d* is added when the infinitive ends in *e love/loved*
• When the verb ends in a consonant + *y*, the *y* changes to *i* and you add *-ed. study/studied*
• When the verb ends in vowel + *y*, you add *-ed. play/played*
• Verbs spelt with a single vowel letter + single vowel consonant double the consonant. *stop/stopped*

▬▬▬▬▬▬▬▬▬▬▬▬▬▬▬▬▬▬ p. 16 ▬

Listening

The photographs and the discussion activity introduce the theme of hidden talents.

1 • Spend a few minutes as a whole class discussing the differences between the two rooms to establish the ideas of tidiness and messiness.
• Students then discuss the questions in pairs or small groups.
• Elicit a few ideas. It is important that students say which room they prefer and why, as this will give them a point of view when they listen to the recording.

2 • Check that students understand the two while-listening questions and the adjectives listed in **b**.
• Elicit the meaning of *Hidden Talents* (an ability or skill someone has that is not generally known about by others).
• You may wish to teach these words before students listen to the recording: *vanish, materialize.*
• **2.2** Play the recording, allow students time to exchange ideas, then elicit their answers.

Answers

a • The speaker's talent is that she is able to make things disappear and re-appear.
• The recording mentions keys, pens, glasses, documents, a hairbrush, a T-shirt, a screwdriver, certificates, and a sandwich.
• She has different feelings about her talent. At first she was *not altogether happy about it*, she envied tidy people. Then she began to see the advantages of losing things. It made life unpredictable and exciting.

b The general tone is *amusing, humorous, ironic,* and *light-hearted.* It is partly the fact that the speaker describes a personal failing as a mysterious talent, over which she has no control, that makes the talk funny. This is a person who has tried to change, has not succeeded, and is now making the best of the situation.

2.2

I have a secret power. I can make objects vanish into thin air. I can put keys, pens, or glasses on to surfaces or into drawers, and a few seconds later they have disappeared. Unfortunately, I don't have quite so much control over the re-appearance of these objects.

Sometimes my secret power makes an object invisible, so that it only looks as if it's disappeared – after a few days, weeks, or months, it becomes visible again, and there it is, exactly where I first put it. Once I spent a whole day looking for an important document that I knew I'd left in an obvious place on the table. Although I couldn't see the document, it was there. Medical experts might say this was a case of temporary blindness, but, erm I'm not so sure.

More often, objects disappear to special parts of the house. They particularly like hiding in my daughter's bedroom. She can never understand how my hairbrush or T-shirt materialize in her room. Another favourite hiding place is my car. Objects I'm certain I left on top of the fridge turn up under the driver's seat.

My most remarkable experience was when the last remaining key to the kitchen door disappeared and we had to leave the door unlocked and banging in the wind for several weeks. One day, as I was unpacking the food I had just bought at the local supermarket, I discovered the missing key under a bag of potatoes. I have to say I was puzzled by this, but grateful, of course, to be able to lock the door again.

When I first became aware of my talent, I was not altogether happy about it. I began to envy people whose keys always hung on special hooks and whose papers were always neatly put away in cupboards and drawers. Then I realized that the tidiness of these people's houses reminded me of old-fashioned museums with their carefully labelled exhibits.

In my opinion, a good house is an unpredictable house, with objects in all kinds of unexpected places. It's nice to be able to open a kitchen cupboard without having the slightest idea of what's inside.

Another advantage is that unpredictable houses don't appeal to burglars. In the last few months every house in my street has been burgled except mine. Admittedly I don't have a video or a hi-fi system but I feel the unusual combinations of objects in my house might have made the burglar think that my house had already been broken into.

It is true that the pleasure of finding things is far greater than the inconvenience of losing them. The things I find are hardly ever the things I'm looking for. While I was looking for a screwdriver recently, I found my daughter's birth certificate which I'd been searching for for months. On another occasion, while I was looking for my glasses, I came across a sandwich I'd lost the previous weekend.

The happiness you feel when you find a missing object is worth every minute of the time you've spent searching for it. Of course, even as you smile to yourself, you know that the object will not be staying for long.

■ Interpretation

- Check that students understand the idea of 'listening between the lines' (the listening equivalent of 'reading between the lines') and the importance of interpreting what they hear in order to get the full meaning of someone's words.

1 a Give students time to discuss the extracts in pairs, then elicit their ideas.

Possible answers

1 The speaker is so sure she left the document on the table, she convinces herself that it is still there but has become invisible. She prefers to pretend that the document is hiding from her than to admit that she has forgotten where she left it.
2 The *unusual combination of objects* refers to the untidiness of her house. Nothing is where it should be.
3 The object will disappear again: in other words, she will lose it again.

b Elicit any advantages and disadvantages students can remember, then play the recording again, pausing to allow students to make notes.
- Check answers.

Answers
Advantages
- The speaker's house is unpredictable and therefore exciting.
- Untidy houses will not be burgled – they do not appeal to burglars.
- It is a good feeling when you find something you had lost.
- A tidy house with everything in its place is like a museum, i.e. dull, old-fashioned, and boring.
Disadvantages
- You cannot find what you want.
- Your house is untidy.

2 a Students discuss their choices in pairs.
- Elicit answers, asking students to explain their choices.

Answers
a All these adjectives except *impatient* could apply to the speaker:
 – *untidy* she never knows where anything is; she puts things on the table or on top of the fridge
 – *disorganized* people lose things – they never know where anything is
 – *inefficient* she uses her time inefficiently because she spends so much of it looking for things she has lost
 – *careless* she is careless with her own possessions.
b The opposites of these five qualities are: *tidy, organized, efficient, careful, patient.*

■ Speaking personally

1–3 Students discuss these questions in pairs or groups.
- Allow about five minutes for this, then finish the activity by eliciting any 'hidden talents' students will admit to.

Grammar – Past perfect

■ Exploring concepts

Students will almost certainly have met the Past perfect before. They will know how it is formed and that it is used to refer to actions which were already completed at a particular time in the past. The focus here is on common contexts for, or uses of, the Past perfect.

- Remind students that they can refer to the **Language Commentary** on p.125.

1–2 Allow students time to work through the questions individually or in pairs before eliciting their answers.

Answers

1 **a** *I spent a whole day looking for an important document that I knew I'd left in an obvious place on the table.*
b *As I was unpacking the food I had just bought at the local supermarket, I discovered the missing key under a bag of potatoes.*
c *While I was looking for my glasses, I came across a sandwich I'd lost the previous weekend.*

2 **a** The main actions in the sentences are:
1a *I spent a whole day*
1b *I discovered the missing key*
1c *I came across a sandwich.*
The main action is in the Past simple.
b The actions that took place first were:
1a *I'd left (an important document) on the table*
1b *I had just bought the food at the supermarket*
1c *I had lost a sandwich at the weekend.*
The verbs are in the Past perfect.
c In each example the Past perfect phrase provides background information relevant to the main action.

Note It is interesting to note that all three Past perfect verbs are in relative clauses.

3 • Students match four more Past perfect sentences with the most appropriate use.
• Explain before they start that sometimes more than one of the uses listed is appropriate.

Answers

3 **a** 4 the particular time in the past is *seven o'clock this morning*
b 1 the sequence of events is *finished working / had breakfast*
c 3 *I was hungry because I had eaten hardly anything*
d 2 the background information is *it had been a tiring day, I hadn't slept well the night before*. This information sets the context for a story in the Past simple.

4 • Before students begin, remind them of the concept of *aspect* on p.7.
• Check answers.

Answers

4 The choice of the Past perfect continuous shows that an action was still in progress. In sentence **a** the speaker was still searching (i.e. had not given up the search) when she found the birth certificate.
In sentence **b** the search for the passport had been called off. The speaker was not actively searching when it turned up.

Pronunciation ■■■■■■■■■■■■■■■■■■■■■■■■ p. 17 ■

5 **a** Students work in pairs and spend a few minutes practicing the pronunciation of *had*.

Note If students need more help give them the weak form /həd/ or /əd/ and the strong form /hæd/ and see if they can decide when to use each form.
• Elicit some ideas but don't confirm whether these are correct or not.
b **2.3** Students listen and check.
• Check answers.

Note You could write the answers on the board in phonetic script if your students are familiar with it.

2.3

1 After John had (əd) finished he left.
2 What had (əd) he done to deserve that?
3 Had (hæd) the party finished by two?
4 No, I don't think it had (hæd). No, it hadn't (hædnt).
5 I had (hæd) thought of that, you know.

• Students can either work out the rules of pronunciation in pairs or you can elicit ideas from the class.

Answer

a See tapescript **2.3** .
b In normal speech we use the strong form of *had* /hæd/:
• in short answers (Sentence 4)
• in negatives (Sentence 4)
• for emphasis (Sentence 5).
We use the weak form of *had* (hæd) or (əd) at other times. (Sentences 1, 2, 3)

Note When *had* is the first word of the sentence, we can use either form. (Sentence 3)

■ Exploitation ■■■■■■■■■■■■■■■■■■■■■■■■■■■■■■■■

1 • Explain the task, work through the examples with the class, then ask students to make individual lists of activities. Monitor carefully, correcting where necessary.
• Once students have their lists, get them to work in pairs. Help them to phrase Past perfect questions, again correcting any errors you hear.
• Finally, pairs should try to agree on a few of the most interesting or unusual experiences they have been talking about. These could be retold to the whole class.

2 • Check that students understand the task, then elicit a few more possible explanations for the example situation.
• Students work through situations **a–f** writing answers, then comparing their ideas in pairs.
• Monitor and correct.
• Check answers.

Possible answers

• These answers could begin with any of these subjects: *Someone, Somebody, People, They.*
a Someone had broken into the office. They had had to force / break the lock.
b People had been having a party. They'd been drinking red wine.
c Someone had been eating sandwiches.
d They'd been playing football. They'd broken a window.
e Someone had been opening and reading other people's letters.
f Someone had been looking for (secret) information.

3 This is a more open-ended activity which requires students to use their imagination to explain the situations described.
• Check they understand the task and suggest they think of a real person when they are making up their explanations.
• Students can work individually or in pairs.
• Elicit a few ideas to finish the activity.

4 The strict definition of a mini-saga makes this activity fun, but also acts as a limitation which gives students a reason to write carefully and accurately.

- Check that students understand the idea of a mini-saga and read through the example with them.
- Set the task. Students could work individually or in pairs to write their mini-saga.
- Monitor, help, and correct.
- You could finish the activity by displaying the mini-sagas in the classroom.

Additional activities

- If students need more practice of the form of the Past perfect simple, try this game.
- Working in groups of four or five, students take turns to add to a list of imaginary household jobs they had done by a certain time yesterday.
  Example
  A *By midday, I'd cleaned the floor.*
  B *By midday, I'd cleaned the floor and done the shopping.*
  C *By midday, I'd cleaned the floor, done the shopping, and fed the cat.* If anyone forgets one of the jobs, they are out of the game. The rest continue until one student is left.
- Here are some variations on the same idea. Instead of household jobs, you could ask students to talk about:
  – office jobs
  By 5 o'clock yesterday afternoon, I'd written a report, arranged a meeting with my boss, dictated six letters, etc.
  – holiday activities
  We arrived on Saturday. By Tuesday afternoon, we'd swum in the sea, visited six islands, taken photographs of the castle, played volleyball, etc.

— p. 18 —

Reading

The text, *My single ticket to freedom*, is based on an autobiographical account of a young woman leaving home. The author is the well-known author, lecturer, and feminist, Germaine Greer, who first came to public attention in 1970 with her book *The Female Eunuch*.

1 • Students discuss the question in pairs for two or three minutes.
- You could elicit one or two of their memories, or move straight on to the first reading task.

2 • Explain the first reading task.
- You may wish to teach these phrases before students read the text: *be entitled to housing* (have the right to free or subsidized public accommodation), *be eligible for the dole* (have the right to receive state unemployment benefit).
- Students read the first paragraph only.
- Check answers to questions **a** and **b**.

Answers

a The writer left home. She went by train.
b Words and phrases
the happiest day of my life, l.1; *the brightest afternoon I had ever lived*, l.3; *I sang...*, l.5; *I feel the warm afterglow of that afternoon*, l.6.

3 • Allow students four to five minutes to read the rest of the text and underline words or expressions which show whether or not she was happy. (They will get other opportunities to read the text more carefully and look more closely at the language used.)
- Check their ideas.

Answers

The general answer is *Yes, she did remain happy.* Here are some of the phrases which suggest this:
l.21 *it was perfect*
l.34 *I was living in a shed and I liked it fine.*
l.37 *If I'd been gathered up and forced to return to my parents' clean, warm house, I would have gone berserk, beaten up my warders, and thrown myself under a truck. I needed that space just as it was.*
l.50 *It was certainly better for me.*

- At this stage you could ask students how they react personally to this story.

Note Do not spend too long on this discussion – there are other opportunities for more considered personal reactions to the text.

■ Close up

- Allow students time to work through the questions individually or in pairs.
- Check answers.

Answers

- l.3 *I had no baggage **but** a briefcase, and nothing in it **but** a night-shirt. but* here is used as a preposition and means *except* or *apart from.* This meaning is commonly used in expressions like these: *nobody but you / nothing but the best / anything but that.*
- l.11 to *keep something under your hat* means to keep something secret.
- l.13 *house-sit* means to stay in a house and look after it while the owners are away. It is obviously related to or derived from *baby-sit.* These activities are *house-sitting* and *baby-sitting* and the people who do them are *house-sitters* and *baby-sitters.*
- l.33 *let alone* means *without considering.* Another example *There isn't enough room for us, **let alone** a dog.*

■ Interpretation p. 19 ■

1–4 Students work individually or in pairs. They may need to use dictionaries to understand the full meaning of some of the words.

- Elicit ideas.

Suggested answers

1 The opposite of a *single* ticket is a **return** ticket. She has bought a *single* ticket because she is not planning to return home.

2 – *to dump* means to throw away, to leave, or abandon. It suggests that what is *dumped* has no value and is not wanted.
 – *unceremoniously* means *roughly, rudely, or without consideration*.
 The whole expression suggests that whoever did the *dumping* considered the writer and her belongings to be worthless.

3 The fact that her new home was *freezing* and *insecure* emphasises how different it is from the warm, suffocating atmosphere of her parents house. It is *perfect* because she is now independent and she has chosen to live in these conditions.

4 *Dozens of people* suggests a number of possibilities:
 – she was popular and had lots of friends
 – lots of people came to visit the writer in her home
 – like her, lots of people she knew didn't have much money
 – the people who came to visit her probably shared her ideas about living independently of their parents.

Speaking personally

1–4 Students now discuss their ideas about the article in detail.

- Students think about whether they agree or disagree with each statement before discussing their ideas in pairs or small groups.
- Finish off with a short, whole-class discussion. Is there a general consensus in the class on any of these questions?
- You could extend their discussion with these questions:
  What does freedom mean to you?
  How far would you go to find personal freedom?

Grammar – used to, would

Exploring concepts

It is almost certain that students will be familiar with *used to* to refer to past habits, but they may not have come across *would* with a similar use.

- Remind students that they can refer to the **Language Commentary** on p.125.

1–2 Students work through the two tasks independently or in pairs. Monitor the discussions and give help if necessary.

- Briefly check through answers with the class. Don't spend too much time on this but check that students have understood the main grammar points.

Answers

1 These verbs should be underlined in sentences **a–g**.
a *walked*	**e** *they'd burn*
b *would keep, was*	**f** *used to drink*
c *found*	**g** *used to suffer*
d *used to burn*	

2 a Past habits or typical behaviour are referred to by all the extracts with *used to* or *would*: (b, d, e, f, g).
 b The only single past actions are: *walked* (a), and *found* (c).

 Note In *I was at university*, **was** refers to a past state.

3 The distinction between *used to* and *would* introduced in this section may not be known to your students.

- Let them work through the questions **3a** and **b** for themselves to start with, but be prepared to answer any questions they may have.

Answers

3 a *Used to* can be used for states as well as actions, but *would* cannot. Sentence 2: *I would have long hair* is not possible.
 b *Used to* suggests that the past habit no longer takes place. Sentence 1 suggests that the speaker no longer smokes.

Pronunciation

4 a Ask students to work in pairs or elicit ideas from the class.
 b **2.4** Students listen and check.

2.4

1 I used to (juːstə) go out more.
2 I used to (juːstuː) eat meat.
3 No, but I used to (juːstuː).
4 Yes, but I didn't use to (juːstuː).

Answers

a See tapescript **2.4**.
b *Used to* is pronounced
- /juːstə/ before consonants
- /juːstuː/ before vowels and when it occurs at the end.
The final consonant of *used* is never pronounced.

Exploitation

Although this is intended primarily to be an oral activity, you could give students time to think and make notes about the aspects of life in the past specified.

1 • Elicit an example for each topic before students continue talking in pairs or groups.
- Monitor and correct.
- Encourage them to add their own ideas.
- Do a brief whole-class feedback on some of their ideas.

2 This is a writing follow-up to the last speaking activity. It may be done in class or set for homework.
- Check that students understand the task, and set a word limit of 100 words.
- Students could exchange work and suggest improvements or additions to their partner's writing.

3 This is a personalised activity to practise *used to* and *would*.
- Elicit a few examples from the class, then let students continue in pairs.
- Monitor and correct.
- You could do whole-class feedback if necessary.

Free speech

4 • This is fluency activity, so monitor, but do not correct students' discussions.
- Give students time to think of their ideas individually before they begin the discussion.

▶ **Photocopiable activity 2 p.159**

Collocations

Collocations were introduced in the Vocabulary section of Unit 1, so you could start by checking that the class remembers what they are.

Explain that sometimes there is a logical reason for the pairing of words, as in example **a** *burst* is used in other contexts referring to a sudden break resulting in a leak of something (e.g. air or water). In many cases, however, there is no obvious explanation, as in sentence **b**.

■ Verbs and nouns

1 • Let students work through the list, matching the verbs with appropriate nouns.
 • Check answers.

Answers

answer the door / the telephone	*play the piano*
do the housework	*suffer from an illness*
lock the door	*take medicine*
make a loss	*tell a lie*
(this is the opposite of to make a profit.)	*watch television*

Additional activity

• You could find out how many other nouns students can think of that collocate with these verbs.

Verb	Examples
lock	*a car, a case, a bicycle, a house*
tell	*the truth, the time, the difference* (between two things)
watch	*a film, the clock, your step* (to be careful)

2 This mini-discussion activity allows students to practise these collocations.
 • Explain the task and elicit a few possible answers to **a** to demonstrate. Encourage students to use full answers.
 • Set a time limit of two minutes for each topic.
 • Monitor and correct.

3 One of the commonest collocation problems in English involves the choice between *make* and *do*.
 • Explain the task.
 • Check answers.

Answers

do *aerobics, your best, the cooking*, a crossword, an exercise / exercise*, someone a favour, your homework, research, a subject at school, the shopping**

Note

1 *an exercise* (countable) normally refers to a single activity, as in *The first exercise in the book was really difficult*; *exercise* (uncountable) refers to use of the body or mind that involves effort, as in *The doctor said I should do more exercise.*

2 All *the … … -ing* expressions which refer to jobs or activities collocate with *do*. More examples include: *do the washing, the ironing, the cleaning*, etc.

make *a complaint, a decision, an effort, an excuse, friends, living, a mistake, money, a noise, notes*

4 • Students make word webs with *answer, play,* and *take*.
 • Set a time limit and then compare as a whole class.

Possible answers

answer	the door	a letter
	a question	the teacher
	an advertisement	the invitation
play	an instrument	a joke
	a game	a trick on someone
	a part (in a film)	
take	a photograph	advice
	time to do something	medicine
	the blame	part in something

■ Adjectives and nouns

1 • Explain the task and let students work through the list, matching the nouns with appropriate adjectives.
 • Check students understand that the adjectives have different meanings when they collocate with different nouns, but don't go into detail on the different meanings at this stage.
 • Check answers.

Answers

A	B	
bare	facts	simple
	feet	no shoes
	room	empty, with no furniture
	walls	without decoration
bitter	beer	taste of typical English beer
	chocolate	dark, not milk
	feelings	resentful
	person	with resentful feelings
	taste	sharp
	wind	very cold
hard	bed	uncomfortable
	exercise	tiring or difficult
	facts	strongly expressed, to the point
	feelings	bearing a grudge
	person	cold, unfeeling, not emotional
rich	chocolate sauce	
	taste	having a sickly taste, because it has a lot of sugar, cream, eggs, etc.
	country, person, town	having a lot of money
single	bed	for one person
	person	unmarried
ticket	single	in one direction (not return)
strong	beer	
	feelings	
	person	not weak
	taste	
	wine	
wind	strong	not light
sweet	potato	yam
	sauce	
	taste	sugary, not sour
	wine	not dry

2–3 Elicit answers to **a** *a hard exercise*, then ask students to continue through the rest of the exercise and question 3.
 • Check answers.

Answers

		Meaning	Opposite
a	*hard exercise*	difficult	easy
	hard bed	solid	soft
b	*rich person*	with a lot of money	poor
	rich sauce	containing a lot of butter, sugar, eggs, etc.	plain, simple
c	*single person*	unmarried	married
	single room	for one person	double
	single ticket	one way	return
d	*strong coffee*	with a lot of taste	weak
	strong wind	with a lot of force	light
e	*sweet apple*	tasting like sugar	sour
	sweet wine	tasting like sugar	dry

■ Verbs and adverbs

1 This is a fairly open-ended exercise, as there are many possible answers.
- Read the example and elicit students' suggestions for the second adverb in the list, *dangerously*, then ask them to continue.
- Monitor, giving help and correcting.
- Check answers.

Answers

dangerously	drive, live, play (a game)
honestly	speak, write, live
loudly	talk, snore, play (music)
neatly	write, work, dress
quickly	walk, think, move
seriously	talk, think, work
simply	live, write, dress
slowly	drive, walk, move, speak, talk, work

2 This is an open-ended, free practice exercise which gives students the chance to use some of the collocations they have come across in this section.
- Students work in groups, each student talking about a subject for twenty seconds before the next student takes over. Each student in the group should talk only once about each subject.
- Monitor conversations, but do not interrupt.

Additional activity
- You could develop this exercise further by organizing a mini debate. Some possible subjects:
  – Single beds are more comfortable than double beds.
  – Rich people are more unhappy than poor people.
  – Driving dangerously is more exciting than driving carefully.
  – It's better to play sport than watch it on TV.

Language in action

■ Eavesdrop! p. 21 ■

The questions could be done as a whole-class activity or as pairwork. Students listen, check their ideas, and find the answers to the additional questions.

- Direct attention to the picture and the three questions.
- Remind students that there are no right or wrong answers to these questions. They are interpreting what they see and should come up with a number of different possible answers.
- Elicit possible answers but don't confirm or deny them at this stage as students will check their guesses in *Listening* 1.

■ Listening 1

1
- Draw attention to questions **a** and **b**.
- **2.5** Students listen to check their *Eavesdrop!* ideas and think about answers to **a** and **b**.

2.5

A Well, that's everybody. What do you reckon?
J Personally, I wouldn't even consider Jackie or Rachel – they just wouldn't fit in, but I quite like the look of Christina and I'd say Robin sounds OK from his letter.
A Charlie?
C It's difficult to say. Several of them sound OK from their letters.
J So, you're not keen on Christina or Robin?
C I didn't say that.
A So, what do you think?
C I don't have any very strong feelings, really.
J But we've got to decide this together. There's no point in one of us being unhappy – I mean we'll probably have to live with our choice for the next six months at least.
A How do you feel about having another man about the place, Charlie?
C I don't really mind. I wouldn't be jealous if that's what you're getting at.
J Come on, Charlie – no one's suggesting that. We just want your opinion, that's all. It's difficult enough deciding who to interview. We need all the ideas we can get.
C But it's not up to me to decide, is it?
J Why not?
C Well, it was you two who found this place originally, wasn't it? It's up to you.
A Look, Charlie, you've been here for over a year now, you and Jo have been going out together for half that time and you pay a third of the rent. It's your decision just as much as it is ours.
J Well, if you ask me, I think we should talk to Christina, Robin, and possibly Ed.

- Allow students time to discuss their ideas in pairs, then elicit their answers to questions **a** and **b**.

Possible answers
Eavesdrop!
- student's, friends, people who share a flat or house, members of a family
- in students accomodation, at one of their homes, in their shared flat
- a holiday, someone they all know, their plans for the future

Listing 1

a Three people who share a house or flat. The two girls found the place originally but Charlie, who is Jo's boyfriend, has been living there for a year and pays his share of the rent. They are discussing finding a fourth person to share the flat / house with them. They are trying to decide which of the applicants they should interview.

b Charlie is unwilling to express an opinion. This is because he feels less important than Jo and Amy. He did not originally find the flat.

2 • Students now listen and note down the functional language used by the three speakers.

• Check that students know what to do by eliciting a few examples of each type of language they are listening for.

• Allocate tasks, and play the recording again, once or twice as necessary.

• Students note down the expressions and then compile lists. They help and correct each other at this stage.

Note Students add to these lists during the next listening task.

Answers
See full list of expressions after *Listening 2*, question 2.

▮ Listening 2 ▮

1 • Ask students to read through the questions.

• **2.6** Play the recording, pausing after the first conversation to elicit answers.

2.6 including **2.7**

Conversation 1

B Well, how much money have we got?

J What is it?

T **2.7** About seventy quid, wasn't it?

J Is it? Have you any ideas, Roger?

R No, nothing, no, nothing springs to mind, no.

T I think we ought to get a picture or a print, something, you know, something she can actually put on the wall – it'll be there to remember us by.

B Well, she's keen on art. I mean she went to that art course this, this year, so …

T That would work, yeah. What sort of things does she like, then?

B Well, I don't know. It'd be nice to get something original, but I don't know if we've got enough money for that.

T No, seventy quid's not much for an original, is it?

R No, it's not much for that.

J I suppose so. Might be able to get a nice piece of pottery, though, or glass, or something like that.

T Yeah, there's quite a good place down, is it down the end of … the High Street somewhere …?

J That's right, that's right, they're lovely.

T … that's very often got some stuff there.

B She's got quite a lot of pottery already, I mean …

T Oh, has she?

B Well, she's … it's quite a small house – a bit limited space really.

J Roger, come on, what do you think?

R No, I can't really think.

B You know her well, you know her well, I mean.

R I really don't have any strong ideas on it, I mean … I don't think pottery or glass, as you say, she's got a lot already.

B … Well, why don't we have a … ? Why don't we … ? Why don't two of us go down and have a look at that shop that you were mentioning … ?

J That's a good idea.

B … and just what there is.

T That the Gallery?

B Yeah.

T Yeah, all right.

B We could come back and report and see what there is, but I mean … Roger are you going to come down?

J Oh come on!

T Yeah, come on down …

R No, really, really, I'll leave it up to you, honestly. I don't, I really don't have any strong ideas, I mean I'll go along with what you, what you decide.

J But you made a big contribution, Roger. You know you should.

R No, I'll go along with what you decide.

Conversation 2

B What do you suggest, then?

J Well, I think we should go round, look at a lot of places – something of interest, something sort of … that will er, um, educate you.

B Like what, for example?

J Well, bit of um, historical sightseeing er … maybe somewhere like erm, Cambridge or a … to a nice er … castle somewhere.

K Oh … I …

B Oh, I don't know – sounds like hard work, all that walking around and things – I'd rather something a bit more rela … relaxing. Erm …

J Well, … I'd, well … I don't really like the idea of that very much – not really.

K What, going to the health farm?

J **2.7** No, no. I think if you want something relaxing, perhaps we ought to do something a bit more active, but relaxing.

B Yeah, but with the health club you can do both, I mean you can do exercises in the gym, you can do aerobics, or you can do swimming, or you can just lounge around and do nothing.

K Mmm, sounds all right.

B What do you think?

K Well, you know, it's … we're going away. I don't mind really where we go or what we do.

J Well, don't you think you might waste your weekend if you were just lazing around?

K Well, I don't know. It's difficult to say, I mean once we get there we might find that, you know, there's all sorts of things we could do.

B Well, in the end, I mean, I don't suppose I really mind, I mean, you know, whatever you two decide, I mean, if we can all decide … if two of us decide on something …

K Yeah, fine, that's OK with me.

J Well, how about … Well, I think perhaps then we ought to then choose a neutral erm … one that we all …

B Karen, can you suggest something?

K Well, I'm quite happy with any of these suggestions really, I mean the health, the health club, that sounds fine.

B Yeah, but Julie's not keen on that, so …

• Check answers.

Possible answers

	Conversation 1	Conversation 2
a	Two men, two women	Three women
b	Work colleagues	Friends
c	Buying a present for a colleague who is leaving	Deciding where to go away for the weekend

2 • **2.7** Play the recording, while students follow the extracts on p.22 of their books, marking the examples of the functional language.
• Students add the expressions to their lists.
• Check through the lists with students.

Answers
(This includes expressions from **Listenings 1** and **2**)
Asking for opinions
.5
What do you reckon?   So you're not keen on ....   So, what do you think?   How do you feel about ...?
.7 Extract 1
Have you any ideas ...?   What do you think ...?
.7 Extract 2
What do you think?   Well, don't you think ... (you might waste your weekend)?   Can you suggest something ...
(From full conversation
What do you suggest, then ...?)
Expressing opinions
.5
Personally ...   I'd say ...   Well, if you ask me, I think ...
.7 Extract 1
I think we ought to...
.7 Extract 2
I think we should ...   perhaps we ought to do something ... Yeah, fine, that's OK with me.   Well, I think perhaps then we ought to ...
Avoiding expressing an opinion
.5
It's difficult to say.   I didn't say that.   I don't have any very strong feelings, ...   I don't really mind.   But it's not up to me to decide, ...
.7 Extract 1
No, nothing springs to mind ...   No, I can't really think. I really don't have any strong ideas on it ...
(From full conversation
I mean, I'll go along with what you decide.)
.7 Extract 2
I don't mind really ....   Well I don't know.   I don't suppose I really mind, ...

© Oxford University Press **PHOTOCOPIABLE**

■ **Features of natural conversation** ▬▬▬▬ p. 22 ■

Vague language

Vague language is a term for words and phrases which help people to avoid being too precise. It is common in everyday speech. Vague language may be used because speakers cannot or do not want to be exact. In the past *vague language* was often thought to be lazy or sloppy language used because speakers could not be bothered to be more precise.
• Read through the definition of *vague language* with the class and go through the list of reasons why people use it. Point out that when we hear people using *vague language* we cannot usually tell their real reason for using it.
• Students look at the highlighted examples of *vague language* in the two extracts. They should think about two things for each word or phrase: *What could this mean? Why is the speaker being vague?*

• Go through the example with students to demonstrate. *About seventy quid* could be either £69 or £72 as both amounts are close to £70.
• Check students' answers and ideas.

Note If you not wish to spend too long on this activity, do it as a whole-class oral activity and focus on the first extract only.

Answers
Extract 1

Word/phrase	Possible meaning	Reason for use
something original	work of art print, picture, etc.	the thing is less important than its originality.
might * be able to get	it's possible	speaker not sure, doesn't know.
something like that	a decorative, artistic, handmade object	speaker has given two examples of the type of present he is thinking of.
the end of the High Street *somewhere*	on the left or the right the last shop, next to the last shop?	the speaker doesn't know precisely where the shop is. It is not very important.
some *stuff* there	glass, pottery, and similar pieces	the speaker doesn't know exactly what the shop has.
quite a lot of pottery	a significant amount (for an ordinary house.)	the exact amount doesn't matter. Maybe 10 or 20 pieces – it seems a lot in this house.
quite a small house	not very small – but not large	the exact size is not important.

Extract 2

something relaxing, a bit more active, etc.	a type of activity or weekend break	at this stage in the conversation the friends are trying to get general agreement.
all sorts of *things we could do*	activities, sports, entertainment	the speaker is talking generally and cannot be specific.
perhaps we ought to choose	this is a gentle way of making a suggestion	the speaker doesn't want to give too strong an opinion.

Note Modal verbs used to express uncertainty or possibility can be defined as vague language.

■ **Practice** ▬▬▬▬▬▬▬▬▬▬▬▬▬▬

1 • **2.8** Play the recording. Stop after each expression and drill chorally and individually.
• Ask students to identify the syllable in each expression which carries the main stress. Check answers as you go along.

2.8

a What do you think?
b How do you feel about it?
c Have you any ideas?
d What do you reckon?
e Don't you think we should discuss it?

Answers

See tapescript **2.8** for stress.

Note There are other possibilities depending on the context.

2 a Students spend a few minutes in pairs saying the expressions and deciding which syllable carries the main stress.

Note In sentences 2 and 6 there are two main stresses.

b **2.9** Students listen and check.

2.9

1 I'd say it's a good idea.
2 If you ask me, I think it's fantastic.
3 I don't really mind.
4 I don't have any very strong feelings.
5 I think we ought to stay in.
6 It's not up to me to decide, is it?
7 I don't think we should.

Answers

See tapescript **2.9** for stress.

Note Depending on the context, there are other possible variations. Use your own judgement if students' answers are different from these.

■ Exploitation

This section gives students a chance to use the functional language introduced in the recordings and the pronunciation points they have just practised.

- Students should read both situations and choose one.
- Divide the class into groups. Explain that one member of each group should be unwilling to express opinions, and that others should try to persuade them to say what they think.
- In both situations, it is important that groups decide on the kind of person they are looking for **before** reading about the four candidates. The people in the photographs relate to both situations, although some details are more relevant to one situation than the other.
- Monitor their conversations. Make a note of errors in their use of functional language, but do not interrupt. Feedback on these errors at a later stage.
- You could finish the activity with a brief feedback session to find out which of the four people had been chosen for the two situations. Students should give reasons for their choices.

■ Writing ■■■■■■■■■■■■■■■■■■ p. 23 ■

1 • Read through the opening rubric with the class to check that they understand the task.

a Students compare the conversation extract and the semi-formal spoken language (the talk) and discuss the similarities and differences in pairs.

- Elicit their ideas.

Possible answers
Similarities
- both speakers express personal opinions
- both use contracted verb forms
- both use *vague language*
Differences
- The semi-formal spoken language uses longer, more formally constructed sentences.
- The semi-formal spoken language uses more formal expressions of opinion (see below).

b–c Students read the notes on which the talk was based. They should look for the language that has been added to the bare notes to produce the talk.

- Elicit their ideas.

Answers
- Opinion language has been added:
  My own view is … It seems to me … I don't think, In my opinion … I feel sure … I must say … From my point of view … as far as I can tell …
- Verbs and articles have been added.
- Some expressions have been expanded:
  little experience of sharing – hardly any experience of living with other people.

2 The two situations relate directly to the Situations on p.22.
- Remind students to refer to the **Writing guidelines** on p.155 of their books.
- Refer them back to the situations and get them to choose one. Tell students to keep their notes factual and brief.
- Set the note-writing activity, monitor and give help where necessary.

3 • Students now work with someone who chose the other situation and use their notes to explain their situation and give their opinion.
- Monitor these conversations, listening for the use of the more formal expressions of opinion.

■ Summary ■■■■■■■■■■■■■■■■■■■■■■■■■■

- Encourage students to use the tick boxes to help them keep a record of their learning.

3 It'll never happen

Theme

The thread running through this unit is time.
Preview 1890 and 1990 predictions compared
Listening The short and long term future
Reading Time-bandits and attitudes to time

Grammar

- *will, going to* (LC p.126)
- Future continuous and Future perfect (LC p.126)
- The language of contrast: *but, however, although* (LC p.126)

Vocabulary

- Adjectives to describe feelings
- Using a dictionary

Functional language

- Asking for and giving reasons

Conversation strategies

- Changing the subject of conversations

Features of natural conversation

- Repetition of words or phrases (sometimes with changes)

Pronunciation

- *going to / will have*
- Sentence stress
- Sounding angry, frustrated, sympathetic, surprised

Writing

- Letters and notes of explanation (WG p.155)

Workbook

- The effects of global warming
- Topic vocabulary: the environment; *bring* + particle; Word-building
- Futures review; *will, will* and *going to*; Future continuous and Future perfect; The language of contrast
- Topic sentences; Describing a holiday resort

Preview

The first theme of the unit is visions of the future – and presents examples of *will* future and *going to* in context.

Your thoughts ▬▬▬▬▬▬▬▬▬▬▬▬▬▬▬▬▬ p. 24 ■

1 • Give students time to look at the illustrations on the left of the Student's Book showing how past generations saw the future. In pairs, or as a whole class, students discuss how accurate these predictions were.
  • Elicit their ideas.

Possible answers
- Aerotaxis in Paris – Obviously science hasn't quite caught up with this idea, although it is possible to fly by helicopter into the centres of big cities.
- Multi-storey car park – This is very similar to many modern multi-storey car parks.
- 1950s house in a bubble – Many outdoor pursuits can now be done inside. Double glazing allows people in cold climates to live in warm indoor surroundings.

2 The illustrations and texts are present-day images of the short- and long-term future.
  • Give students time to look at the pictures and read the texts before they discuss what they see.
  • Students read the text about Marinopolis. Discuss the issues raised with questions like these:
    Is this a realistic idea?
    What kind of people would live in a floating city?
    What would life here be like?
  • Now move on to the text and image which predicts the long-term future of the planet and its inhabitants. Elicit students' reactions.
    What do you think of these ideas? How realistic are they?
    What other possible long-term predictions can you think of?

Note It is likely that students will use future verb forms in their discussions. Gauge how well students already know and can use *will* and *going to* forms. You can correct errors now if you wish, but there will be later opportunities for students to revise and practise these forms.

Reading ▬▬▬▬▬▬▬▬▬▬▬▬▬▬▬▬▬▬▬▬ p. 25 ■

1 • Students read the newspaper headline and the paragraph of text, then discuss the question in pairs.
  • Monitor discussions, listening for how well students use future forms, especially *will*.
  • Elicit a few ideas before moving on.

2 • Students read the *Futuropolis* text. Is this one of the ideas they came up with in their previous discussions?

• You could pre-teach these words before students read the text: *cavern*, *shaft*, *gimmick*.

3 • Students discuss the questions about life in Geotropolis.

• Monitor their conversations, but do not interrupt. This is mainly a fluency activity.

• Elicit their ideas.

Possible answers

a *In general it will be claustrophobic and may be rather stressful. On the other hand, it may be less crowded than conventional cities because its population may be limited by the authorities.*

b Personal reactions from students.

c • *health problems – illnesses may spread quickly*
• *stress may cause antisocial behaviour or even crime*
• *people may feel alienated and alone*
• *people may suffer from lack of natural light and may not get enough exercise.*

■ Person to person

1–2 Students discuss these ideas in pairs.

• Elicit a few ideas from the class and finish this part of the unit with a discussion of how students see the future.

— Grammar – Futures review, *will*, *going to*

• Students work through questions 1–3 individually or in pairs.

• Allow them to work straight through, referring when necessary to the **Language Commentary** on p.126, or impose time limits and check after each of the questions.

• Monitor, giving help where necessary.

• Check answers.

Answers

1 a *will* indicates that these are simple predictions or expectations.
b *going to* is used to make a prediction based on present evidence.
2 a *will* is used to refer to a future fact or certainty.
b *will* is used to make an offer, or a spontaneous decision.
3 The other main use of *going to* is for future intentions or plans.

■ Check

4 • Students work through a–e individually, then compare answers with a partner.

• Check answers and the reasons for students' choice if helpful.

Answers

a	*I'm going to*	a prediction based on present evidence – the speaker knows they are tired
b	*I'm going to*	the speaker is stating an intention or plan
c	*You'll*	a simple prediction
d	*It'll*	a future fact or certainty
e	*I'll*	an offer

■ Pronunciation

5 a Students discuss ideas in pairs.
b **3.1** Students listen to check their ideas.

3.1

1 Polls suggest that the President is going to (/ɡaʊɪŋ tə/) win the next election by a wide margin.
2 I don't know what I'm going to (/ɡənə/) do, Fran, I really don't.

c Play the recording again. Students listen and repeat.

Answers
See tapescript **3.1**.

Note The use of *gonna* /ɡənə/ is very informal.

— p. 26 —

Listening

1 • In this recording students hear the reactions of two people (David and Tanya) to what they hear in a programme about the future. Make sure students understand this before they hear the recording.

• Elicit ideas about what the experts will say about some or all of the topics listed.

• If students are working individually or in pairs, they should note down their ideas. If you are eliciting ideas from the class, write them up on the board.

• You may wish to teach these words before students listen to the recording: *a visionary* (someone who can imagine what the future will be like), *science fiction* (type of writing based on imaginary or invented views of the future / world).

2 • Tell students to listen for their predictions and for the threat that is mentioned.

• **3.2** Play the recording for the first time.

3.2

T Look, there's a really interesting programme on tonight – it's called *Visionaries* – it's about the future.
D What time's it on?
T Eight-thirty – oh, it's just started. I'll switch it on.
'… then the most important natural threat we should be concerned about is asteroids or comets. In the next 100 years there's a one in a thousand chance of a kilometre-sized object hitting the Earth. The effect would be devastating – probably half the population would die.'
D Half the population?
T Yeah, that's incredible, but I definitely won't be worrying about comets in a hundred years' time.
D I wouldn't be so sure. Some scientists are predicting that we'll all be living to the age of 130 or more.
T Oh, that's scary.
'… even more exciting than that, we'll start seeing intelligence in computers – not the kind of intelligence people claimed for *Deep Blue* when it became the world chess champion. No, I mean genuine intelligence. By about the year 2200 humans will almost certainly have merged with computers, though I have to say I don't like the idea much. In fact it'll be very embarrassing, because it means we won't be the most intelligent beings on the planet …'

T What does he mean 'we'll have merged with computers?'. That sounds terrifying!

D I don't know – it sounds like science fiction to me.

T Perhaps he means we'll be spending more and more of our time working on computers – you know, we'll be more dependent on them.

D I'm not so sure – it doesn't sound as simple as that. You know, like nowadays people have pacemakers fitted to control their heartbeat – well, maybe in a hundred years' time, we'll all have been fitted with other kinds of devices, like those virtual reality helmets you wear on your head.

T You mean like some kind of brain implant. So we'll all be walking around with computer chips in our brains – telling us what to do.

D Yeah, and what to think.

T That sounds horrendous.
'The impact of information technology means enormous change. In the fairly short-term, half of the entire workforce will be working from home, for at least part of their time. It also means that there will be massive unemployment, and so fewer people will be paying tax. It is my estimate that by the year 2100 nations as we now know them will have broken up and been replaced by smaller economic units – regions, states possibly, or even independent large cities. I see no reason, for instance, why London should not become independent.'

D Incredible – I don't believe any of it.

T It's too frightening even to think about.
'This means, of course, that there'll be first- and second-class citizens. The identity card of the future will be a credit card, and the better your credit, the higher up the citizen ladder you will be.'

D I haven't even got a credit card so where does that leave me, I wonder?

T Better off than me! I've got a credit card, but at the moment I'm nearly up to my limit.

D I've had enough of this – I'm turning it off.

- Check answers.

Answers
Main ideas mentioned by speakers
computers
intelligence will be developed in computers / humans will have merged with computers
employment
in the short term half the workforce will be working from home, for part of their time / massive unemployment
wealth and poverty
fewer people paying tax / nations will have broken up – smaller economic units
Threat mentioned
asteroids or comets. In the next 100 years there's a one in a thousand chance of a kilometre-sized object hitting the Earth.

Interpretation

a–d Students do this exercise in pairs or as a class activity.
- Elicit ideas.

Suggested answers
a The speaker means she'll be dead by then.
b Maybe human behaviour and body functions will be controlled or regulated by computer. David suggests something like a virtual reality helmet; Tanya thinks this might involve a brain implant.

c Throughout history human beings have been the highest form of life, more intelligent than any other species. Intelligent computers, ironically created by humans, may become more intelligent – this is embarrassing.
d Social status will be measured by financial stability or reliability. People with a bad credit record will be lower down the social scale than those with a good record.

Vocabulary

1 a Explain the task.
- Play the recording again and if necessary refer students to Tapescript **3.2** on p.142 of their books.
- Check answers.

Answers

incredible	that half the population could die if the Earth was hit by an asteroid
	that nation states will break up and be replaced
scary	the idea that humans might live to the age of 130
exciting	the scientist's view of intelligence in computers
embarrassing	humans being merged with computers
terrifying	humans being merged with computers
horrendous	having computer chips implanted in human brains
frightening	that nation states will break up and be replaced

- Get students to work through questions a–d in pairs.
- For **a**, suggest that they work out the answers for themselves, then check their ideas in a dictionary.
- Check answers to **a**.

Answers
a *frightening, scary, terrifying, horrendous*
b Personal answers.

b–d These questions allow students to re-use the words in a personalized way.
- Monitor their conversations but only interrupt if you hear a completely wrong use of one of the adjectives.
- Elicit one or two answers to each of the questions.

2 • Ask students how many different meanings of *like* they can think of.
- Students match a–d with 1–4.
- Check answers.

Answers
a 1, b 3, c 4, d 2 + 3 (or 2)

Speaking personally

1–3 Students work in pairs or groups through some or all of these discussion questions.
- Groups can report back on their conclusions.

Additional activity

Groups could list the advantages and disadvantages of living in an independent city. Get them to think of a city in their own country or a world city like Paris, London, or Tokyo.

▶ Photocopiable activity 3 p.160

Grammar – Future continuous and Future perfect

Exploring concepts

1–3 Students work through this section in the usual way.

- Remind students that they can refer to the **Language Commentary** on p.126.

Answers

1 a *won't be worrying*   **d** *we'll (all) be walking*
b *we'll be spending*   **e** *will be paying*
c *we'll (all) have been fitted*   **f** *will have broken up*

Extracts a, b, d, e – Future continuous
Extracts c, f – Future perfect

2 a In the first sentence oil will be in the process of running out in the year 2100. In the second sentence the process will take place in the year 2100.
b In the first sentence 2100 is the date by which the breaking up will be complete. In the second sentence 2100 is the year in which the breaking up will take place.
c In the first sentence 2100 is the date by which the breaking up will be complete. In the second sentence the breaking up process will be in progress during the year 2100.

Note The Future continuous and the Future perfect both use *will*. This means that both verb forms express future predictions or expectations.

3 a The Future continuous
b The Future perfect

4 • You could start by checking that students understand the words and phrases in the box.
- Allow time for students to decide on the correct position for the words and phrases in the two sentences.

Note This will be quite time-consuming, so you could begin with a couple of examples in class and set the rest for homework.
- Check answers.

Answers

I'll probably	
I'll definitely	be a millionaire.
He'll almost certainly	be running his own business.

Maybe	
It's possible that	
Perhaps	I'll be a millionaire.
I'm sure	he'll be running his own business.
I've no doubt	
It's (un)likely that	

Note the following alternative forms:
I'm (un)likely to be a millionaire.
He's (un)likely to be running his own business.

Pronunciation p. 27

5 a Students discuss ideas in pairs.
b **3.3** Students listen to check their ideas.

3.3

1 In the future, we'll (/wɪl/ or /wil/) all be (/bi/) working from home.
2 By 2100 the world as we know it will have (/wɪləv/) changed completely. War, however, won't have (/wəʊntəv/) disappeared.

Answers
See tapescript **3.3** .

Note *we'll* and *will* can sound the same in fast natural speech. The *h* of *have* is not normally pronounced when speaking quickly. When one word finishes with a consonant and the next word starts with a vowel, the words are run together. Consequently *will have* and *won't have* sound like one word rather than two.

c Students practise saying the sentences with a partner.

Exploitation

This exercise gives controlled practice of *will* for predictions. There is also practice of the Future perfect and continuous.

1 a Discuss the meaning and the implications of the newspaper headlines with the class. Make it clear that the headlines themselves are 'real reports in the future', not predictions about the future.
- Students decide individually when they think these events will take place. They can add their own dates, or decide whether the headlines will *ever* come true or not.
- Monitor carefully, correcting any mistakes.

b Read through the example with students.
- Students make Future perfect sentences for the three dates, saying what *will* and *won't have* happened, before comparing ideas in pairs.
- Monitor and correct.
- Elicit a few ideas from the class and discuss any differences of opinion.

Note If this becomes a full discussion, treat it as a fluency activity and do not interrupt the flow of the conversation with corrections.

c Read through the example with students.
- Students now speak and write sentences about the implications of three of the headlines, using Future continuous verbs.
- Monitor and correct.
- Elicit a few ideas from the class to finish the activity.

Additional activities

- Each student in the class thinks of a future headline and writes it on a small piece of paper. All the pieces of paper are displayed in the classroom and form the basis of new class discussions.
- Students choose a headline, either one listed or one they have made up, and then write a short newspaper story.

2 • Check that students understand this construction with *there*. Write these two sentences on the board:
Fewer people will be paying tax in the future.
There will be fewer people paying tax in the future.
- Give brief practice by reading out more examples and ask students to transform them into *There'll* constructions. Examples
  - *More young people will be going to university.*
    (*There will be more young people going to university.*)
  - *Fewer people will be going to work.*
    (*There will be fewer people going to work.*)

- Students could work in pairs. If they are from different countries they could each think about their own country, then compare ideas.
- Monitor and correct.
- Finish by eliciting a few ideas from the class.

3 This is a personalized practice activity – students think about their personal and professional future.
  a Work through the expressions listed, checking understanding.
  - Read through the example and elicit a few more ideas.
  - Students write down their own thoughts on the subject using the expressions.
  b Give them time to think about their partner before they make guesses or predictions.
  - Monitor and correct.
  - You could have a brief class discussion to see what things students think they *will* or *won't have* done.

■ Free speech

4 • Get students to write down on a small piece of paper one thing they would like to know about the future and one thing they would not like to know. They could be personal or about the world in general.
  - Collect all their ideas, mix them up, then select a few at random and use these with the whole class as discussion starters.
  - Students then form groups to discuss their ideas.
  - Monitor. Listen for students' use of the future verb forms, but do not interrupt.

— p. 28 —

Reading

This section looks at the subject of time, and the speed of modern life. The text considers the possibility of slowing down time. The language point contextualized is link words and phrases which are used to express contrast.

1 • Introduce the pre-reading questions. Question **a** requires students to think about their own lives, while **b** relates to the text.
  - You may wish to teach these words before students read the text: *a race, speed*.
  - Allow them to spend three or four minutes on this opening activity.
  - Elicit a few answers to the two questions.

Possible answers
a Students may mention:
  - travelling
  - communicating: phones, mobile phones, e-mail, faxes, Internet
  - working practices – especially computers
  - buying things by phone, credit cards
  - convenience foods which take little time to prepare – microwave cooking.

b Students will have their own ideas about what or who *Time-bandits* are. Elicit some of these but do not confirm or deny them. They will find out when they read the text. *Time-bandits* are people who steal time, i.e. they refuse to live at the modern pace of life. Text l.29–l.32 *Time-bandits committed to slowing down any part of their lives where blind action has replaced thought-out deeds.*

- You could find out students' attitudes to time and the speed of modern living. Is it something that they are aware of or worry about? Discuss these questions for a few minutes before moving on to the text.

2 • Ask students to read questions **a–c**.
  - Students check whether they were right about *Time-bandits*, the aspects of life mentioned, and the meaning of *Tempus*.
  - Set a strict time limit for students to scan the text for the answers to these first questions, say three or four minutes. (There will be a chance for detailed reading later.)
  - Check answers and ideas.

Answers
a *Time-bandits* – see answers to **1b**.
b Aspects of life mentioned in the text:
  leisure time (l.20), *travel* (l.35), *work* (l.37).
c Tempus is *'the society for the slowing down of time'* (l.11).

■ Close up

- Students work through the questions individually or in pairs.
- Check answers.

Answers
- l.14 + l.21 Here *ever* means *more and more* or *increasingly*. Possible rephrasings:
  The wheel of time is turning faster and faster,
  Leisure time is getting more and more packed / increasingly packed.
- l.24 *hot air* – pointless and unnecessary talk leading nowhere.
- l.31 *blind* here means without reason or thought. The opposite would be: *considered, well thought-out, logical, reasonable, rational*.
- l.52 *blurts* something *out* – they say something suddenly without thinking.

■ Interpretation ■ p. 29 ■

The aim of this exercise is to get students to think about the main message of this text. There is no definitive list of five correct words and phrases, but you should expect all students to include the word *time* in their list.

1 • Students read the text again to select their five key words and then compare their choices with a partner.
  - Monitor conversations between pairs, but do not interrupt.
  - Elicit a few answers – write the most commonly agreed five words and phrases on the board.

Possible answers
time, speed, to slow down, slowness, Tempus, Time-bandits

2 • This exercise gets students to relate some of the main ideas from the text to their own lives and experience.

a Students work individually, then compare ideas in pairs.

• Elicit students' suggestions.

b This question could be used for a brief class discussion.

Speaking personally

1 • Allow students time to read the ten points mentioned in the text and decide which of the ideas could relate to them personally.

• You may want to pre-teach the following words: *Bedouin* (nomadic tribe which wanders the Sahara Desert, or a member of this tribe), *monastery* (place where monks live), *to delegate* (to allocate responsibilities or jobs to someone in a lower position than yourself).

• Do a quick class survey to find out which of the pieces of advice are relevant to most students.

2a–b Students work in pairs or groups and discuss the questions.

• Monitor the discussions but do not interrupt.

c Elicit a few of the tips, write them on the board, and use them as the basis of a rounding-off discussion.

Grammar – The language of contrast:
but, however, although

1–3 Check that students understand the idea of contrast language by going through the example sentence with them. The contrast language is *not … but*; the contrasts here are between doing the 100m in a few seconds and taking an hour over it.

• Remind students that they can refer to the **Language Commentary** on p.126.

• If necessary, elicit their ideas for sentence **a**, before getting them to work independently.

• Monitor, giving help where necessary.

• Check answers.

Answers

1	**Language**	**Contrast between**
a	*rather than*	slowness and speed and patience and power
b	*not / in fact (quite the opposite)*	people obsessed with time and speeding it up and the German novelist Sten Nadolny
c	*however*	(two ideas of Nadolny): people want to slow down their lives and speed has its place.
d	*instead*	doing lots of things at once and doing one thing at a time

2 *not* could replace *rather than*

• Possible rephrasings:
Instead of doing lots of things at once, do one thing at a time and do it well.
Do one thing at a time and do it well *instead of* doing lots of things at once.

• *However* could start the sentence:
However, he is keen to point out that speed does have its place.

3 *but*
Nadolny believes in slowness **but** he insists that speed has its place.
however
Nadolny believes in slowness. **However,** he insists that speed has its place.
Nadolny believes in slowness. He insists, **however,** that speed has its place.
Nadolny believes in slowness. He insists that speed has its place, **however.**
although
Although Nadolny believes in slowness, he insists that speed has its place.
Although he believes in slowness, Nadolny insists that speed has its place.
Nadolny believes in slowness, **although** he insists that speed has its place.

Pronunciation

This exercise demonstrates the use of stress in English to indicate contrast.

4 • Before the students work on the sentences, work through the example sentence with them.

Note The example on the page is also included in the recording. You could use this first to demonstrate the idea of stress for contrast.

• Ask them which words in the sentence are the most important and which are being contrasted, these will be the ones that carry the main stress.

• If necessary, work through the sentences one by one, checking answers as you go.

b **3.4** Students listen and check their ideas.

Note Although other words will be stressed in the sentences, students are only asked to identify the most important stressed syllables.

3.4

Example The challenge is not to cover 100 m in the shortest time, but to cover it in one hour.

a Slowness rather than speed, patience rather than power, are the qualities needed to win the Calw challenge.

b Not all of us are obsessed with time in terms of increasing speed: in fact quite the opposite in the case of the German novelist Sten Nadolny.

c Nadolny believes that many people want to slow their lives down. He is keen to point out, however, that speed does have its place.

d Stop doing lots of things at once; instead, do one thing at a time and do it well.

Answers
See tapescript **3.4** for stress.

Exploitation

1 • Use sentence **a** as an example. Elicit as many different endings as possible from students, stressing the idea that what they add must be a contrast with the beginning.

• Students work individually through sentences **b f**, then compare their ideas with a partner. Together, pairs could think up one or two more endings for each beginning.

• Elicit sample answers from the class.

Possible answers

a *I can't afford one / the service is poor in our town.*
b *help me to get it right. / tell me what I'm doing wrong.*
c *they're very expensive. / I prefer to travel by car or train.*
d *I don't work as much as my best friend. / I'd retire tomorrow if I could.*
e *it's not particularly healthy. / I prefer traditional food.*
f *rich or famous. / to have a high-status job.*

- You could ask students to make up three more sentence beginnings. They then exchange these with their partner. Each student completes their partner's sentences.
- Monitor, helping and correcting as necessary.

■ Role play

2
- This activity based on Tip 5, should allow the natural use of contrast words and phrases. Do not force the use of the language.
- Check that students understand the task and allocate roles. If necessary, have a quick brainstorm to get suggestions for possible three-day breaks. Some ideas:
  Monastery / Watch a sporting event / A hotel in a remote country area / An educational workshop / Walking
- Suggest a time limit of five minutes per conversation.
- Monitor, but do not interrupt.
- Pairs take turns to be Student A.

▶ **Photocopiable activity 4 p.161**

Using a dictionary

The purpose of this page is to get students to think about the range of information their dictionaries contain and how they can exploit them fully.

■ Investigation   p. 30 ■

1a–b In pairs, students make lists of the information they can find out from a dictionary. An example is taken from the *Oxford Advanced Learner's Dictionary*, but students may use their own dictionaries (although small dictionaries do not contain the full range of information).
- Monitor students' conversations, helping where necessary. Don't spend time on abbreviations now, as there is a follow-up exercise on these.
c Allow students a few minutes to compare their lists with another pair.
- Check answers.

Answers

Dictionaries contain this information:
- spelling   (including alternatives or variations, e.g. American / British)
- different forms   for example of verb, *predict – predicted*
- pronunciation   sounds and stress *pri'dikt*
- part of speech   *v = verb / adj. = adjective*, etc.
- meanings   *to say in advance that something will happen.*

Note If there are different meanings, these are numbered.

- examples of the word   *She predicted that the election*
  in context   *result would be close.*
- related words   *predictable / predictability / predictably*
- notes on usage   *e.g. often derog. (this is a negative thing to say)*
- collocations, fixed   *(no example here)*
  phrases or idioms
  using the word
- synonyms and antonyms

Note Although dictionaries often contain more than this, these are the most important points for students to be aware of.

2
- Students work out the meanings of the two sets of abbreviations. They could do this individually or in pairs.
- Check answers.

Answers

a	1	*v*	verb
	2	*V.n*	verb + noun phrase
	3	*sth*	something
	4	inf	infinitive
	5	*adj*	adjective
	6	*derog*	derogatory insulting, critical
			If someone said you were *predictable* you could interpret this as *boring*.
	7	*n* [U]	uncountable noun
			The opposite of U is C countable.
	8	*adv*	adverb
b	1	*Brit*	British English. The main alternative is US American English.
	2	*def art*	definite article. The other is *indef* art.
	3	*infml*	informal. The opposite is *fml* formal.
	4	*sl* slang	very informal language, sometimes restricted to particular groups of people.
	5	*sing*	singular. The opposite is *pl* plural.

■ Practice

1–4 Students now work through the tasks using their dictionaries. It will be easier if students are all using the same dictionaries, but this may not be possible.
- Students work through exercises one at a time.
- Checking answers after each question.

Answers

1 a
- *predict* to say in advance that something will happen
- *foresee* to see or know that something is going to happen in the future
b
- *resident* person who lives or has a home in a place, not visitor
- *citizen* 1 person who has full rights as a member of a country
  2 person who lives in a town or city
c
- *extinct* no longer in existence: extinct is used to describe a species of plant or animals.
- *dead* not living: dead is used to describe individual living things.

2 Rhyming pairs

This gets students to practise using their dictionaries to check the pronunciation of words which contain *ough*.
The three rhyming pairs are:
- *tough / enough* **ough** /ʌf/
- *borough / thorough* **ough** /ʌrə/
- *ought / bought* **ough** /ɔːt/.

The other words are pronounced like this:
- *though* **ough** /əʊ/
- *bough* **ough** /aʊ/
- *through* **ough** /uː/
- *cough* **ough** /ɔːf/.

3 Stress patterns

a *device*   The others are stressed on the first syllable.
b *exciting*   The others are stressed on the first syllable.
c *technology*   The others are stressed on the third syllable.

Note Get students to practise saying these words with the correct stress pattern to emphasize that dictionaries can help your speaking.

4 Common meanings of *ring*

verb
1 phone – *I'll **ring** you tonight*
2 make a long clear sound – *the doorbell **rang** loudly*
3 make a bell sound – *they **ring** the church bells*

noun
1 band of (precious) metal worn on the finger – *wedding **ring***
2 circular band of any metal – *key **ring***
3 a circle – *to dance in a **ring***
4 group of people working together – *spy **ring***
5 enclosed space where people or animals perform – *circus **ring***
6 phone call – *Give me a **ring** later.*

▧ Different dictionaries ▧

These discussion points are intended to get students to think about the value of dictionaries and how they are best used.

1–5 Ask students to work individually, thinking of their own answers to the five questions.
- Either give students a few minutes to compare their ideas in pairs or groups, or move on to a whole class discussion of the questions.

Answers

1

	Advantages	Disadvantages
Monolingual dictionaries	• Give practice in reading comprehension • Avoid the dangers of literal translation	• Students may not understand • Students don't know what to look up E.g. they may only know a word in their own language
Bilingual dictionaries	• Students can find an English word by looking up a word in their own language • Students feel more confident because they understand the language of explanation	• Students may not choose the correct English word from those listed • Students may get the impression that there is a one-to-one correspondence between their language and English

2

Electronic dictionaries	• They are easy to carry around • They seem easy to use • They often do not include examples of words in context	• They do not include as much information as larger dictionaries • They often lack the full range of meanings

3 Electronic dictionaries are popular because:
  – they are easy and light to carry around
  – they work very quickly
  – you can hear the words (although pronunciation is not always reliable)
  – they can help if you don't have all the letters in a word.

4 • Many teachers prefer students to work out meanings from context.
  • Constant use may mean students spend too long checking the meaning of every word.
  • Students may look up words that are unimportant to overall meaning, individual words do not always help students to understand overall meaning.

5 Personal answers.

Language in action

▧ Eavesdrop! ▧ p. 31 ▧
- The questions could be done as a class activity or as pairwork.

1 • Ask students to look at the picture and answer the questions.
  • Remind students that there are no right or wrong answers to these questions. They are speculating about what they see and should try to come up with a variety of answers.

2 • Answers to this question will depend on how students interpreted the relationship between the two people in the picture.
  • They should look at the expressions of the man and the woman and try to imagine how they feel about each other.
  • You could check possible answers to 1 and 2 now or move straight on to *Listening 1.*

▧ Listening 1 ▧

1 • **3.5** Students listen to check their *Eavesdrop!* ideas and think about answers to **a** and **b**.

3.5

W So, Stuart, let's go over this again, shall we? Mr Johnson phoned you at three-thirty yesterday afternoon? Right?
M Yes.
W And what did you do?
M I took his telephone number.
W What did you say to him?
M I said someone would ring him back.
W And did they?
M Did they what?
W Did someone ring Mr Johnson back?
M I don't know.

W What I can't understand, Stuart, is why you told him someone would ring him back. Why didn't you deal with it then and there?

M Mainly because I didn't really know what he was talking about, I suppose.

W So why on earth didn't you pass him on to someone who could deal with his problem?

M Because I don't actually know who does what around here yet.

W Well, you should know by now – you've been here nearly a month.

M Sorry. It won't happen again.

W I hope not. Anyway, to get back to Mr Johnson. What exactly did he want?

M I'm not sure – I didn't ask him.

W Why not?

M Well, he didn't really give me a chance – that's why. He just kept saying it was a disgrace and that he'd had an account here for nearly forty years and it was the first time anything like this had happened and he wanted to speak to the manager.

W So why didn't you pass him on to me?

M I didn't want to bother you.

W OK, OK. Perhaps you could find out if anyone has phoned Mr Johnson back. On second thoughts, phone him back yourself.

M What, now?

W Yes, now!

W2 Sorry to interrupt, Mrs Harper, but a Mr Johnson has just rung to say that as no one's phoned him this morning he's taking his account elsewhere.

W Oh no! Well, I suppose it's not really surprising in view of …

M Shall I still phone Mr Johnson?

W Of course. Why not?

M I just thought that if he's taking his account …

W Phone him now! See what you can do!

M Right, OK. Oh yes, before I forget, Mrs Harper, I'm, er, I'm going to a party tonight. Would it be OK if I came in late tomorrow morning?

W No, it would not be OK. You're here on time or you can start looking for a new job. OK?

- Allow students time to discuss their answers in pairs.
- Check answers.

Possible answers
Eavesdrop!

1 • The two people are an employee and his boss / manager. The young man is the junior in this relationship.
- They are in a financial institution of some kind – possibly a bank. There is mention in the conversation of the customer having had *an account* with the company for a long time.
- They are discussing the way in which Stuart dealt with a long-standing customer.

2 The woman feels superior to the man / the man feels inferior.
The man dislikes the woman.
The woman is impatient with the man.
The man is fed with being criticized by the woman.
The man has respect for the woman.
The woman feels responsible for or motherly towards the man.

Listening 1

1 **a** The young man's attitude: he is apologetic but seems unprepared to take the blame (because of his lack of experience) for the problem with the customer, Mr Johnson. In addition, he seems rather insensitive. Even after having admitted to being responsible for the likely loss of a customer, Stuart still asks if he can come to work late the following morning because he is going to a party.
b This is a question of personal opinion. The two extremes would be:
- Give him the sack. / Fire him. / Ask him to leave.
- Give him extra training and treat him patiently.

2 • Students now listen again and note down the functional and conversational language used by the two speakers.
- Check that students understand the task, especially to change the subject.
- Allocate tasks and play the recording again, once or twice.
- Students note down the expressions and compile lists. They help and correct each other at this stage.

Note Students add to these lists during the next listening task.

Answers
See full list of expressions after *Listening 2*, question 2.

■ Listening 2

1 • **3.6** Ask students to read questions **a** and **b** and then play the recording.

Note There are no extracts in Unit 3. You need to play the full conversation again.

3.6

B Yeah, uh–huh …

T What on earth for?

B Well, I mean, the main reason is, I mean, on terrestrial television, you've just got five channels, erm, if you've got satellite, then you get about forty.

S But why d'you want more, more channels?

B Well, there's more choice, you know, you've got lots of films, you've got sport, lots of live sport.

T You'll never have, you'll never, never have the … all the time to watch all that TV.

B No, but, but you, I mean you've got more choice, so you can watch, you can choose what you want to see, I mean a lot, now a lot of the time there's nothing you want to see at a time you want to see it, there's much more choice. You can see films when they're out much more quickly, erm …

T Do you really think you're going to have the time to sit down and go through all the choices and do all the recordings and watch the recordings afterwards? Come on, you'll never make it.

B No, I mean a friend of mine's, a friend of mine's got it and he's really pleased with it, you know, and I've watched it and I think it's really good – it's not that expensive either.

T I don't understand why it's, you know, why it's so popular, why it's the thing to have. Four channels of terrestrial TV is fine.

B Well, five, Tony. Well, for the simple reason that it's, it just gives more choice, that's all. And I mean, I think it's really good for the sports, you know, because you can't get live sports now on a lot of, erm terrestrial television.

S There must be another reason than sport, though, because there … there's quite a lot of sport on television already.

B Well, yes, certain sports …

T Too much sport …

S Too much, yeah.

B It depends, you know, there are certain sports you, you can only get if you've got satellite …

S By the way, did you see the tennis yesterday?

T Tennis?

S Yeah.

T Yeah. Who won?

S Erm … Can't remember who won …

- Check answers.

Possible answers

a The speakers are talking about television. The woman has got, or is thinking of getting, satellite TV. The conversation is about the pros and cons of all the extra TV-watching choices that this provides.

b The two men cannot understand why the woman wants to have satellite TV. They seem to be ridiculing her. They don't believe she will have time to watch more TV programmes than she already does.

2 · Play the recording again, while students follow the conversation on p.32 in their books, marking the functional language used by the speakers.
· Students add the expressions to their lists.
· Check through the lists

Note Students will have a chance to practise some of this functional language as part of Pronunciation and in the Exploitation section.

Answers

(This includes expressions from *Listening 1* and *2*.)
Asking for reasons or explanations
3.5

What did you do?   What did you say to him?   What I can't understand, (Stuart), is why you told him …   Why didn't you …? (So) why on earth didn't you pass him on …?   Why not? (So) Why didn't you pass him on to me?

3.6 Extract
What on earth for?   But why d'you want more channels? I don't understand why it's so popular.   There must be another reason …

Giving reasons or explanations
3.5

Mainly because I didn't really know …   Because I don't actually know …   Well, he didn't really give me a chance – that's why.

3.6 Extract
The main reason is …   Well, for the simple reason that it's …

Changing the subject
3.5

Anyway, to get back to …   Oh yes, before I forget, …

3.6 Extract
By the way, did you see …

Note Using *anyway* is a clear indication that a speaker wants to change the subject. It can sometimes sound quite impolite if it is used to interrupt another speaker. It implies that you are not interested in what the speaker is saying.

© Oxford University Press **PHOTOCOPIABLE**

Features of natural conversation ▬▬▬ p. 32 ▬

This section focuses on the repetition and rephrasing of words or phrases in conversation. The aim is to draw attention to them rather than to get students to incorporate them into their use of language.
· Read through the introduction with the class. Make comparisons with what happens in students' own language(s) if this is appropriate.
· Play **3.6** again.
· Allow students a few minutes to compare ideas, then check their answers.

Suggested answers

· The speaker is making a case for having satellite TV. She thinks of two advantages over terrestrial TV: *lots of films* and *lots of sport*. She refines this to *lots of live sport*, because to her this is what the real advantage of satellite TV is.
· This is probably the way this speaker speaks. His repetition of *you'll never* and *never have* adds nothing to the meaning.
· The rephrasing of *watch* to **choose** to watch helps the speaker to be precise about the benefit to her of satellite. It allows *choice*.
· This repetition has no meaning. The speaker may be thinking of what to say next.
· The speaker doesn't know how to finish what he is saying, he is searching for words that he is happy with.

▬ Practice ▬▬▬▬▬▬▬▬▬▬▬▬▬▬▬

1 a **3.7** Play the recording without stopping. Ask students to write down how the speakers sound.

3.7

1 Why on earth are you here?
2 Why did you lie to me? There must be a reason.
3 Can you tell me exactly why you came?
4 What I don't understand is why you didn't phone.
5 Why didn't you tell me?

· Students compare answers.
· Play the recording again for students to check their ideas.

Answers

1 surprised   3 angry   5 sympathetic
2 frustrated   4 frustrated

· You could play the recording again and drill chorally and individually.
b Read the example with the students, and if necessary give a further example to demonstrate the task. Elicit possible explanations for the first question,
Why on earth are you here?
Mainly because … I wanted to see you again.
Well, you see … I thought you'd be upset.
· Students work together to create mini-dialogues.
c **3.8** Play the recording to hear some possible dialogues.

3.8

1 A Why on earth are you here?
  B Mainly because we had arranged to meet.
2 A Why did you lie to me? There must be a reason.
  B The main reason was I thought you'd be angry.
3 A Can you tell me exactly why you came?
  B For the simple reason that I wanted to see you again.
4 A What I don't understand is why you didn't phone.
  B The phone was broken. That's why!
5 A Why didn't you tell me?
  B Well, you see, I thought you'd be upset.

· You could play the tape again for choral and individual pronunciation practice. Students can also practise with a partner without the tape. Remind them that they should sound angry, surprised, etc.

2 · **3.9** Play the recording, pause after each expression and drill chorally and individually.

- Elicit the expressions used to change the subject.
- Students add the expressions to their lists.

3.9

1 **Oh, by the way,** I've invited John.
2 **Oh yes, I nearly forgot,** the meeting's been cancelled.
3 **Just to change the subject for a minute,** I saw Pete the other day.
4 **Going back to what you said** about David, I'm sure he wouldn't mind.
5 **Incidentally,** I'll be at a meeting all day tomorrow.

- Play the recording again. This time pause after each expression. Drill chorally and individually.

Exploitation

- Students should form groups of three for this role play.
- Check that they understand the two situations and the different roles, then ask them to choose a situation and decide on their roles. Point out that students **A** do not want to give the real reasons for their decisions – maybe they have secrets. It is for this reason that they want to change the subject of the conversation.
- Remind them to refer to their lists for *asking for and giving reasons* or *explanations and changing the subject* expressions.
- Monitor this preparation stage, giving help.
- When students have prepared, they can start the role play.
- Monitor conversations, listening for the correct use of the functional language. Do not interrupt conversations unless the language is completely incorrect.
- You may need to prompt student **A** to change the subject.
- If there is time students can repeat the role play, changing roles.

Writing   p. 33

This writing section follows a slightly different pattern to the one established in Units 1 and 2. Two different types of written explanation are focused on separately: formal letters and brief notes.

1 • Allow students time to read through the two examples, then elicit their ideas about the differences between the conversation and the formal letter.

Suggested answers
a The tone of the letter is very polite and quite formal, whereas the conversation is casual and very informal.
  - The writer uses full, not contracted verb forms.
  - The writer has to provide the context for the explanation, whereas the spoken explanation in the conversation is a direct result of a question and a comment from the other speaker.
  - The writer has time to think carefully about what to write, so there is no repetition or rephrasing as there is in the conversation.
  - The writer can include convincing details in his letter.
b The letter writer is probably not responding directly to anything. However, the professional context demands that an absence of this kind is apologized for and explained.
c *I am writing to explain why I …*
  The reason I did not phone was that …

2 a Read through the description of the situation with students. Suggest that they write a letter of 100–120 words.
  - Remind students to refer to the **Writing guidelines** on p.155 of their books.
  - Allow students time to plan their letters, following the suggested paragraph plan in their books.
  - Since students will take different lengths of time, the writing itself is probably best set as homework.
b Students exchange letters and discuss possible improvements.
c Students then write a final draft of these letters.

Sample letter

> I am writing to inform you (let you know) that I will not be able to come to New York for our sales meeting next week. I know that the arrangements were made several months ago and I am very sorry to have to cancel my visit at such short notice.
> The reason for my change of plan is that my brother has suddenly had to go into hospital and I have to help sort out the family crisis that this has caused. As soon as this emergency is over, I will contact you again to arrange a new date for my visit.

3 a Students read the explanatory note and say how it is different from the formal letter.
  - Elicit their ideas.

Suggested answers
- The note is more casual or informal than the letter. It is more like conversation.
- It contains the main points of information, but there is no polite, functional language explaining the background. The reader would be left wondering exactly what had happened.
- The language itself is note form: some pronouns and articles have been left out.
- It is very short and factual.

b Let students write their own explanatory note in class, but set a time limit of five to six minutes. (This reflects the hurried situation in which many brief notes like this are written.) Suggest twenty to thirty words for this note.
c Again, students exchange pieces of writing and read and suggest improvements.

Sample note

> Sorry, can't make lunch today – urgent report to write. Tried to phone you but couldn't get through. How about next week? Will phone.
>
> Best wishes, Alex

Summary

- Encourage students to use the tick boxes to help them keep a record of their learning.

4 Children, parents, and ancestors

Preview

This introduces the first theme of the unit – early childhood – from two angles: adults looking back on their own childhoods, and parents trying to cope with difficult infants.

Theme

The overall theme of this unit is *different generations*.
Preview Coping with difficult infants
Listening Older relatives, grandparents, etc.
Reading Neanderthal Man

Grammar

- Rules, needs, duties, and advice (LC p.127)
- Modal verbs: prohibition / no obligation (LC p.128)
- Modal verbs: speculating about past events (LC p.128)

Vocabulary

- Word building: suffixes
- Pairs of words: *remind, remember, grow up, bring up*

Functional language

- Remembering the past, reminiscing

Conversation strategies

- Telling someone to keep to the subject of conversation

Features of natural conversation

- Unfinished statements
- Question tags

Pronunciation

- *must, should, ought to*
- *have, have to*
- Third conditionals
- Word stress
- Reminding politely / sounding exasperated

Writing

- Short narratives (WG p.156)

Workbook

- An extract from a short story by Judah Waten
- *go, give, throw, put, take + away*; Topic vocabulary: ways of looking; Word-building
- Rules, needs, duties, and advice review; Prohibition / no obligation; Mixed patterns; Speculating about past events
- Adjectives, describing a person; Writing a description

■ **Your thoughts** ▨▨▨▨▨▨▨▨▨▨▨▨▨▨▨▨▨▨▨▨▨ p. 34 ■

- Before reading the short texts, students think and talk about memories of their own early childhood and their relationship with their parents. The aim here is to introduce the theme in a personalized way.

1–2 Students discuss the questions in pairs or small groups.
- Elicit a few memories, but don't push students to reveal personal information if they are reluctant.

■ Reading

- Before getting students to read the texts and think in detail about the difficult situations, spend a few minutes discussing the photographs.
- You could ask pairs or groups to discuss the pros and cons of having children.
- You may wish to teach these words before students read the text: *a toddler* (young child who is learning or has just learnt to walk), *a nervous wreck* (a person suffering from stress).

1–2 Students read the three reading texts which describe difficult situations for parents of young children.
- Individually students note down answers to the questions.
- They compare ideas in pairs.
- Elicit a few ideas in answer to each of the questions. Obviously there are no right or wrong answers. You could ask students to vote on which is the most difficult situation to deal with, and then discuss different ways of solving the difficulty.

3a–b Students read the *Golden Rules* text and decide which, if any, of the rules would help a parent to deal with Situations 1–3.
- Students compare ideas in pairs. Monitor their discussions, listening for their use of modals and other verbs expressing obligation. Do not interrupt at this stage, as this is a fluency, not an accuracy activity.
- Elicit and discuss students' ideas.
- **c** Elicit a few suggestions for more rules from the class. Note these on the board and use them as a basis for further class discussion if you have time.

- Students discuss this question in pairs.
- Elicit a few ideas from the class and finish this part of the unit with a general discussion on the subject of children's behaviour.

Grammar – Rules, needs, duties, and advice review

Students can work through questions 1–2 individually or in pairs. You could allow them to work straight through, or you could impose time limits and then check after each question.

- Remind students that they can refer to the **Language Commentary** on p.127.
- Explain the task and monitor, giving help where necessary.
- Check answers.

Answers

1 **Note** Comparing pairs of verbs by meaning is an attempt to simplify a difficult area. Obviously not all the meanings of the six verbs are dealt with in this way; many of the subtle differences are ignored. If you feel this is an oversimplification, spend more time on the **Language Commentary** notes, which go into more detail. You may also wish to compare other pairs of verbs, for example *must* and *should*. If you do this, however, beware of overloading students with too much information.

a	*need*	physical necessity
	want	a desire
b	*have to*	an obligation resulting from an external situation or rule
	must	strong advice, or an order to be obeyed
c	*should*	to give advice
	ought to	to suggest a duty or obligation

2 This raises the issue of the past tense of modal verbs.

a	1 *we needed*	2 *we wanted*
b	3 *had to*	4 *had to*
c	5 *shouldn't have asked*	6 *ought to have set*

■ Pronunciation ▰▰▰▰▰▰▰▰▰▰▰▰

3 **a** Students discuss ideas in pairs.
   b ▪ **4.1** Students listen and check their ideas.

▪ **4.1**

1 You must (/məs kæri/) carry on as usual.
2 You must eat (/mast i:t/) less if you want to lose weight.
3 You should go (/ʃʊ(d) gaʊ/) and see the new Bond film.
4 You should ask (/ʃʊd ɑːsk/) for help if you don't understand.
5 You ought to (/ɔː(t) tə/) do as you are told.

Answers

a See tapescript ▪ **4.1** .
b In the weak form, the final letter of the modal verb is not normally pronounced when the next word begins with a consonant (1,3,5) but it is pronounced when the next word begins with a vowel (2,4).

Note Point out to students that any of the modals will have the last letter pronounced if the word is stressed for emphasis or comes at the end of a sentence.

■ Check ▰▰▰▰▰▰▰▰▰▰▰▰▰▰▰▰▰▰▰▰▰▰▰▰▰▰▰▰

4 • Students work through the *Check* exercise individually, then compare answers with a partner.
   • Check answers.

Possible answers

Note As is often the case with modal verbs, there are several possible answers here. These are listed below. When correcting and commenting on students' answers, make sure they understand the difference in meaning between the different verbs.

a	*need to*	(This is physical necessity.)
b	*must*	(This is strong advice, an order spoken with the authority of the speaker.) *should* and *ought to* are also possible. *should* suggests advice.
	ought to	suggests that the speaker thinks the person being spoken to should feel a moral obligation to get to work on time.
c	*wants to*	(The child has a desire to go to bed, doesn't have to be forced, and so is no problem.) *Needs to* is possible and suggests that the child is tired and needs sleep.
d	*ought to*	(The speaker is pointing out a moral obligation, trying to make whoever they are talking to feel guilty.) *Should* is also possible as advice.
e	*should*	(This is simple advice.) *must* and *ought to* are also possible. *must* suggests stronger advice. *ought to* suggests moral pressure by the speaker.
f	*have to*	(The contract is the external rule.)

Listening

The purpose of looking at the photograph is to introduce the new theme, older relatives, and to revise family vocabulary.

1 • Students discuss who is who in the photograph.
   • List words for older relatives on the board. Acknowledge all vocabulary suggested by students, but list only the words relating to older generations.

Note There are no right or wrong answers for this activity, but the following family words will probably occur.
parents father / mother / father-in-law / mother-in-law
grandparents grandfather / grandmother
great-grandparents great-grandfather / great-grandmother.
uncle / aunt / great-uncle / great-aunt / cousins

Additional activity

- Students could discuss this question:
  If your family gathered for this sort of photograph, who would be there?
- They could bring in their own photographs and / or draw a family tree, concentrating on older generations.

2 • Give students time to prepare and then ask them to tell their partner about an older relative.
   • Monitor their conversations, but do not interrupt.

3 a Give students time to read through questions **1–4**. Make it clear that they should complete the chart as they listen to the recordings for the first time.

- **4.2** Play the recording, pausing for a few seconds between each of the speakers.

4.2

Speaker 1

I remember my grandad really well – although he died nearly twenty years ago. He was one of the kindest people I've ever known – he never got angry or shouted at me or anything like that, you know, and he'd often take my side in arguments I had with my Mum and Dad. When I was about seven or eight, he came to meet me from school and walk home with me even though he had rheumatism in one of his knees. I mean, he needn't have done that – I could easily have got home on the bus. And it was him that started me off smoking – he got through about forty a day and he used to give me the odd cigarette when I was quite young – you know about ten or eleven, and said I mustn't tell anyone. That made me feel really grown-up. My Mum always said he spoiled me, and looking back, it's fairly obvious I was his favourite grandchild – he had seven altogether – but I was his first and I suppose that made me sort of special. People have always said I look like my grandad. In fact, my Mum even says that I remind her of him when he was the age I am now – that's a strange thought, isn't it?

Speaker 2

My mother's amazing – she'll be ninety this year and she's incredibly independent – in fact, she still lives on her own, cooks all her own meals, and that kind of thing. She has loads of visitors, though, and a nurse who comes in every two days or so to check she's all right. She's not that good on her feet and she moves around pretty slowly, but at least she lives in a bungalow, so she doesn't have to climb any stairs. When she was in her mid-eighties, she went to live with my youngest sister and her family, but she couldn't stand them fussing around her all the time, so after a couple of years she moved back into a place of her own – the place she's in now. As I say she's got lots of friends who pop in regularly, so she's never lonely and she doesn't have to do too much for herself. She spends most of the time listening to the radio – mainly the news and talk programmes. She's got a TV but she still thinks of it as a new invention – and she's never really got used to watching it regularly.

Speaker 3

There's Nanna, my great-grandmother. She's my mother's grandmother. She's ninety-two but she's still pretty fit, she still goes on walking holidays with her youngest daughter – my great-aunt –and until recently she drove everywhere in her own car. Unfortunately, she's got problems with her eyes now and the doctor's said she mustn't drive any more. From the personality point of view she's amazing too – probably the most patient person I've ever known. You know, when we were younger she'd spend hours playing games with us, reading us stories, taking us for walks –anything we wanted to do really. She couldn't be more different from her eldest daughter, my Grandma, who's nearly always grumpy – she never has any time for us – not even now we're older. The thing is she paints in her spare time – and as far as she's concerned we're just in the way. But Nanna – she's just amazing for her age.

Speaker 4

My grandparents are really young – they're both forty-nine and they hate being called Grandma and Grandad – so we have to call them Aunty and Uncle. It still surprises everyone 'cos most people our age have got grandparents in their late fifties or early sixties at least. Some people assume they're our parents – that makes them feel really good! They live on the coast, so we quite often go and stay with them especially in the summer when we can go down to the beach. They're both great swimmers – when he was younger grandad was quite famous apparently, and he still swims every day in the summer and once a week all through the winter. We get on pretty well with them,

but they're always having arguments with Mum and Dad about how we should be brought up. They think Mum and Dad are too easygoing – Grandma thinks we have far too much freedom.

- Unless students find the task very difficult, check their answers now rather than playing the recording again. (It is important that they do not become too dependent on hearing recordings several times.)

Answers

	Speaker 1	2	3	4
a	grandfather	mother	Nanna great-grandmother	grandparents
b	✗ – dead	✗ – lives alone ✓ moves slowly	– but eye ✓ problems	very fit
c	✓ – ninety ✓		– ninety-two ✗	– both forty-nine
d	✓ – smoking ✗✗✗			

b Students discuss in pairs any similarities between the people described and their relatives.

Interpretation

1
- Students could do this exercise in pairs or as a class activity.
- Explain the task, then elicit ideas.

Possible answers

1 Smoking is a bad habit. Grandfather didn't want the boy's parents to know he'd been getting their son into bad habits.

2 Dresses and washes herself / Light housework, e.g. making the bed, dusting, washing-up, etc. She probably doesn't do her own shopping or heavy housework, etc.

3 She won't talk to them, answer their questions, play games with them, read them stories, take them places. She may tell them to go away or stop making a noise. She may suggest they watch TV etc. She may tell them to go to bed early.

4 Note Deal with **a** and **b** together, as they are on the same subject.

a Let them stay up late instead of going to bed. / Let them watch TV instead of doing homework. / Say Yes to everything they ask for. / Let them eat what they like when they like.

b Stay up late. / Smoke and drink. / Have friends to stay or stay with friends. / Have parties at home. / Wear any clothes.

Vocabulary

1
- Explain the task. Impress upon students the value of making a guess before checking in a dictionary.
- Students can work individually or in pairs.
- Check answers.

Answers

a – *remember* have a recollection
   – *remind* make someone remember

Note There are two different uses of *remind*:
– remind someone of + noun
I remind her of my grandad I make her think of her grandad (because I look or behave like him)
– remind someone to do something
I reminded her to post the letter I made her remember to post the letter (I told her not to forget)

b – *favourite* most liked
– *special* different from others (not necessarily in a good way)

c – *grow up* intransitive verb referring to what children do
– *bring up* transitive verb referring to what parents or adults do for children

> **Note** The passive form *I was brought up…* is often used to mean the same as *I grew up …*

d – *patient* being able to stay calm when you are annoyed
– *easygoing* not worrying, being relaxed about life. *Easygoing* people are often *patient*, but *patient* people are not necessarily *easygoing*.

e – *angry* cross, very annoyed at something / someone
– *grumpy* generally irritable or bad-tempered

2 • Students now use some of these words in personal contexts.
• Monitor their conversations, but do not interrupt unless you hear a wrong use of one of the key words.
• Finish the exercise by eliciting a few answers to each question.

■ Speaking personally

1–2 Students can work in pairs or small groups to discuss these questions.
• Before students exchange ideas, check that they know the opposites of the qualities listed.
patient – impatient, kind – unkind, funny – serious / humourless, intelligent – unintelligent / stupid
• Again monitor the conversations and finish by eliciting a few descriptions of people with the positive and negative characteristics.

Additional activity
• You could ask students to write a brief pen-portrait of one of the people they have talked about.
• These could be displayed in the classroom.

— Grammar – Modal verbs: prohibition / no obligation

This grammar section focuses on the negative forms of some of the verbs introduced in the Preview: *mustn't, don't have to, needn't, needn't have, didn't need to.*
• Remind students that they can refer to the **Language Commentary** on p.128.

■ Exploring concepts ■ p. 37 ■

1–2 Students work through this section in the usual way.

Answers

1 a	1	*mustn't*	this is prohibited / not allowed / against the law
	2	*don't have to*	there is no obligation to, but you can if you like
	3	*needn't*	it isn't necessary for some reason
b	1	5	
	2	4 (6 is also possible)	
	3	6 (4 is just about possible)	

> **Note** There is little difference between *don't have to* and *needn't*.

2 a 1 the person came, even though it wasn't necessary
2 the person didn't come because it wasn't necessary
b 1 3, 2 4

■ Pronunciation

3 a Students can work in pairs or you can elicit ideas from the whole class.

> **Note** This exercise focuses on the pronunciation of *have* as a main verb and as a modal of obligation *have to*. When *have* is a main verb it is pronounced /hæv/, and /hæz/ in the third person singular. Although *have to* can be pronounced in the same way it is often pronounced /hæf tə/ and /hæs tə/ in the third person singular.

b **4.3** Play the recording so that students can check their ideas. They can then practise the sentences in pairs.

4.3

1 I have two brothers. (/hæv/)
2 I have to go. (/hæf tə/)
3 He has a problem. (/hæz/)
4 He has to work hard. (/hæs tə/)
5 You don't have to come. (/hæf tə/)

Answers
See tapescript **4.3** .

■ Exploitation

This exercise gives controlled practice of *mustn't, don't have to*, and *needn't* in the personalized context of the students' own country.

1 • Elicit one or two more completions of the example sentence about underground trains to check students understand the task.
• Students should work individually, writing their answers.
• Elicit one or two answers for each beginning.

2 This exercise practises *to have to do something* in its past, present, and future forms.
a Divide students into pairs. Make sure they know that student As have to prepare questions about the past and Bs have to prepare questions about now.
• Set a time limit for preparing the questions and conducting interviews.
• Students swap roles and prepare their own questions.
b When you feel the first practice phase is coming to an end, ask pairs to move on to discussing the future.

Possible questions
a *… do much homework? / … wear school uniform?*
b *… take exams? / … pay fees? / … live away from home?*
c *… work hard. / … look after my family.*

■ Free speech

This is an opportunity for students to use some of the grammar of the unit in a more natural way to talk about an club or organization they belong to.

3 · You could start by telling the class about a club you belong to. Include a number of examples of *must, have to, don't have to*, etc., but don't make these too obvious.

· Get all students to think of a club or organization they belong or belonged to and elicit a brief description of one or two of these, following the list of points in the Students' Book.

· Monitor conversations, but do not interrupt this free production activity.

—— p. 38 ——

Reading

The text is about our far-off ancestors, Neanderthal Man.

Note Each student reads only part of the text, and then pairs of students pool information.

1 · In pairs, students discuss any information or ideas they already know about Neanderthal Man and make brief notes. Unless the class seems particularly knowledgeable, don't spend more than a few minutes on this activity.

2 · All students now read the introductory paragraph which contains some of the basic facts about Neanderthal Man. As they read, they should check whether their answers in **1** were correct and make a mental note of any new information.

3 · Each student in the pair now reads a different part of the text to find further information and note additional ideas.

■ Close up

· Students can work on these points together even though they have not read the whole text.
· Check answers.

Answers
· l.7 **maximize**
   Check that students understand the meaning of these prefixes:
   mini small
   maxi large / largest.
   Other words:
   minimum / minimal / minibus / miniskirt
   maximum / maximal.
· l.12 a **vegetarian** (also an adjective)
   The animal equivalents of these words are *carnivore* and *herbivore* (adjectives: *carnivorous / herbivorous*).
· l.12 **immense, huge**
· l.16 Two-syllable adjectives which have two comparative and superlative forms: *common*, gentle, handsome, happy*, narrow, pleasant*, quiet, shallow, stupid, tired.*

Note The negative forms of these adjectives* also have two comparative and superlative forms. Example *unhappier / more unhappy*

■ Interpretation ━━━━━━━━━━━━ p. 39 ■

1–2 Referring to the notes they have made, students now tell each other the main points of information that came out of their part of the reading text.

3 · Encourage students to use the evidence in the texts to speculate about why Neanderthal Man disappeared.

· Monitor their discussions, helping or prompting where necessary. Listen for the use of modal perfect forms, which are a natural way of speculating about past events. Do not correct at this stage as these forms are the focus of the next grammar section.

· Elicit the main ideas and list them in note form on the board.

Answers

1 Part 1 of the text suggests that Neanderthal Man was able to: *exist in a cold climate (body-heat minimized – l.7); hunt animals – l.14; make stone tools – l.18; control fire – l.19; communicate in a limited way – l.20.*

2 Part 2 of the text suggests that Cro-Magnons were good at: *making efficient weapons – l.25; measuring time – l.27; controlling their environment – l.28; building villages – l.29; creating art – l.36.*

3 The texts suggests three possibilities:
· The Cro-Magnons (may have) killed the Neanderthals.
· The Cro-Magnons (may have) interbred with the Neanderthals.
   interbreed means *have children with*. In other words, the two races became mixed.
· The Cro-Magnons (may have) forced the Neanderthals into environments where they could not survive and eventually they died out.
   Students might suggest that a combination of all the above contributed to the disappearance of Neanderthal Man.

Additional activity
· Write these on the board or photocopy this section.
· Students then match the words and their definitions.

Match these words with their meanings:

a	*compact* (l.7)	1	not central, relatively unproductive
b	*prominent* (l.8)	2	sudden increase
c	*humidify* (l.9)	3	solid, able to be compressed into a small space
d	*co-ordination* (l.14)	4	images which represent other things
e	*marginal* (l.33)	5	large, standing out from, easily noticed
f	*coexistence* (l.35)	6	make damp or wet
g	*explosion* (l.37)	7	living peacefully together in the same area
h	*symbols* (l.38)	8	the organisation of people or things so that they work efficiently together.

Answers
a–3, b–5, c–6, d–8, e–1, f–7, g–2, h–4

■ Speaking personally ━━━━━━━━━━━━━━━━
· Students discuss this question in pairs and groups.
· Elicit their ideas and, if you have time, broaden this out into a class discussion.

Possible answers

Humans will be more dependent on technology, computers, etc., and so less able to survive in completely natural environments. Human characteristics which may affect the future success or failure of the race:

- widespread addiction to drugs
- uncontrolled aggression (leading to world war)
- uncontrolled population growth
- uncontrollable diseases related to modern lifestyle (e.g. AIDS)
- consistent choice of easy living style leading to bad diet, lack of exercise, etc.
- the effects of genetic engineering

Grammar — Modal verbs: speculating about past events

▉ Exploring concepts ▉▉▉▉▉▉▉▉

1–3 You could allow students to answer questions 1–3 in the usual way, or work through 1 with the whole class. Doing this would allow you to draw students' attention to the form of modal perfect verbs.

- Remind students that they can refer to the **Language Commentary** on p.128.
- Check answers.

Answers

1 a The speaker is almost certain.
   Modal forms *must have / can't have* show near certainty.
   The speaker is asserting what he feels sure, but cannot prove, is a fact.
   b The speaker is sure – he is conveying factual information about the past. The verb *was* shows this.

2a+c The writer is almost certain of what they are saying (*must have evolved*) and (*can't have been*).
   b (*may have killed*) This is pure speculation – the writer is putting forward one possible explanation (the use of *may* indicates this).

3 a 1 The writer is almost certain about something positive:
      Neanderthal Man *was* artistic.
      2 The writer is equally certain about something negative:
      Neanderthal Man *was not* artistic.
   b The continuation sentences provide supporting evidence for the writer's near certainty.
      1 3, 2 4

Note Before moving on to the *Exploitation* section, draw students' attention to the **Language Commentary** p.128 which introduces *might have* and *could have* as alternatives to *may have*. Point out:
1 that *might / could have* express greater uncertainty than *may have*.
2 that *could have* refers to a physical possibility.
3 The negative forms *might not* and *could not have* do not have the same meaning.
   He might not have been to work today. I am not sure. It is possible that he went or that he didn't go.
   He could not have been to work today. I am almost sure that he did not go. This means almost the same as *He can't have gone.*

▉ Pronunciation ▉▉▉▉▉▉▉▉▉▉▉▉

4 a Ask the class how *have* is pronounced. You could write it on the board to avoid saying it yourself.

Note This exercise focuses on the pronunciation of *have* as an auxiliary verb.

- Students discuss their ideas.
b 🔲 4.4 Students listen and check their ideas.

🔲 4.4

a Neanderthal Man had a large, broad nose which must have (/mʌst əv/) evolved for warming and humidifying cold, dry air.
b Cro-Magnons may have (/meɪ əv/) killed them off …
c … the evidence indicates that their language can't have been (/kɑːnt əv/) very sophisticated.

Answers
See tapescript 🔲 4.4 .

Note Point out that *been* is usually pronounced /bɪn/ or /bin/ but not the strong form /biːn/.

▉ Exploitation ▉▉▉▉▉▉▉▉▉▉

1 a Elicit a few sample explanations for the first comment based on the prompts given and on students' own ideas.
   She could have had a car accident.
   She might have overslept.
   She might have gone to bed late last night.
   She could have decided to stop work.
   She might have run off with her boyfriend.
- Students work on **2–5** individually, writing down their answers.
- Monitor this stage carefully, correcting mistakes.
- Elicit a few answers to each of the comments but do not spend too long on this as the next exercise gives further practice with some prompts.

Answers

2 *He might have / could have won a competition; had a letter from his girlfriend; got a pay rise; had some good news.*
3 *He could / might have lost his razor; had no sleep; got up late; thought it was Sunday; forgotten to shave; had to work all night.*
4 *She might / could have bought her own car / got her own car back from the garage / passed her driving test / got up too late to catch the train. She might not have wanted to walk.*
5 *He could / might have worked late / fallen asleep with the light on / been reading an exciting book. He might not have been able to get to sleep.*

b Explain the task to students. Take them carefully through the example in their books.
- Students work in pairs.
- For each item in exercise **a**, each student chooses one of the explanations they thought of.
- They tell their partner and suggest a possible explanation:
   *Ella **might have** overslept. She's been working very hard recently.*
- If their partner agrees with this idea, they confirm this and add their own supporting evidence.
   *Yes, she **must have** overslept. She looked very tired yesterday.*
   If their partner disagrees with this idea, they refute it with their own evidence.
   *She **can't have** overslept. She rang me at 8 o'clock this morning.*

- Monitor this exercise carefully, correcting where necessary.

Additional activity

Do an activity similar to the one above, but about people all the students know, for example, pop stars, politicians, film actors, etc. Students could bring in photographs.

- Each students thinks of a *why* question.
  Why do you think the president has suddenly left the country?
- Others think of possible explanations, using *might / could have*.
  He might have gone on holiday.
- Others think of why these suggestions are not possible.
  He can't have gone on holiday. Presidents have to plan their lives months in advance.

Free speech

2 This activity is intended to provide free practice in the language of speculation. This may include the modal perfects, *must have*, *could have*, etc., but also other ways of expressing this idea, like *perhaps*, *probably*, *maybe*, etc.

  a Elicit a few ideas about the pictures from the people in the class. Do not force the use of modal perfects here. Students may use them because they have just done related controlled practice, but encourage other forms as well.

- Monitor discussions, but do not interrupt or correct.

  b When pairs have discussed the pictures, they then discuss the appearance or behaviour of someone they know.

Word-building: suffixes

Suffixes and word class   p. 40

This introduction reminds students that suffixes can show whether words are verbs, nouns, adjectives or adverbs.

1 a Students decide whether the words in the box are nouns, verbs, adjectives, or adverbs.

- Check answers. Don't correct stress at this point.

Answers
a–b

competitive (adj.)   *membership* (noun)   *personality* (noun)
decision (noun)   *visitor* (noun)   *personalize* (verb)
famous (adj.)   *technologically* (adverb) *punishment* (noun)
humidify (verb)   *organization* (noun)   *responsible* (adj.)
independent (adj.)   *personal* (adj.)   *suggestion* (noun)
intelligence (noun)

  b Students then think about and mark the main stress on the words.
  c **4.5** Play the recording. Students listen and check.
- Check answers.

4.5

competitive   independent   technologically   personalize
decision   intelligence organization   punishment
famous   membership   personal   responsible
humidify   visitor   personality   suggestion

Answers
See tapescript **4.5** for stress.

2 • Students make lists of suffixes related to each type of word.
  • Elicit answers and write up lists on the board.

  Note You could get students to think of any other suffixes they know which are not included in the words in the box. Add these to the list.

Answers

noun	verb	adjective	adverb
-ion	-ize	-ous	-ly
-ence	-ify	-ive	
-ship	-ent		
-or	-al		
-ity	-ible		
-ment			
Others			
-er	-able		
-ness	-ible		
-ee		-less	
-ist		-ish	
-hood		-ful	

Noun suffixes

1–3 Students form nouns from the verbs. Give them a short time to try and work out rules of pronunciation and spelling before going through the answers with them.
- Students work through the verbs in 2.
- Check answers.

Answers

1 *associate associa**tion**, invent inven**tion**, explode explo**sion**, invade inva**sion***
If a verb ends in -ate, a noun can be formed by taking off the -e and adding -ion.
If a verb ends in -t a noun can often be formed by adding -ion. This -tion ending is pronounced /ʃn/.
If a verb ends in -ode or -ide, a noun can be formed by removing the final -e, then changing the -d to an -s and adding -ion. This -sion ending is pronounced /ʒn/.

2 *communicate communica**tion**, include inclu**sion**, infect infec**tion**, react rea**ction**, regulate regula**tion***

3 a Students compile their own lists of pairs of jobs and related verbs.

  Note Point out to students that words for the majority of people who do things end in -er rather than -or.

Possible answers

verbs		jobs	
sail	*act*	*sailor*	*actor*
write	*supervise*	*writer*	*supervisor*

  b The two endings (-er / -or) are pronounced in exactly the same way: /ə(r)/

Verb suffixes

- Students answer questions **a–d** using *-ize* verbs.
- Check answers.

Answers

Note The suffix *-ize* can also be spelt *-ise*.

a *hospitalize*

Note This is often used in the passive.

Seven of the accident victims were hospitalized.

b *industrialize*

c *privatize*

d *popularize*

Note These verbs can be turned into nouns which refer to processes: *hospitalization, industrialization, privatization, popularization*

Adjective suffixes

1–2 Students work through the exercises individually, then compare answers with a partner.

- Check answers.

Answers

1 The suffix *-ous* is pronounced /əs/.
The suffix *-al* is pronounced /əl/ or /l/.

2 a See tapescript **4.6** .

b In most cases the stress does not change when the suffix is added. The exception is *mysterious*.
Usually the vowels in the adjectives are pronounced the same as in the nouns except for *nature* (/ˈneɪtʃə/) or *natural* (/ˈnætʃ(ə)rəl/).

c **4.6** Students check pronunciation of adjectives.

4.6

adventure	adventurous
fame	famous
humour	humorous
mystery	mysterious
nature	natural
nerve	nervous
profession	professional
religion	religious
season	seasonal
tradition	traditional

d This activity gives students practice in using the adjectives.

- Elicit their ideas about which of the adjectives can describe people.
- Monitor students' conversations about people they know, helping out and correcting where necessary.

Answers
Only *seasonal* and *traditional* CANNOT be used to describe people.

Mini-discussions

This is a brief practice activity recycling some of the words from this page. The time limit makes this a game-type activity.

- Remind students of the time limit.

- Monitor the conversations, but do not interrupt.
- You could finish with a brief class discussion of one topic.

▶ **Photocopiable activity 5 p.162**

Language in action

Eavesdrop! ▨▨▨▨▨▨▨▨▨▨▨▨▨▨▨▨▨ p. 41 ▨

The questions could be done as a class activity or as pairwork.

- Direct attention to the picture and the two questions.
- Remind students that they are speculating about what they see and should try to come up with a variety of different answers.
- You could elicit possible answers to the first question now or move straight on to *Listening 1*.

Listening 1

1 - Draw attention to question **b**.
- **4.7** Students listen to check their *Eavesdrop!* ideas and think about an answer to **b**.

4.7

A OK, so that's agreed then. Let's move on to the next item on the agenda, shall we? I think we all agree with the suggestion, don't we, that in future all requests for time off should be made in writing and made six months in advance of the proposed starting date? Fiona?

F Yes, I think that's perfectly reasonable. After all, we're a growing business – these things need to be formalized more than …

D That's right. I mean, it was OK when we only had ten or so staff, for people to ask their manager a couple of weeks before they wanted to go. It's a much more serious matter with a staff of over three hundr …

R I think there's a danger of too much bureaucracy here, Andrew. I remember, when I first started here nearly forty years ago, me and a mate of mine in accounts decided to go to Greece – it was, you know, a spur-of-the-moment decision, and I was quite happy to…

A Can we stick to the point, Richard? Things have moved on since you first started here.

R I can still see the look on my boss's face when I said I was taking a couple of weeks off. But he didn't really mind – everything was much easier …

F Look, Richard, we're supposed to be talking about a new system which will be fair to everyone.

R As far as I can remember, we left on the Friday night. I put a few clothes in a rucksack and we were off.

D I'm sorry, Richard, but we're not here to talk about the good old days. If we're going to survive and grow in a competitive world, we've got to move with the times. You know the company motto – 'Plan or perish'.

R I can remember as if it were yesterday. We went by train to Brindisi in Italy and then got a boat across … (fade)

b - Give students time to discuss how they would deal with someone like Richard.
- Elicit ideas and discuss as a class.

Possible answers
Eavesdrop!
The board of a growing company. They are colleagues of different ages.

They are trying to introduce a measure to make the company more efficient: they want employees to give advance notice of when they want to take holidays. One of the older employees, Richard, is not keen on the new idea and remembers the more easygoing old days nostalgically.

Listening 1
b Many answers are possible. The two extremes are, to tolerate the older employee who is set in his ways, knowing that he will retire soon, or to make his life difficult unless he accepts the new ideas.

2 • Students listen again and note down the functional and conversational language used by the two speakers.
  • Check that students understand the task, especially t*o keep to the subject of conversation.* You could elicit ideas for expressions to fit into each category.
  • Allocate tasks and play the recording again, once or twice as necessary.
  • Students note down the expressions and then compile lists. They help and correct each other at this stage.

Note Students add to these lists during the next listening task.

Answers
See full list of expressions after *Listening 2*, question 2.

■ Listening 2 ■

1 • **4.8** Ask students to read the questions, then play the recording.

4.8 including **4.9**

Conversation 1
R Well you're lucky – 'cos I, I work on my own now, so …
K Ah, do you? – so it must be very different.
R Well, it's a bit, bit lonely at times, you know, but er …
K That was one of the best things, I think, erm, just that there were so many people that you could get on well with.
R Yeah, well, I can remember those impromptu drinks and things we used to have …
K **4.9** Well, there was always so many things to do, weren't there, I mean you could always just sort of nip round the corner and go out for a drink or …
R 'Cos it was so central.
K That's right.
R But it's a bit difficult now.
K Is it?
R Yeah, well …
K I suppose if you …
R It's only me.
K Yeah, that's true …
R Nip out with myself round the corner, but … I'll never forget the time we all went to the restaurant together … about ten of us, weren't there?
K Oh, that was wonderful, wasn't it? Yeah, I really enjoyed that. It just doesn't hap … , the people I work with now are not the same, I mean they're a lot older …
R They don't like …
K Well, they just have different interests, erm, and it's a lot harder to sort of get people together …

R I mean, that's the problem when you work with a lot of people – sometimes it clicks and sometimes it doesn't click and er, you know, you're lucky if it does, and you're in a group of people that you can do those things – those those times were good, I'll never forget those times – it was a good period.
K Mmm it was.
Conversation 2
R What about teachers – did you have any strange teachers?
J Oh, yes, – they were all Miss somebody or another and they were very fierce …
R I can remember one – he was a French teacher – he used to put … if you did something wrong he'd put his hands all over your face and – but he was a heavy smoker and it used to choke you …
J Oh, how awful.
R It was either that or he'd hit you with a book – strange people.
J Oh, no, I can't remember anyone as terrible as that – we used to get some funny punishments, though, from our teachers. Did you?
H What sort of punishments?
J **4.9** Well, I used to talk too much, and I used to have to stand in the corner on my chair …
H That's very Victorian …
J I can remember doing that an awful lot.
R One used to make us bang his head, bang our head, bang our head on the blackboard …
J Oh, no – that's awful …
R Yeah, he, he wouldn't do – he'd make us do it.
J He'd make you do it yourself?
R Yeah, auto-punishment.
J Oh, dear.
H We used to get chalk flung at us.
R Oh, yeah …
H Yes.
J That's not very nice, is it, really? Oh, dear …
R And uniforms. Did you, did you have to wear uniforms?
J Yes, we did, that's right.
R I used to hate uniforms.
H Our school was very strict on uniforms.
J Yes, and we couldn't wear our skirts too short.

• Check answers.

Possible answers

	Conversation 1	**Conversation 2**
a	ex-colleagues.	Both are friends (not ex-school mates – now working somewhere else. They don't talk about the same teachers.)
b	The friendly atmosphere of their past workplace.	Memories of school. The man now seems to work alone – maybe freelance.
c	generally happy	generally unhappy

2 • **4.9** Play the recording, while students follow the extracts on p.42 in their books, marking the functional language used by the speakers.
  • Students add the expressions to their lists.
  • Check through the lists with students.

Note In these authentic conversations there are no *keeping someone on the subject of conversation* expressions.

Answers

(This includes expressions from *Listening 1* and *2*.)

Remembering the past

4.7

I remember, when I ... + past   I can still see ...   As far as I can remember, ...   I can remember as if it were yesterday.

4.9 Extract 1

I'll never forget the time ...

4.9 Extract 2

I can remember + -ing

Note In this conversation the speakers use *used to* and *would* to talk about past memories. Examples
I used to talk too much.   He wouldn't do – he'd make us do it.

Keeping someone on the subject of conversation

4.7

Can we stick to the point ...?   ... we're supposed to be talking about ...   ... we're not here to talk about ...

© Oxford University Press **PHOTOCOPIABLE**

■ Features of natural conversation p. 42

This section focuses on the way in which speakers break off what they are saying in conversation, leaving statements and thoughts unfinished. The aim is to make students aware of this as a feature of speech rather than to suggest that they incorporate it into their own speech.

1 a Elicit general ideas, making comparisons with students' own language(s) if appropriate.
  • While students are marking examples in the extracts, you could play the recording again.

Note Students should concentrate on why sentences are left unfinished generally rather than specifically, as this is covered in **1b**.

  • Check answers.

Answers

a – The examples of unfinished statements are listed in **1b** in the Student's Book.
  – Speakers leave statements unfinished for a number of different reasons.
  • They lose their thread of thought – they can't remember what they were going to say.
  • They decide to say something different – because they have had a new idea.
  • They don't know how to finish what they started or they can't think of a particular word or phrase.
  • Another speaker interrupts them or finishes their statement for them.
  • They think of a better way of expressing their idea, so start the statement again.

b • Give students a few minutes to discuss in pairs what these speakers were going to say. There are no right or wrong answers, of course.
  • Elicit their ideas.

Possible answers

1 *a meal / go to a film straight after work*
2 *are working on your own you can't expect it to be the same as it was / miss the company you could always get another job*
3 *the same things as me / going out together*
4 *it himself*

2 • Work through this question with the whole class.
  • Elicit ideas about the use of question tags in this context.

Answers

The question tags add to the nostalgic tone of the conversation. They refer to shared memories and are a way of involving the listener as well as speaker. The speakers use them to confirm that their own memories are true.

■ Practice

1 • **4.10** Students listen to the expressions. Drill chorally and individually.

4.10

a I can clearly remember saying goodbye at the school gates.
b I can still see my mother standing there crying.
c I can remember walking into the classroom as if it were yesterday.
d I'll never forget the time we played a trick on Mr Jones.
e I remember when we had outside toilets.
f As far as I can remember we got homework most nights.

2 • First check that students understand the words *exasperated* (very irritated or annoyed), and the phrase *a gentle reminder* (remind sb politely about something).
  • **4.11** Play all four sentences before checking students' ideas.

4.11

a We're supposed to be talking about school uniforms.
  We're supposed to be talking about school uniforms.
b We're not here to talk about school rules in general.
  We're not here to talk about school rules in general.
c Can you stick to the point?
  Can you stick to the point?
d Keep to the point.
  Keep to the point.

Answers

The first speaker in each sentence is giving a gentle reminder, they speak softly and fairly quietly. The second speaker sounds exasperated, they speak in a louder voice and emphasizes the stressed syllables more.

■ Exploitation

Here the exploitation activities are discussions, in which students express ideas and include memories related to the subjects.
  • Check that students understand how the discussions work. In each case Student A wants to talk about memories, or to move away from the subject. Students B and C try to get A to keep to the subject.
  • Students form groups of three and decide on their roles. Before each discussion, they should spend a few minutes thinking about what to say. In A's case, this preparation time should be spent thinking of related memories.
  • Monitor discussions, listening for use of the functional and conversational language. Do not interrupt unless the language is incorrect or inappropriate.
  • You may need to prompt Students **B** and **C** to get **A** to keep to the subject.

1a–d Draw attention to the questions **a–d** then allow students time to read through the two examples, and think about or discuss their ideas.

- Elicit their ideas.

Suggested answers

a • The most obvious difference is that in the conversation two people are exchanging memories. This means they are reminding each other about incidents in their past. The writer, on the other hand, has to create a picture in the mind of the reader, by including all kinds of physical details.
- The speakers focus on the action, whereas the writer describes the background as a build-up to the action.
- The sentences or ideas are longer in the written account.

b Words and phrases which show the writer is recalling a personal memory:
I am back in the car   (I am in the car again)
I can see the road   (this is a clear memory)
… all I remember now is …

c The writer describes what the driver of the car saw, felt, heard, and smelt before and after the accident.

d The other car was *a black BMW* / there was damage to one or both of the cars *breaking glass*. We can also infer a number of possibilities: the accident may have happened on a *sharp bend* in the road / because of the *wet surface*.

2 a Check that students understand they are writing a first paragraph, not a complete story. Suggest 80–100 words.

Note If students choose Suggestion 2, they should still write as if they are describing a personal memory.

- Remind students to refer to the **Writing guidelines** on p.156 of their books.
- Allow students time to plan their first drafts, stressing the importance of making the event 'come alive'.
- This piece of writing may be short enough to be written in class, but if class time is precious, set it as homework.

3 a Students exchange paragraphs and decide whether what their partner has written 'comes alive' and makes them want to find out more information. What they are doing at this stage is assessing the effectiveness of the descriptive build up to main event.

b Students discuss possible improvements.

c Again, the writing of the final draft of these paragraphs may be done in class or as homework.

d Students tell each other how their stories end.

Additional activity

- If students need more writing practice, suggest that they write the ending or continuation of their stories. They could add another two or three paragraphs of similar length to the first.
- Any completed stories could be displayed in the classroom.

■ **Summary** ■■■■■■■■■■■■■■■■■■■■■■■■■■■■

- Encourage students to use the tick boxes to help them keep a record of their learning.

5 Judging by appearances

Preview

Theme

The topics of this unit are all related to *appearances*.
Preview Married couples and first impressions
Listening Labels and brand names
Reading Human beings as zoo exhibits

Grammar

- Conditionals review (LC p.128)
- The verb *wish* (LC p.129)
- Mixed conditional sentences (LC p.129)
- Past verbs with present or future meaning (LC p.129)

Vocabulary

- Learning new vocabulary
- Vague language

Functional language

- Making instructions clear
- Checking instructions

Features of natural conversation

- Ways of replying positively (alternatives to *Yes*)

Pronunciation

- Intonation of complaints and regrets

Writing

- Instructions (WG p.157)

Workbook

- A newspaper article about the jeans industry
- Topic vocabulary: employment; *get* + particle
- Conditionals review; The verb *wish*; Mixed conditional sentences; Past verbs with present or future meaning
- Connecting ideas; Describing similarities and differences between people

■ Your thoughts ▬▬▬▬▬▬▬▬▬▬▬▬ p. 44 ■

1–3 Students could discuss the three questions in pairs or groups *before* they open their books. Questions could be written on the board or given to students on cards.

- Before they start, you could check that students understand *get on with* and *first impressions*.
- Students discuss the questions and note down points of agreement.
- Finish the activity with a whole-class exchange of ideas.

■ Reading ▬▬▬▬▬▬▬▬▬▬▬▬▬▬▬▬▬▬▬▬▬▬

1 • You may wish to teach these words and phrases before students read the intoductory text: *Cupid* (Roman god of love), *opposites attract* (People who are very different from each other often make good couples), *match-making skills* (ability to recognize that two people are romantically compatible).

- Students read the text and initially try to guess the couples simply from the photographs.
- They could then read the biographical information and, if necessary change their guesses.

2 • Students compare ideas with a partner.

- Monitor the discussions to ensure that students give reasons for their suggestions. Only when they have done this should they check their guesses by turning to p.159.

Answers

The couples are *Nelson & Ruth / Matthew & Lucie / Pip & Helen*

3 • This discussion could be done in pairs, groups, or by the whole class. This is in preparation for the listening exercise which follows.

■ Listening ▬▬▬▬▬▬▬▬▬▬▬▬▬▬▬▬▬ p. 45 ■

1 • **5.1** Students listen to a psychologist talking about the three relationships. This provides a check on the ideas they discussed in **3**.

- Make sure students A and B know which information they are listening for.
- You could play the recording once before students take notes.

Lucie and Matthew married fairly recently. They've been together now for two years and they are expecting their first child. They met when Matthew shared a flat with Lucie's friend, Jane. Lucie says her friends didn't expect her to go for someone like Matt. He was older than her and he was divorced. But she thinks he's very typical of the kind of men she likes – older and professional. Matthew feels they get on well because they want the same things out of life.

Matthew and Lucie look as if they come from well-off backgrounds. Their choice of holidays and the desire for children are an excellent fit. If Matthew's idea of a perfect weekend is watching football, it's just as well Lucie likes staying at home doing nothing, otherwise she might get bored or nag him to take her out.

Nelson and Ruth met through a friend and have been together for seven years. They think they make a good couple because, although they are very different, they are both easygoing and give each other a lot of space.

Both Ruth and Nelson have artistic, creative personalities which seem to complement their home and working lives. Even though Ruth comes from a large family, neither Ruth nor Nelson really seem to want children. I suppose Ruth could see Nelson's need to save as meanness, but she may also find that this more cautious approach is a useful curb for her own concerns, as she worries when things are not under control. Holidays will have to be quite carefully negotiated.

Pip and Helen got married after four years together. They met when Helen was a hairdresser – Pip says she deliberately gave him a bad haircut so he had to go back to have it recut, but Helen denies this. According to Pip, they're best friends, but they're careful not to crowd each other. Helen mentions their sense of humour as being important. Pip and Helen look happy and relaxed. Loyalty is top of their list, so this looks like playing an important part in their relationship, as do creativity, the countryside, and the company of friends. It seems that children will be something for the future, as neither is ready yet. The desire for exotic travel is shared though there may be disputes over modes of transport.

- Play the recording again if necessary.
- If you wish, before moving on, let students check their ideas by referring to the tapescript on p.144 of their books or check answers with the whole class.

Answers
New facts
Lucie and Matthew
married for two years / expecting a child / met when Matthew shared a flat with friend of Lucie's / Matthew divorced / both from well-off backgrounds
Nelson and Ruth
met through a friend / have been together for seven years / Ruth comes from a large family
Pip and Helen
got married after they'd known each other for four years / met when Helen was a hairdresser

Points that might affect the success of their relationship
Lucie and Matthew
Positive   both are from well-off backgrounds / like the same kind of holidays / both want children
Negative   nothing
Nelson and Ruth
Positive   both artistic and creative / neither wants children / Ruth might find Nelson's need to save money reassuring
Negative   they might disagree about holidays / Ruth might see Nelson's need to save money as meanness

Pip and Helen
Positive   loyalty important to both / shared interests – creativity, the countryside, being with friends / feel the same about having children / exotic travel
Negative   they might not agree about how to travel on holiday

2 • Students now compare notes and, in the light of the new factual information and the psychologist's ideas, they decide whether they think the three relationships will be successful or not.
   • Monitor conversations, then have a final class discussion about the relationship most likely to succeed.

■ Person to person ■▬▬▬▬▬▬▬▬▬▬▬

1–2 Students discuss these personal questions in pairs or groups.
   • You could finish this section by asking a few individual students to tell you about occasions when their first impressions were wrong.

▶ **Photocopiable activity 6 p.163**

─ Grammar ─ Conditionals review ──────────

Students will be familiar with the three main conditional patterns in English (plus the zero conditional) and their knowledge should simply need checking here. In the next grammar section, mixed conditional patterns are introduced, so revision here is important.
   • Remind students that they can refer to the **Language Commentary** on p.128.

1–3 Students work through the concept questions in the usual way. If you wish, stop after **1**, **2**, and **3** to check answers and understanding.
   • Students should not move on to the *Check* exercise until questions **1–3** have been checked.

Answers

1 a 1 This is something that usually happens.
        When / whenever I get money I always put it in the bank. (Zero)
     2 The speaker is saying what he will do if he gets money – this is quite possible. (First)
  b 1 The speaker thinks it is quite possible that he will win the lottery, and if he does he will spend the money on a luxury holiday. (First)
     2 The speaker doesn't believe he will win the lottery, but in the unlikely event of winning he would spend the money on a luxury holiday. (Second)
  c 1 The speaker doesn't believe he will win the lottery, but in the unlikely event of winning he would buy a new house. (Second)
     2 The speaker has played the lottery, but did not win. He's speculating about what he would have done if he had won. (Third)

2 a b2 / c1 (Second)   **c** a1   (Zero)
  b a2 / b1 (First)   **d** c3   (Third)

3 a This section draws attention to the fact that the second conditional can refer to an unlikely possibility or to an unreal situation.

1 *If **I were** a woman, …*
The speaker is not a woman, so having children is not possible.

2 *If **I won** the lottery, …*
Winning the lottery is unlikely, but it is possible.

b This question points out that *might* can be used as an alternative to *would* in second conditional sentences and that it shows less certainty.

1 The speaker is certain. (***I'd buy** a Caribbean island.*)

2 The speaker is uncertain. (***I might buy** a Caribbean island.*)

▉ Pronunciation ▉

4 • **5.2** Students discuss the pronunciation of *had / have* and *wouldn't* in the sentences, then listen to the recording to check their ideas.

5.2

1 If he'd (ɪd) won the lottery, he'd have (hiːd əv) bought a Ferrari.

2 If he (ɪ) hadn't come, you wouldn't have (wʊdnt əv) known.

• Draw attention to the contractions and the weak form of *have* in *he'd have* and *wouldn't have*.

Answers
See tapescript **5.2** .

Note The *h* of *have* is not pronounced, and the *h* of *he* is frequently not pronounced. There is also linking between words when one word ends in a consonant and the next word begins with a vowel.

▉ Check ▉

5 • Students could work through this short controlled practice individually and then compare answers in pairs.

Answers
a *I'd go* d *came up*
b *I want* e *I'd have lost*
c *you promise*

— p. 46 —

Listening

The new theme is brand names, including designer labels in clothes, etc. The conversation contains examples of the verb *wish* and mixed conditional sentence patterns.

1 • Students look at the pictures, and discuss the questions in pairs or small groups. If you have a small class, this could be done as a whole-class brainstorming session.

Possible answers
a
Haagen Dazs ice-cream (sexy image)
Ford popular, inexpensive cars
BMW prestige (expensive) cars
Apple Mac computers
Levi's casual clothes, particular jeans
Body Shop environmentally friendly cosmetics, soaps, shampoos, etc. natural ingredients used and nothing tested on animals
KFC (Kentucky Fried Chicken) fast food: chicken
Virgin pop recordings (CDs / recordings) / cheap air travel

Harrods exclusive, expensive clothes and other goods
Volvo cars (reliable image)
McDonald's fast food: burgers
b–c Personal answers.

2 This is a pre-listening activity in which students check vocabulary and predict what the speakers are going to say.
• Do the first one as an example to check students understand the task.

3 • Draw attention to the first two listening tasks. Students listen to find out whether any of their ideas from **2** were correct.
• **5.3** Play the recording.

5.3

A Did anyone see that article in the paper the other day about brand names?

C Not sure – what did it say?

A Well, it said how important brands are to young people.

P It sounds pretty boring to me.

J What sort of brands?

A Well, you know, clothes, drinks, food, cigarettes – things like that. It said that lots of young people need them to create an identity for themselves.

P Sounds really heavy.

A No, it wasn't – it was interesting.

C I think there's something in it. I remember when I was about thirteen, I wanted a pair of Levi jeans. I mean they had to be Levi's – I went into this shop and they had Wranglers but not Levi's – I remember storming out and then getting home feeling depressed. I wouldn't go out with my friends until I'd actually got some real Levi's – they had to have that little orangey label.

J That was like me when I was only about twelve – everyone had Nike shoes – so that's what I wanted. I didn't care whether they were comfortable or not – or what my Mum and Dad thought about them – as long as they had that Nike symbol on them – that was all that mattered.

P My parents were always broke, so I got what I was given. If they'd had more money, I'd probably be more worried about what I wear now. As it is, I don't really care.

C **5.4** It's a bit the same with drinks – I mean Coca-Cola and Levi jeans are fairly similar, aren't they?

P 'Cept you can't drink jeans!

C You know what I mean, Pete. I wish you'd stop being so childish. Jeans are a sort of uniform – if you're young and you don't drink Coke, there must be something wrong with you.

P I don't drink Coke and there's nothing wrong with me.

A Well, you're not exactly young, are you? Anyway what do you drink?

P Fanta, Seven-Up – I'm just not keen on Coke. And I really like the Fanta adverts on telly.

A Exactly – it's all a question of image.

P Rubbish.

J It's not rubbish, Pete. Image is important. Think of how many people want a Mercedes or a BMW – they're status symbols.

P I don't see what cars have got to do with drinking Coke.

A Anyway, this article I was reading said it isn't just kids that are obsessed with brands – it said that strong brands reflect people's deepest emotions – like people are attracted to Volvo cars because they have a safe dependable image.

C It's funny though – 'cos you can buy things without really being aware of their image. I mean, last year, I bought myself a new coat in Harrods. It wasn't particularly expensive – but every time anyone saw the Harrods label inside, they'd say – 'Oh, you're going up in the world', or 'Has someone died and left you some money?'. Irritating remarks like that. I really regret buying it now. I wish I'd gone to Marks and Spencers' instead – you know, somewhere more ordinary like that.

J   When I bought my Armani shirt – I knew how people would react – so as soon as I got it home I cut the label off.

P   Blimey! I wish I had enough money to buy an Armani shirt – I wouldn't cut the label off – I'd make sure everyone could see it.

J   Actually, to be honest, I wish I hadn't cut the label off now – it's not quite the same somehow.

A   Look, you lot, stop side-tracking me. What was I saying? Oh, yeah, this article also said that brands give young people something to believe in – it makes them feel more adult.

C   It's a bit like The Body Shop – I know loads of teenagers who buy soap and stuff there because they believe that the Body Shop cares about animals and the environment.

- Check answers.

Answers

Young people need brand names *to create an identity for themselves ...*
Image is important to people. / Volvo cars have a strong *image*.
The jeans had to have a particular *label*.
Jeans are a sort of *uniform*.
A Mercedes or a BMW are *status symbols*.
Not only kids are *obsessed with* brands.

4 • Students could work through **a–h** in pairs to see what they remember.
   • Play the recording again if necessary.
   • Check answers.

Answers

a Levi's / Nike
b Coca-Cola / Seven-Up / Fanta
c Mercedes / BMW
d Marks and Spencer
e Armani
f Harrods
g Body Shop

■ Interpretation ■

1 • **5.4** As you play this extract from the recording, let students follow the tapescript on p.144 at the back of their books.
   • Elicit students' ideas about the speakers' attitudes towards each other and the subject of brand names.

Answers

Three of the speakers, Clare, Anne, and John, seem to take seriously the idea that brand names appeal to young people and can be important. Pete is the odd one out; he deliberately misunderstands what the others are saying: *You can't drink jeans.* The others think he is being childish.

2 The concept *Vague language* was introduced as a feature of natural conversation in Language in Action in Unit 2.
   • Briefly remind students of the idea and elicit a few examples from them.
   • They then work through extracts **a–f**, underlining the vague terms and thinking about what each could mean.
   • Check answers.

Answers

a	*anyone*	any of the other speakers
	the other day	yesterday, a few days ago
b	*pretty*	*quite* or *fairly* (less than *very*)
c	*things like that*	consumer goods where there is always a lot of choice
	lots of	possibly between fifty per cent and ninety per cent, a large number
d	*about thirteen*	between twelve and a half and thirteen and a half
	orangey	a shade of orange
e	*somewhere more ordinary like that*	a shop which caters for ordinary people and doesn't sell expensive designer clothes
f	*loads of*	(probably) a majority of the teenagers I know
	stuff	the kinds of thing you can buy there – cosmetics, shampoo, etc.

■ Speaking personally ■

1–2 Students can now express their personal opinions on some of the ideas from the conversation.
   • Students work in pairs or groups.
   • Monitor, but do not interrupt conversations.
   • You could have a brief whole-class discussion on their opinions.

—Grammar – The verb *wish*; mixed conditional sentences

■ Exploring concepts ■ p. 47 ■

1–3 Students work through the questions individually or in pairs.
   • Remind students that they can refer to the **Language Commentary** on p.129.
   • Monitor, helping if necessary.
   • Check their ideas and answers before they move on to question 4.

Answers

1 a The speaker doesn't want the person she is talking to, to keep behaving like a child.
    b The speaker can't afford an Armani shirt, but he would like to be able to.
    c The speaker has cut the label off, but regrets it now.

2 1 1b   2 1d   3 1a

3 1 1c   2 1a   3 1b / 1d

4 • You could work through this section with the whole class. Read through the rubric and examples, then elicit students' ideas about how the two sentences differ in form and meaning.

Note Students are reminded that some *conditional* sentences refer to a past situation which cannot be changed. (In this respect it is similar to *wish* + Past perfect.)

Answers

a (Third conditional: this speculates about a *past* result of a past action.)
if + Past perfect / *would have* + past participle
b (Mixed conditional: this speculates about a *present* result of a past action.)
if + Past perfect / *would* + infinitive

Note Point out that the main clause of a mixed conditional sentence can have a variety of verb forms. Examples: *would* / *might* / *could* infinitive, *be* + *-ing* form.

Additional activity

To give students some immediate practice of mixed conditionals, get them to think of as many endings as they can to these If clauses:
If I had passed my driving test, …
If he hadn't eaten so much, …
If it hadn't snowed last night, …

▮ Pronunciation ▮

5 a **5.5** Play the recording and get students to repeat. Pay particular attention to correct intonation.

5.5

1 I wish you wouldn't do that!
2 I wish you'd stop interrupting!
3 I wish I had hair like yours.
4 I wish I were twenty years younger.
5 I wish you'd listen when I'm talking to you.
6 I wish I could go.

b Students work out which are complaints and which are regrets.

Answer

b Sentences 1, 2, and 5 are complaints. 3, 4, and 6 are regrets.

Note In complaints the stressed syllables usually have more emphasis. The intonation is HIGH on the main stressed syllable and then falls. In regrets the main stressed syllables are less strong. Sentence 6 is an exception to this pattern.

▮ Exploitation ▮

1 a Students listen to six extracts of conversation and work out what the situation is and what was said before each one.
   • **5.6** Play them one at a time, eliciting students' ideas.

5.6

1 Unfortunately, I can't take you anywhere at the moment. I've had my licence taken away for dangerous driving.
2 I know I'm stupid – I should never have started smoking – now I can't stop.
3 Yes, I'd love to work abroad now – I shouldn't have refused that job in Malaysia when they offered it to me.
4 I hope it tastes all right. I never went to cookery lessons when I was at school.
5 I'd like to, but I can't swim. Everyone else I know learned when they were four or five years old.
6 Sorry I can't, I'm completely broke. I spent most of it on an expensive French meal.

Possible answers

1 The speaker is replying to someone who has asked for a lift in his car. The request could have been:
Could you possibly take me to the airport tomorrow morning?
2 The speaker is admitting that he is addicted to smoking. What he says could be a response to:
I think you're stupid. Smoking is really dangerous, you know.
3 The speaker regrets turning down a job in Malaysia because he wants to work abroad. What he says could be a response to this:
Wouldn't you like to work abroad?
4 The speaker has given someone something she has just cooked. What she says could be a response to this:
That looks delicious – I didn't know you could cook.
5 The speaker has probably been invited to go swimming, but has to decline the invitation. What he says could be a response to:
Would you like to come swimming with us this afternoon?
6 The speaker is probably apologizing because he can't lend a friend some money. What he says could be a response to this:
Can you lend me some money until the weekend?

b Before listening again, work through the example in students' books to make sure the class understands the next stage of the exercise.
• Students listen again and produce two *wish* sentences for each snippet. Allow them plenty of time to produce their sentences and to compare their ideas in pairs.
• Check answers.

Possible answers

1 *I wish I could take you to the airport.*
I wish I hadn't lost my licence.
2 *I wish I didn't smoke.*
I wish I'd never started smoking.
3 *I wish I could find a job abroad.*
I wish I hadn't turned down that job in Malaysia.
4 *I wish I was a good cook.*
I wish I had learnt cookery at school.
5 *I wish I could swim.*
I wish I had learnt to swim when I was younger.
6 *I wish I could lend you some money.*
I wish I hadn't spent so much money on an expensive French meal.

2 • Elicit suggestions for the kinds of things students would find irritating in someone they were on holiday with. Write a few ideas in note form on the board. For example, *stay in bed all day / smoke in the bathroom / talk too much.*

a Once the idea is established, students write sentences about things they find irritating. They should not show their partner at this stage.
• You could provide some prompts if students find it difficult to think of their own ideas: personal habits, food and drink, household jobs, music, daily routine, smoking.

b Read through the example with the class which shows how the original sentences have been converted into *wish* sentences.
• Using the ideas they thought of in a, pairs of students now take turns to complain about aspects of each other's behaviour. They should make conversations like the examples in their books.
• Monitor conversations, correcting any mistakes involving the use of *wish.*

3 This is a fluency activity, which should naturally involve students using a variety of the structures from the grammar sections.

- Monitor conversations, but do not interrupt them with corrections at this stage.

Note The personal subject matter of this exercise should interest students and encourage them to talk openly about themselves. An over-emphasis on specific grammatical structures is likely to affect student interest and involvement, and thus reduce the value of this activity as fluency practice.

▶ **Photocopiable activity 7 p.164**

— p. 48 —

Reading

The theme of the text is about human beings as zoo animals.

1 The questions help students predict ideas in the text.

- Students could discuss the questions in pairs, groups, or as a whole-class brainstorm.

Possible answers

a *typical behaviour* could be eating, drinking, sleeping, working, relaxing, watching TV, gardening, etc.
b Students' personal reactions: surprise, curiosity, amusement, shock, fascination, etc.
c To understand the human race better, to make comparisons and question the way we live.

2 • You may wish to teach these words before students read the text: *Homo sapiens* (modern human beings regarded as a species), *inhibited* (unable to express feelings in a natural way).

- As students read the text for the first time, they should check their predictions and note down anything they find surprising, interesting, or funny. They should write notes, NOT whole sentences.
- Get quick feedback on the points they have noted. You could establish a class consensus on the most surprising, interesting, or funny thing.
- You could check that students have understood the main points of the text by asking a few comprehension questions:
  1 *Who are the couple on display at the zoo? What do we know about them?*
  2 *How do children and adults react differently to the couple?*

■ Close up ■■■■■■■■■■■■■■■■■■■■■■■■

- Students work through the questions individually or in pairs.
- Check answers.

Answers

- l.3   other *primates – animals of the monkey or ape families (chimpanzees, gorillas, gibbons, baboons, orang-utans)*
- l.4   the non-literal meaning of *make an exhibition of yourself* is to draw attention to yourself in any situation. *Literally* is used to show that this couple is part of a real exhibition, not a metaphorical one.
- l.34   *continue*
- l.51   a *cage* is a structure, made from bars or wire in which animals are kept. A *cubicle*, on the other hand, is a small room with three walls and a door (or curtain) typically used for dressing / undressing. For example, swimming pools often have *changing cubicles*.

■ Interpretation ■■■■■■■■■■■■■■■■ p. 49 ■

1–3 Students answer the questions in pairs or as a whole-class activity.

- Set the task, then elicit ideas.

Suggested answers

1 • Adult humans have been taught to avoid staring at others. It is taboo. (Children are often told that it is *rude to stare*.)
- Staring could be interpreted as aggressive or challenging behaviour.
- People's homes are traditionally regarded as private places.
- Children, however, are more instinctive; if they find something interesting, they will look closely at it.

2 • People often compare themselves with others in terms of their material possessions.
- Possessions can be used as a measure of relative status.

3 • It is unlikely there would be enough humans willing to appear in a zoo.
- Humans might also be expensive to feed and look after.
- The novelty value of seeing people in a zoo may wear off eventually.

■ Speaking personally ■■■■■■■■■■■■■■■■

1–2 Students work in pairs or groups on these discussion questions.

- Monitor, but do not interrupt.
- You could finish the activity with a short whole-class discussion of the second question.

Additional activity

The Danish couple live in a cubicle like a typical Danish home, with a tiny kitchen, a hi-fi, etc.

- Students talk and / or write an answer to this question: *What would a typical home in your country look like?*

Grammar – Past verbs with present or future meaning

■ Exploring concepts ■■■■■■■■■■■■■■■■■■

1 • Go through **a** and **b**, which are taken from earlier grammar sections in the unit, to check that students understand the task.

- Remind students that Past simple tense verbs do not always refer to past time.
  - a *If I won* … is an unlikely, but possible future happening.
  - b *I wish I had* … refers to an unreal present situation.
- Remind students that they can refer to the **Language Commentary** on p.129.
- Students now work through sentences c–j, deciding whether the Past simple form refers to past, present, or future.
- Monitor, giving help where necessary.
- Let students compare answers in pairs before they begin work on question 2.

2 • Students work independently through the explanations.
  • Check answers.

Answers

1	a	Future	2	1 a	3
	b	Present		1 b	1/2
	c	Present – they do exist		1 c	1
	d	a possible, if unlikely future action		1 d	3
				1 e	2
	e	Present / future. It means people should be or should become more aware.		1 f	2/3
				1 g	4 *
				1 h	1
	f	Present		1 i	2
	g	Present			
	h	Present / future			
	i	Present			
	j	Past			

Note This use*, which is dealt with in Unit 6 (6C), includes expressions like:
*I **wondered** whether you'd like to go for a drink.*
*I **was hoping** you'd phone.*

■ Exploitation

1 • Students could work through this exercise individually in writing and then compare answers with a partner.
  • Check answers.

Answers

1 I'd rather we *didn't sail* – it makes me feel sick. / I'd rather *we flew*.
2 He behaves *as if he was / were* a single man.
3 I wish people *weren't* always in a hurry these days.
4 It's time *we left*. Hurry up! We're going to be late.
5 If you *didn't eat* so quickly, you wouldn't always feel ill.

2 This exercise encourages students to use their imagination (and their sense of humour).
  • You could discuss what is going on in the scenes from old films before eliciting ideas from students. Although this exercise is intended to be fun, encourage students to use the structures listed and correct errors.

Note *Supposing (that)* can be used instead of *Suppose*.

Possible answers

Photograph 1
Man on left *I wish I didn't have to wear this hat.*
             Supposing you ordered the drinks this time.
Man on right *I'd rather you ordered the drinks. I can't speak Russian.*
             It's time we went home. Mother will be worried.
             Imagine I wasn't your father.

Photograph 2
Man   *I wish you weren't my sister.*
      Imagine we were on a tropical island.
Woman *If we're going to dance, I'd rather you stood up first.*
      Suppose you tried speaking to me in English.
      It's time you bought a new jacket.

■ Role play

3 • This activity gets pairs of students to role play a conversation between the characters in one of the photographs. Point out the last part of the rubric – that the people would like things to be different.
  • Monitor but do not interrupt conversations.

Learning new vocabulary

This is one of only two overt 'learner training' focuses in *Landmark Upper Intermediate*. (Using a dictionary was the Vocabulary focus in Unit 3 on p.30.) It is likely that your students will already have their own effective way of learning words. This is acknowledged before various methods are introduced.

Note The two lists of six words to learn have been chosen because they are current and colloquial and will probably not be known to students. *Gobbledegook* is pronounced (ˈgɒb(ə)ldɪˌguːk).

■ Experiment   p. 50 ■

Students are given six new words to learn as an experiment.
  • Allow them about five minutes to do this in any way they wish. It is important at this stage that you do not discuss different ways of learning, but that students use ways they are familiar with.
  • Do not feed back on this stage, but move straight on to the questionnaire.

■ Methods

1 a Students work through the questionnaire individually. Set a time limit of five minutes for students to answer the questionnaire and compare their answers.
  b In comparing their answers with a partner, students may discover that there are different methods of learning and dealing with vocabulary.
  • Finish with a class discussion of questions 3, 4, and 6. This is a preparation for the next stage.

2 • Students now read the checklist of different methods of learning words, ticking any they have tried.

- When they have finished, find out how many students have tried each of the methods. This may lead to a discussion about the pros and cons of each method.

▭ Test

1 • Students now test each other on the six words they learnt in *Experiment*.
- Students could work in pairs or groups. They read out the words and the other students give the definitions. Alternatively, they could read the definition and the other students have to guess the words.
- You could have a brief class discussion on the relative effectiveness of the different methods used.

2 • Students now use a new method to learn the second list of six words.
- You could test the whole class on these words at the beginning of the next lesson or on the following day.

Additional activity

- Make a list of ten words students have had difficulty with in recent lessons and ask them to learn these for homework.
- Remind them of the different methods of learning words.
- Test them two or three days later.

Language in action

▭ Eavesdrop! ▭▭▭▭▭▭▭▭▭▭▭ p. 51 ▭

The questions could be done as a class activity or as pairwork.
- Direct attention to the picture and the three questions.
- Remind students that they are speculating about what they see and should try to come up with a variety of different answers.
- You could elicit possible answers now, or move straight on to *Listening 1*.

▭ Listening 1

1 • Ask students to read questions **a** and **b**.
- **5.7** Students listen to the recording, check their *Eavesdrop!* ideas, and listen for the answers to questions **a** and **b**.

5.7

A OK, so let's try that again. The car will stop here.
B Where?
A Here. Exactly where I'm standing now. OK?
B Yeah, OK.
A The front door will open and one of the detectives will get out and take a good look round.
B So that's when I start to walk forward, is it?
A No, you don't start wa …
B I'm nervous just thinking about it.
A Try not to worry.
B I can't help it.
A Anyway, when the detective is satisfied everything's safe, he'll open the back door and that's when you start to walk forward.

B In other words, I don't move until the door's open?
A Right. Oh, and don't forget, you won't be wearing jeans tomorrow, so you'll need to allow a little more time to reach your meeting point. Does that make sense?
B Yes, that's fine. I'll just need to practise walking in the dress a bit before tomorrow.
A Right, so, then, at the meeting point you look her in the eye, smile, and present her with your gift. Right?
B I just hope nothing goes wrong.
A Don't worry. Everything will be just fine.

- Check answers.

Possible answers
Eavesdrop!
- The young girl is going to present something to a famous visitor. The man is in charge of organizing the event and is explaining the arrangements.
- Outside a public building, an airport, town hall, a church etc.
- It's a dress rehearsal for a ceremony to welcome a famous person.

Listening 1
a The celebrity is going to arrive by car and be presented with a gift by the girl.
b Somebody famous, probably royalty or an important politician, because she will be accompanied in her car by detectives.

2 • Students work in pairs, listen again and note down the functional language used by the speakers.
- Check students know what to do by eliciting examples of the kind of language they are listening for.
- Allocate tasks and play the recording a second and third time if necessary.
- Students note down the expressions and then compile lists. They help and correct each other at this stage.

Note Students add to these lists during the next listening task.

Answers
See full list of expressions after *Listening 2*, question 2.

▭ Listening 2 ▭

1 • **5.8** Ask students to read questions **a**, **b** and **c** and then play the recording.

5.8 including 5.9
Conversation 1
H Right, Julie, you'll find a lot of this job is to do with answering people's queries. People will come in with lots of different queries and they'll expect you to know the answer to them. Now, I know that's not always possible, but you've really got to just try and answer, erm, everything that you can and if you don't know the answer, then you'll have to find out the answers and get straight back to them.
J Erm – Do you … Do you mean that, erm, we, we can't or that I can't ask other people? Will there be somebody else about apart from you that I can ask?
N **5.9** Well, it depends on the time of day really, erm, I'll be here most of the time so you don't have to worry about that. Sometimes there will be questions which I can't answer, so we'll really have to find out the answers together, because you never know what people are going to ask you.
J So what you're saying, is I've got to learn as I go along.

H   Yes, that's right. A lot of it is is just learning, as you say, as you go along. You will also be asked by people for various documents – erm – now, you'll find in the file over in the corner that I have put a lot of specimen documents there – they are also on the computer, but the file will just give you the layout of the documents.

J   Yes …

H   Is that all right?

J   Erm, yes, I think so. Erm, I think I'd like to, erm, do as much as I can of, of speaking to people, erm, so I can learn what to do.

Conversation 2

K   **5.9** Right, OK.

B   … and, erm, the ones in the kitchen – they need watering every other day really.

K   Oh – right, OK.

B   Is that clear?

K   Yeah, I think so – that's fine. Yeah.

B   I mean, it's not the end of the world, but … there are more important things. Erm, the washing machine …

K   Right …

B   … erm, just be careful that you close the door properly.

K   Right – what, what, what do you mean?

B   Well, er, I've had a few problems with it, so just make sure it's properly closed.

K   Er, OK.

B   … and, erm, try to avoid using that long programme.

K   Do you mean I shouldn't use it?

B   Well, it might be better if you didn't, yeah. Aha.

K   Right. OK. Fine.

B   OK, and erm, I've given you some keys,

K   Yes.

B   All right. Check when you leave that the back door's locked.

K   Right, OK.

B   And one of the keys is a bit dodgy …

K   Right …

B   … erm – you've got to sort of put it in quite, er, erm, hard and then turn it – so if you, if you don't get it the first time just try again.

K   Right. OK.

B   Are you all right with that?

K   I'm fine, yeah. That's fine.

B   Erm. Right. Do you just want, just to, just see if there's anything else?

K   You mentioned something about the cleaner.

B   Yeah.

K   When does she come in?

B   She comes in on Mondays – all right?

K   Right.

B   All right? She's got her own key so you don't need to worry about her.

K   Right. So, do you mean – do I have to lock up after she's gone or will she … or do I have to stay while she's there?

B   No, no, no, no, not a problem – I mean she'll probably come when you're out anyway, and I mean, she can arrange to come on another day if it suits you better …

• Check answers.

Possible answers

	Conversation 1	**Conversation 2**
a	Not very well.	They are not close friends, probably neighbours.

b   Someone explaining a job to a new colleague – it's an office job. | One person is going away, perhaps on holiday; the other person is going to come in and look after the house while the first person is away.

c   She sounds positive and seems prepared to learn. | She sounds very matter of fact – not particularly keen on the things she has to do.

2   a   **5.9**   Play the recording, while students follow the extracts in their books on p.52, marking the functional language used by the speakers.

b   Students add the expressions to their lists.

• Check through the lists of functional language students have compiled from the conversations.

Answers

(This includes expressions from *Listening 1* and *2*.)

Making instructions clear

5.7

OK?   Does that make sense?   Right?

5.9   Extract 1

Is that all right?

5.9   Extract 2

Is that clear?   Are you all right with that?   All right?

Checking instructions

5.7

So, that's (when I start to walk forward), is it?   In other words, … (This expression precedes a paraphrasing of an original form of words.)

5.9   Extract 1

So, what you're saying, is …

(From full conversation

Do you mean that …?)

5.9   Extract 2

What do you mean …?   Do you mean …?

Note *So* often precedes a question used by someone to check they have understood. The expression *In other words* precedes a paraphrasing of an original form of words.

© Oxford University Press **PHOTOCOPIABLE**

■ Features of natural conversation ▬▬▬▬ p. 52 ■

This section focuses on ways of replying positively to a question (alternatives to *Yes*). It is useful to have a range of alternatives so as to avoid having to repeat the word *Yes*.

1–2   Play the extracts again, while students follow them in their books to find all the words and expressions for replying positively.

• In pairs, students spend a few minutes pronouncing these words and expressions correctly.

• Check answers.

Answers

Extract 1

Yes, that's right.   Yes, I think so.

Extract 2

Yeah /jeə/   That's fine.   Right.   OK.

Practice

1 a **5.10** Students listen and answer the question. They could discuss their ideas in pairs.

5.10

1 Right. / All right. / OK. I'm not sure (Falls then rises)
2 Right. / All right. / OK. Do you understand? (Rise)
3 Right. / All right. / OK. I understand (Fall)

• Check answers.

Answers
See tapescript **5.10** for intonation.

• You could then drill chorally and individually.

b **5.11** Play the dialogue through first, then play it line by line, drilling chorally and individually. Pay attention to the correct intonation of *Right*, *All right*, and *OK*.

5.11

A You need to feed the dog once a day. All right?
B OK.
A The dog food's in this cupboard.
B All right.
A And remember to change the water. OK?
B OK.

2 a **5.12** This exercise gives students practice in identifying and reproducing rising and falling intonation patterns, both of which are possible in these phrases.

• **5.12** Play the recording. Stop after each phrase, and drill the sentences chorally and individually.

5.12

1 Do you see what I mean? ↗   3 Is that all right? ↘
2 Does that make sense? ↘   4 Is that clear? ↗

Answers
See tapescript **5.12** for stress and intonation.

b **5.13** Play the recording. Pause after each sentence and drill chorally and individually.

5.13

1 What exactly do you mean?
2 Do you mean I shouldn't use it?
3 So, do you mean I should be careful?
4 So, what you're saying is, don't use it, right?
5 In other words, I mustn't use it, right?

Answers
See tapescript **5.13** for stress.

Exploitation

• Students form pairs and work through the two situations, taking it in turns to be Student A
• Monitor their discussions, listening for use of the functional language.

• Do not interrupt conversations unless the language is completely incorrect or inappropriate.

Writing p. 53

1 • Allow students time to read through the first two examples, and think about or discuss their ideas.
• Check answers.

Suggested answers

a • With spoken instructions the person being given the instructions can ask for clarification and check their understanding immediately.
  • In the case of written instructions this checking process is not possible, so the writer has to write clear, precise instructions which leave no room for misunderstandings. This means that the instructions must be very clearly staged and simply worded.

b • Informal written instructions are more chatty – they may contain extra, personal information (more like spoken instructions).
  • Formal written instructions are clearly staged, perhaps with numbers.
  • The same instruction words may be repeated (e.g. *choose*).

c • Break the instructions into simple easy stages that leave no room for doubt.
  • Assume the reader knows nothing, if necessary oversimplify the instructions.
  • Use numbers for different points.
  • Show it to someone else to check.

2 • Students quickly read both situations and choose one of the sets of instructions suggested.

Note If students choose the first situation, they must write informal instructions. If they choose the second situation, they have the option of writing formally or informally.

• Remind students to refer to the **Writing guidelines** on p.157 of their books.
• Allow students time to plan their first drafts.
• If the writing itself is too long to be done in class, get students to plan and prepare in class, then write the instructions for homework.

3 a Students exchange written work, read each other's instructions, and ask for clarification of anything they do not understand. This gives the original writer a good idea of what needs improving and clarifying.

b Students rewrite their instructions in the light of their discussions. The writing of the final draft of instructions may be done in class or as homework.

Summary

• Encourage students to use the tick boxes to help them keep a record of their learning.

6 A certain age

Theme

The theme of this unit is *age*.
Preview Important events in peoples' lives
Reading The phenomenon of longevity in an Italian village
Listening The experiences of very old people

Grammar

- Present perfect review (LC p.130)
- Present perfect continuous (1) (LC p.130)
- Present perfect continuous (2) (LC p.130)

Vocabulary

- Homonyms
- Euphemisms

Functional language

- Expressing annoyance
- Calming someone down

Features of natural conversation

- The use of *I mean*

Pronunciation

- *have, been*
- Sounding polite
- Sentence stress

Writing

- A letter of complaint (expressing annoyance) (WG p.155)

Workbook

- Peak ages in different professions
- Word-building; Topic vocabulary: stages of life; *bring up, make up, take up, break down*
- Present perfect review; Present perfect continuous (1 + 2); Present perfect simple and continuous; Past simple and Present perfect tenses
- Expressing an opinion: adverbs (2); Giving an opinion

Preview

The short reading texts introduce the theme, important events in people's lives, and contextualizes the Present perfect and Past simple.

Your thoughts
p. 54

1–2 Students think about and discuss the two questions about the age they are now and the best age to be.

- Elicit their ideas and allow this to develop into a short class discussion if appropriate.

Reading

- You may wish to teach these words before students read the text: *farewell, nun*.

1 • Before they read, ask students to look at the six pictures and elicit ideas about what they depict or represent.
- Do not confirm or deny these ideas at this stage. The purpose of discussing the photographs is to help students think about the content of the texts.
- Students read the texts and match each one with a picture.
- Elicit their ideas.

Answers

Text 1 Picture f	**Text 4** Picture e
Text 2 Picture a	**Text 5** Picture d
Text 3 Picture b	**Text 6** Picture c

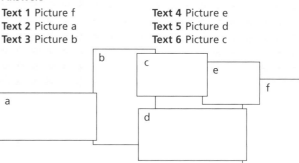

2 • This exercise focuses on idiomatic language from the texts.
- Students could match the sentences and meanings individually, or you could elicit the answers from the whole class.

Answers

a pleased
b because (*cos* is common in everyday speech but not in writing)
c unstable (from the verb *to wobble*)
d not in bed (related to *to get up* – when you have *got up*, you are *up*)
e disappointment
f told me I've lost my job (other slang words for this: *to sack / to fire / give sb the boot* and more formally: *to dismiss / to lay sb off / make sb redundant, give sb their notice*).

1–2 Students exchange opinions and experiences in pairs or small groups.
- Monitor their discussions but do not interrupt.
- Elicit ideas from the class to finish this part of the unit.

Grammar — Present perfect review

1–4 Students work through questions in the usual way.
- Remind students that they can refer to the **Language Commentary** on p.130.

Note

1 You may need to remind students that the contracted forms *she's / he's*, etc. are short forms *she / he has* (not *she / he is*).

2 Students may need to refer back to the short reading texts when they do **4**.

- Monitor, giving help where necessary.
- Check answers.

Answers

1	Present perfect	Past simple
a	*It's been*	
b		*moved on / came out*
c	*has changed / has left / (has) broken*	
d		*was / spent*
e	*has happened*	
f	*It's happened / he's given*	*went / said*

2 **1b** refers to the past, a period of time that is now over.
1c refers to the present and mentions recent past events which affect the present.
The word *now* would make this present reference more obvious:
*All that has **now** changed; she has **now** left her job …*

Note Go through answers for **3a** and **b** together as the continuation sentences help to explain the differences.

3 a 1 • *It's been a really great day.*
  The day in question is today – the day is not yet over.
  This would probably be said towards the end of the day.
  … but I'm really tired now. (C) is the continuation.
  • *It was a great day.*
  The day is over. It could be yesterday, or a day at any other time in the past.
  … but it took me nearly a week to recover. (B) is the continuation.
 2 • *She's left her job.*
  This is a recent event, and probably means she does not have a job at the moment.
  … but she won't tell anyone why. (D) is the continuation.
  • *She left her job.*
  This is old news. It is simply a report of a past fact which has no particular effect on the present.
  … last December. Now she's self-employed. (A) is the continuation.

4 There are many possible present results related to these three sentences.
  a *So now Charlie can walk / doesn't need to crawl.*
  b *Now, I think more about the baby than myself / my career is less important than my baby.*
  c *So now I haven't got a job. / I'll have to look for another job.*

5 a Students work in pairs or you could elicit ideas from the whole class.
  b **6.1** Students listen and check their ideas.
  • You could write the different pronunciations on the board in phonetic script.

6.1

1 What have /əv/ you bought?
2 Have /hæv/ you seen Lucy recently?
3 No, I haven't /hævnt/, but Susan has /hæz/.
4 Michael has /əz/ already told me.
5 I have /hæv/ remembered.

Answers

a See Tapescript **6.1**
b **Rules of pronunciation**

1 The strong form of *have* is used:
  • when *have* is the first word of a question (Sentence 2)
  • in negatives and when it is the last word in a sentence (Sentence 3)
  • for emphasis (Sentence 5).

2 The weak form of *have* is used when it is not stressed:
  • in *wh-* questions after *why, what*, etc. (Sentence 1)
  • when it is embedded in a sentence which is not a question (Sentence 4).

3 We usually drop the *h* in the weak form in fast speech and it is linked to words before it.
  What have /wɒt əv/, Michael has /maɪkl əz/.

6 It is possible to use both verb forms sometimes, but there is always one that is more normal or more appropriate.
  • Students complete the *Check* exercise individually, then compare answers with a partner.
  • Check answers.

Answers

a *I've been* (This week is not finished yet.)
b *travelled* (Last year is a finished time period.)
c *she's forgotten* (The meeting is still going on. The woman *is* an hour late.)
d *I've worked* (*all day* refers to today, a present time period. This is reinforced by the word **Now** *I need a rest.*)
e *I was* (This refers to a completed event, located at a precise time in the past: *ten years ago.*)

—— p. 56 ——

Reading

The subject of the article is the Italian village of Campodimele and the remarkable fact that many of its inhabitants live to be very old.

1 • In pairs, students discuss the lifestyle of the old woman shown in the photograph.
  • Elicit a few ideas on each of the subjects mentioned.

2 • Students now look at the headline and the other photographs and make predictions about the text.

Note The expression *time has stopped* means life is as it was in the past; the place has not moved with the times.

 • You could pre-teach the following: *longevity* (living a long life), *cholesterol* (fatty substance in body tissue and blood), *blood pressure* (the pressure at which blood flows through the body).
 • Elicit students' ideas and discuss them, but do not confirm or deny any of their suggestions.

3 • Give students four or five minutes to read the text and check their predictions.
 • Check their ideas.
 • You could ask a few general follow-up questions.
 What is the main subject of the text?
 In what ways has time stopped in Campodimele?

▇ Close up ▇

 • Students work through the questions individually or in pairs.
 • Check answers.

Answers
 • l.1   *it* The fact that she has a good chance of living 100 years.
 • l.21   *at least* a walk taking at least an hour and maybe more.
 • l.39   *yet* means *however, but,* or *despite what has been written already.* It shows that surprising or contrasting information follows.
 • l.41   *womb and tomb, birth and death,* (*womb* is the part of a woman's body in which a baby is carried before birth / *tomb* means *grave*.)

4 • Ask students to read questions **a–c** before reading the text again. As they read, they underline the relevant information to answer the questions.
 • Check answers.

Answers
 a Low cholesterol levels in old people (*lower than in new-born babies*). (l.14)
 Low blood pressure (*rhythmic fluctuations significantly lower than the national average*). (l.42)
 b The inhabitants themselves have their own explanations: *hard work (not lazy); not much meat; no danger; nice weather; exercise (good hour's walk); easygoing nature, sense of balance (no depression, people aren't lonely, live with their families, stress unknown, no traffic, Mediterranean diet (fresh vegetables, little fat and salt, etc.).*
 The experts' ideas are similar: *well-structured lifestyle; regular exercise; regular routines.*
 c Women wear (traditional) scarves; men … gossip and play cards. (l.32)

▇ Interpretation ▇ ▇ p. 57 ▇

1–2 Students discuss these questions in pairs.
 • Elicit their ideas.

Possible answers

1 The village is interesting because it is *unique*. It reflects a traditional lifestyle which has almost disappeared. It is relatively untouched by modern ways of life. Scientists are able to compare lifestyles and the effects on people's health.
 • They visit regularly to monitor any changes; perhaps to find out whether the traditional ways are changing, whether the way of life is being altered by contact with the modern world.

2 A simple, traditional way of life is healthier and more conducive to long life than modern life.
 • Particular lessons: eat a simple diet, take exercise, avoid stress.

▇ Speaking personally ▇

1–2 Students discuss these questions.
 • Elicit their ideas and, if time, broaden this out into a class discussion.

Grammar – Present perfect continuous (1)

▇ Exploring concepts ▇

1–3 Students work through questions 1–3 in the usual way.
 • Remind students that they can refer to the **Language Commentary** on p.130.
 • Monitor and help.
 • Check answers.

Answers

1

	Present perfect simple	Present perfect continuous
a		*have been visiting*
b	*has stood*	
c		*have been studying*
d	*I've found*	

2 a Present perfect simple – B + D
 Present perfect continuous – A + C
 b **1a** C, **1b** B, **1c** A, **1d** D

3 a and **d** refer to repeated actions
 b and **c** refer to continuous actions

▇ Pronunciation ▇

4 • Ask students how the words *have, has,* and *been* are pronounced in **3a–d**.
 Students can work in pairs or elicit ideas from the whole class.
 b **6.2** Students listen and check.

6.2

 a … scientists have been (əv bɪn or bɪn) visiting this remote mountain village regularly.
 b I have been (aɪv bɪn or bɪn) studying the children and grandchildren of the over-85s.
 c He's been (hiːz bɪn) repairing his car all day.
 d I've been (aɪv bɪn) coming to Spain for holidays since I was fifteen.

Answers

See tapescript 6.2 .

Note
1 When personal pronouns are used it is more usual to use the contracted form *I've* /aɪv/, *he's* /hiːz/, etc.
2 The strong form of *been* /biːn/ is never used in the Present perfect continuous form. The weak form /bɪn/ or /bin/ is used instead.

▌Exploitation ▌

This activity provides personalized controlled practice of the two forms of the Present perfect.

1 a To check that students understand the task, read the example and elicit some additional answers to the question. *How have you kept fit?*
  - Students individually write answers to the seven questions.
  - Monitor, checking that students use both simple and continuous forms of the Present perfect.
  - Elicit a few answers from the class.
  - Students now ask each other questions 1–7 and make a note of their partner's answers.
  - Again, monitor, helping and correcting as necessary.

b When students have finished noting each other's answers, they should discuss any similarities or differences between their lives.
  - Finally, finish with whole-class feedback on one or two of the questions, for example 5 and 7.

▌Role play ▌

The two role plays are for fluency practice and should involve students using the Present perfect verbs naturally.

2 • Allow students a few minutes to read and prepare for Situation 1.
  - Monitor discussions, but do not interrupt or correct.
  - When pairs have completed Situation 1, they should change roles and prepare and work through Situation 2.
  - If you hear any interesting conversations for Situation 2, you could ask students to act them out for the class.

▶ Photocopiable activity 8 p.165

— p. 58 —

Listening

This activity introduces vocabulary to prepare students for the following tasks.

1 a Students read the adjectives, deciding which age-group they associate the words with.
  b Students compare ideas in pairs or groups. They should try to agree on adjectives that apply to old people.
  - Elicit their ideas.

Note Obviously there are no right or wrong answers to this question. Many of the words which describe negative qualities are associated with old or elderly people.

2 • Before listening, students note down three questions they would ask people over 100 and then compare questions with a partner. Allow only two or three minutes for this.
  - Before playing the recording elicit a few questions and note them on the board.
  - You may wish to teach these phrases before students listen to the recording: *senior citizen* (a polite term for an old or retired person), *world cruise* (a voyage by sea which stops at various places – a type of holiday popular with old people).

3 • Ask students to read the two questions.
  - 6.3 Students listen and check their ideas.

6.3

P Good morning to you all. If I sound slightly out of breath, it's because I've been running around the studio trying to find my notes for today's programme! That's better. Now, I have with me in the studio two senior citizens: Mary Craig, who is a hundred and two, and Edward Macintosh, who's a hundred and one. Welcome to you both. I've been so looking forward to meeting you. Could I start by asking you, Mary, what you remember about your hundredth birthday?

M Oh, I had a wonderful day. I had a special lunch at a nice hotel in town and then I spent the afternoon and evening with my family and friends. Everything went so well.

P And a, er, telegram from the Queen?

M Oh, yes, in fact I had three telemessages – one from the Queen, one from the mayor of the town where I live, and one from the Minister for Social Security.

P Edward, what was it like for you – crashing through the hundred barrier?

E Fantastic – because we all had free drinks! We had a lovely get-together and I had two hundred and twenty-five letters, postcards, and telegrams – two hundred and twenty-five.

P Sounds wonderful. You certainly both look very relaxed and happy. Tell me – what's good about living so long?

M Well, one of the things I think is you live a selfish sort of life. You've only got yourself to think about. You do what you want, you eat when you want, you go to bed when you want. There's nobody there to ask what time you're coming home – you're free. And of course you can travel.

P When did you start travelling?

M Oh, I've been travelling ever since my husband passed away – I started in my seventies. I had a world cruise in my nineties. I've had other cruises to the Mediterranean and the Caribbean, and in September I'm going on a cruise along the Rhine.

P You've done a fair amount of travelling too, haven't you Edward?

E Well, when I lost my wife in 1970, I sold my hotel and started travelling. I've been round the world – in both directions – I've been to America, Canada, Australia, Morocco, … I've been all over.

P Do you think that people today are happier than you were in hard times?

M Well, they don't appreciate things so much as we do. As far as young people are concerned it's easy come, easy go. You see, we had to make do and mend in our young days. There was no help, nothing.

P Do you think that has made you appreciate what you've got now, Edward?

E Of course I do. Children get taken to school in a bus now. I used to walk four miles to go to school.

M Well, the tragedy now is that parents daren't let their children walk to school. It's not safe any more. They can't be independent. I think the young have a very difficult time nowadays. At a very early age they get introduced to drugs – and we never had that worry. It was a much easier life when we were young. We were always kept on the straight and narrow.

P You two are speaking what many people would say are words of wisdom. Do you think you are wiser now that you are older?

E Oh, sure, you go on learning no matter how old you are – you go on learning. I learn something every day, every month, every year.

P Mary?

M No, I'm sure I'm not wiser. I've been going to various adult education courses recently. I'm still trying to learn things, because I like keeping my brain ticking over, but most of it goes in one ear and out of the other. I enjoy it at the time but my memory's terrible – I just don't remember things. I can't remember names or names of places – it drives me mad. People think I'm going soft in the head.

P I'm sure that's not true. We're sitting here having a perfectly normal, intelligent conversation. By the way, I've been meaning to ask you this: do you find generally that people of your own age are better company than younger people – people like me, for example?

E Oh, no, not at all. I'd much rather talk to younger people – not teenagers or school children – I mean sensible people, business people. I'd rather talk to them than the elderly people where I live. The thing is, we think a lot but we don't say very much.

P And finally, looking towards the future, I was wondering whether you still have any goals – any special things you want to do?

M Well, I take any opportunities that come along, but no, there's nothing I really want to do now. I just live from day to day. I have a great-grandson who's getting married the day before my hundred-and-third birthday and I'm having a champagne lunch party – that's what I'm looking forward to at the moment.

P Edward?

E No, no, no special goals – but I still want to do a little more travelling before I finish – I like travelling. And I've made up my mind I'm going to live to be a hundred and ten – so I'm looking after myself.

- Check answers.

Answers

a Personal answers from students. (See Tapescript **6.3** .)

b The two people interviewed seem generally happy.

■ Interpretation

1 • Working individually or in pairs, students choose one or two of the adjectives to describe Mary Craig and Edward Macintosh.
- Elicit answers from the class. Check reasons for students' choice of adjectives.

Suggested answers

1 Mary Craig
relaxed (interviewer describes her as this) / *selfish*, *independent* (Mary says 'You've only got yourself to think about') / *adventurous* (she has been on world cruises); *stupid* (not *wise*)/ *forgetful* (Mary says she hasn't done very well at education classes; her memory is terrible) / *easygoing* ('I just live from day to day now.')

Edward Macintosh
relaxed (interviewer describes him as this) / *adventurous* (he has travelled round the world) / *wise* (he says he goes on learning every day) / *ambitious* (he's going to live to be a hundred and ten)

2 • Students make notes on what they remember about Mary and Edward's attitudes. If necessary, play the recording again.

Suggested answers

2	**Mary**	**Edward**
a	– she likes to go on learning, but isn't very good at it, she's been taking classes	– he goes on learning all the time
b	– they don't appreciate things like she did – children can't be independent – they have a difficult time	– everything is done for them – he prefers talking to younger people than to people his own age
c	– takes opportunities as they come – no special goals – she lives from day to day	– no special goals – wants to do more travelling – wants to live to be 110

3 • Students think about the meanings of the expressions and then compare ideas. They could use a dictionary.
- Elicit ideas and check answers.

Answers

3 a – *easy come, easy go* money and possessions obtained without difficulty are not thought to be very valuable and may be spent or lost without regret
– *make do and mend* accept things as they are or repair them (an alternative to buying new things)

b *kept on the straight and narrow* stay honest, keep away from crime

c *keep my brain ticking over* keep my mind or brain active
it goes in one ear and out of the other I hear something, but I don't take it in or learn it

d *it drives me mad* it makes me very annoyed

■ Vocabulary

1–2 Students read the introduction to *euphemisms*. Ask if they use similar expressions in their own language.
- Students can work individually or in pairs. Encourage them to guess or work out the meanings from the context.

Note Don't do the first question as an example as **a**, **b**, and **c** have the same meaning.
- Check answers.

Answers

1 a, b, c	*to pass away,*	
	to lose someone,	
	and *to finish*	to die
d	*soft in the head*	mad, insane, crazy
2 a	*plain*	ugly, unattractive
b	*plumper*	fatter
	go thin on top	go bald, lose your hair
c	*not very bright*	stupid, unintelligent
d	*hard of hearing*	deaf

■ Speaking personally

1–2 Students discuss these ideas in pairs or groups.
- Monitor, but do not interrupt.
- Finish with a brief, whole-class exchange of ideas.

Additional activity

- This could be a homework task.
- Students could write a description of an old person who is well-known in their country; a politician or an actor etc.

Grammar – Present perfect continuous (2)

Exploring concepts ▮▮▮▮▮▮▮▮▮▮▮▮▮▮▮ p. 59 ▮

Two uses of the Present perfect continuous are focused on here:
- to explain a current situation
- to sound polite in social situations.
- Remind students that they can refer to the **Language Commentary** on p.130.

Note You might like to work through question **1** and check answers before students move on to question **2**.

1 • Students work through this question in the usual way.
  • Monitor, giving help where necessary.
  • Check answers.

Possible answers

1 a Her eyes are red and swollen. / She looks very unhappy.
  b They're soaking wet. / They're wearing swimsuits.
  c I've lost weight. / I'm not as fat as I was.
  d He's very fit. / He looks strong and healthy. / He's lost weight.
  e The apartment looks very clean and bright. / There's paint on the floor. / There's a strong smell of paint.

2 • Point out that they are now looking at a different use. Students work through the questions in the usual way.
  • Check answers.

Possible answers

2 a 1 The speaker is meeting someone they know a lot about but haven't met.
    2 This is probably a romantic situation of some kind. Boyfriend and girlfriend have just met again after time apart.
    3 This could be an apology at the beginning of a letter, or the speaker may have met or be on the phone to a person they were going to write to. The speaker is making an excuse.
  b The speakers are all trying to impress the listeners with their sincerity or strength of feeling.
  c In general, the Present perfect continuous is used in this way in personal or social situations, to make a good initial impression. The second sentences would be more likely in more formal situations.

Pronunciation ▮▮▮▮▮▮▮▮▮▮▮▮▮▮▮▮▮▮

3 • The aim of this exercise is to focus students' attention on the use of appropriate intonation to sound polite.
  • **6.4** Play the recording and elicit answers.

6.4

1 I've been so looking forward to meeting you.
2 I've been longing to see you again. It seems so long since yesterday.
3 I've been meaning to write but I just haven't had the time.

Answers

a The speaker sounds polite and sincere in Sentences **1** and **2**.
b This is largely achieved by elongating the stressed syllable and using a higher pitch.

- Play the recording again and drill chorally and individually.

Exploitation ▮▮▮▮▮▮▮▮▮▮▮▮▮▮▮▮▮▮▮▮▮▮

This exercise gives controlled practice of the Present perfect continuous to explain present situations.

1 a Elicit one or two more sample answers to the example sentence to check that students understand.
  • Students should work individually, writing their explanations for 1–5.
  b Students compare answers in pairs, then with their partner try to think of some unusual explanations for each sentence.
  • Monitor conversations, correcting any errors in the use of the Present perfect continuous.
  • Elicit one or two realistic answers for each sentence, then ask for some imaginative ideas.

Possible answers

1 I've been working all night. / I've been playing football.
2 I've been feeling ill all day. / I've been reading a ghost story.
3 I've been crying. / I've been trying to get my make-up off.
4 I've been dieting. / I've been eating less fatty food.
5 I've been trying to find somewhere to park. / I've been sitting in a traffic jam for hours.

2 This activity provides controlled practice of using the Present perfect continuous in order to sound polite.
  • Students could write their new sentences, then compare in pairs.
  • Students then make mini-dialogues.
  • Do **a** as an example with the whole class. Elicit ideas for **A** and **B** parts.
    Example
    A *I've been wondering what to get you for your birthday.*
    B *Well, I'd love a new bike.*
  • Students complete **b–h**.
  • Monitor conversations, correcting if you hear errors.
  • To finish the activity, elicit a few example conversations.

Possible answers

b *I've been expecting you since six o'clock.*
c *I've been wanting to ask you how old you are. / I've been wanting to ask you this – How old are you?*
d *I've been hoping you'd phone.*
e *I've been dying to ask you where you bought that hat.*

Note *To be dying to do something* to want to do something very much.

f *I've been trying to remember your name all morning.*
g *I've been hearing all about you.*
h *I've been hoping to meet you. / I've been hoping we'd meet*

Role play

This is mainly a fluency activity, so don't force the use of the Present perfect continuous.

3 • Do only one of the situations if you are short of time.
   • Read through the instructions and the situations with the students to make sure they understand the task.
   • Give them a few minutes to think about what to say.
   • Monitor the conversations, but do not interrupt.

Homonyms

• Read the introduction on definitions with the whole class. The third category (words that look and sound alike but have different meanings) is not given a special name.

Homophones ━━━━━━━━━━━━ p. 60 ■

1 • Do **1a** with the whole class as an example, then let students work independently. Draw attention to the clues.
   • Check answers.

Answers

		Alternative spellings (homophones)
a	forwards	*fourth*
b	watch	*sea*
c	made someone go (past of *send*)	*scent* *cent*
d	e.g. lamb, beef, pork	*(to) meet*
e	prohibited	*band*
f	to have on (clothes)	*where*
g	not cooked colour	*roar* *read*
h	if	*weather*

2 a Explain that the words for the gaps in sentences 1–4 are all homophones.
   • Ask students to think about possible answers before they listen.
   • **6.5** Play the recording. Students listen and fill in the gaps. Play again if necessary.

6.5

1 I heard the weather forecast but I didn't know whether to believe it or not.
2 She didn't know where her glasses were so I had to read the letter to her.
3 When I travel by plane, I prefer to sit in an aisle seat.
4 Four days ago I was fined for speeding.

b Students compare answers and discuss alternative words in pairs.
   • Check answers.

Answers

See tapescript **6.5** . (words underlined)

1 Alternative spellings (and meanings)
herd – group of animals (*herd of cows*), *whether, no, weather, knot*

2 Alternative spellings (and meanings)
wear, sew / sow, reed

3 *plain, isle*

4 *for, daze, find*

Homographs ━━━━━━━━━━━━━━━━

1 • Do **1a** with the class to check that everyone understands the task.
   • In pairs, students work through the rest of the exercise.
   • Monitor, but don't interrupt or correct.

2 • **6.6** Play the recording. Students listen and check their answers.

6.6

a That's a terrible photo of me. Please tear (/teə(r)/) it up immediately.
b I prefer live (/laɪv/) recordings to albums made in a studio.
c When I was younger I liked sitting in the back row (/rəʊ/) at the cinema.
d When it's very hot, bathing (/beɪðɪŋ) in the sea is the quickest way to cool down.
e My watch has a battery, so you don't need to wind (/waɪnd/) it up.
f In the end, the President had to bow (/baʊ/) to public opinion and change his mind.

• Go through answers with the class.

Answers

See tapescript **6.6** .

3 • As this follow-up exercise is likely to be time-consuming, you could set it for homework.

Possible answers

a You cry *tears*. (/tɪə(r)z/)
b Fish *live* in water. (/lɪv/)
c We had a *row* about money. (/raʊ/)
d I'm *bathing* the dog because he's muddy. (/bɑːθɪŋ/)
e The *wind* blew my hat off. (/wɪnd/)
f I put a *bow* in my hair. (/bəʊ/)
   You play a violin with a *bow*. (/bəʊ/)
   Robin Hood used a *bow* and arrow. (/bəʊ/)

Words with different meanings ━━━━━━

• Students may know some of these words, but if they do not, then this is a useful dictionary activity. Encourage students to guess meanings before checking in a dictionary.
• Do question **a** with the class to check that everyone understands the task.

Note If students can work out what part of speech these words are, it will help them check the meanings in a dictionary.

• In pairs, students work through **b–f**.
• Monitor, but don't interrupt or correct.

Answers

a   *trunk* – noun (large case for carrying belongings)
Other meanings: noun – elephant's nose / Amer. English –
place for putting luggage in a car / main part of a tree.

b   *left* – verb (past of *leave*)
Other meanings: adjective – opposite of *right*.

c   *pretty* – adverb (*fairly* / *quite*)
Other meanings: adjective meaning *nice to look at, beautiful*.

d   *nature* – noun (character)
Other meanings: noun the whole universe and every created
thing / the forces that control the physical world.

e   *cross* – adjective (angry, irritated)
Other meanings: noun – mark made by crossing two lines /
crucifix, verb – to go from one side to the other (e.g. *to cross
the road*).

f   *free* – adjective (independent)
Other meanings: verb – to release (e.g. an animal or a
prisoner), adjective – costing no money / available or spare
(e.g. *Is this seat free* / *free time*).

■ Exploitation ■

5   • This activity recycles some words from p.60. The stories
should be short – two or three sentences at most.

• Students work in groups of three or four and choose one
of the sets of words.

Note If you want to ensure that all the words get used, you could
allocate sets of words to different groups.

• Explain that students should write short stories using all
the words.

• Monitor discussions, helping students with meanings and
pronunciation.

• Groups exchange stories and check on the use of the
key words.

• You could finish this activity by getting groups to read out
their stories. Alternatively, students could display their
stories in the classroom.

Language in action

■ Eavesdrop! ■ p. 61 ■

The questions could be done as a class activity or as pairwork.
• Direct attention to the picture and the two questions.
• Remind students that they are speculating about what
they see and should try to come up with a variety of
different answers.
• You could elicit possible answers now, or move straight on
to *Listening 1*.

■ Listening 1 ■

1   • Before they listen students should read **a** and **b**.
   • **6.7** Students listen to the recording, check their
Eavesdrop! ideas, and listen for the answers to **a** and **b**.

6.7

M   What's the matter, Daniel?

D   I'm really fed up with people thinking I'm under age. That's the
second time today. It's really getting me down.

B   Well, you must admit you do look pretty young.

D   Yeah – OK, I may not look eighteen, but surely I look older than
fourteen. It really annoys me.

M   Don't let it worry you. You got what you wanted didn't you?

D   I did in the end, but not until I'd shown him my driving licence.

L   That's OK then, isn't it?

D   No, it isn't. I think the whole system is really stupid. It's OK to leave
school, become a soldier and fight for your country and die if
necessary – when you're sixteen, but you can't vote in elections and
you can't even buy yourself a drink until you're eighteen. It really
irritates me.

M   That's because people under sixteen haven't got a clue what
elections are about.

D   How can you say that? We've been talking about politics since we
were about twelve.

B   Relax.

L   Calm down.

D   I'm quite calm. All I'm saying is that it isn't logical. I mean you can
go into a pub when you're fourteen, but what's the point of that if
you've got to wait for four years before you're allowed to buy
a drink?

L   He's right. There are some really silly laws. The one that really gets
me is that you can't get a part-time job until you're thirteen.

D   Everyone does though, don't they?

M   That's because no one bothers checking how old you are when you
go for that kind of job.

L   Exactly! That's what I mean – it's a really silly law.

• Check answers.

Possible answers

Eavesdrop!
• A bar, pub, hotel, drinking place of some kind.
• Someone thinks he is not old enough to buy alcohol. (In
Britain you cannot buy alcoholic drinks under the age of 18.)
Actually the speaker is old enough, but looks under age.

Listening 1

a   You can do these things at these ages:
   • 13 get a part-time job
   • 14 go into a pub (but not buy alcohol)
   • 16 leave school, join the army
   • 18 vote in elections, buy alcohol.

b   Check answers related to students' own countries.

2   • Students listen again and note down the functional
language used by the speakers.

• Check that students understand the task, especially to
express annoyance and to *calm someone down*.

• Allocate tasks and play the recording a second and third
time if necessary.

• Students note down the expressions and then compile
lists. They help and correct each other at this stage.

Note Students add to these lists during the next listening task.

Answers
See full list of expressions after *Listening 2*, question 2.

Listening 2

1 · **6.8** Ask students to read questions **a** and **b** and then play the recording.

6.8 including **6.9**

Conversation 1

Ju ... break reduced from twenty minutes to ten minutes.
All What?
 I beg your pardon.
 What do you mean?
B What was that? Could you say that again?
Ju **6.9** Well, we're going to have our coffee break reduced from twenty to ten minutes.
R You're joking!
J That makes me really angry. Why?
Ju Well, I wasn't told officially, but that's what I've heard and I think it's right.
R Oh, that's outrageous ...
Ju I know, I, well ...
J I can't believe it. Who said ... ?
R That's not enough time to get your sugar in the cup.
 That's ridiculous.
Ju No, I know, no ...
J Ten minutes, we don't even get back – just haven't got the time for that ...
Ju Well, it's just a money-saving exercise, isn't it?
R Whose, whose brainwave was that?
J Yes.
Ju Well, I don't know. I don't know where it came from.
J Oh, that's so infuriating. Barbara?
B I mean, don't get so worked up about it. I mean, you know, I mean, we've got to be a bit more flexible, perhaps. I mean ...
R Flexible?
B Ten minutes is, ten minutes is ...
J Barbara ...
R Ten minutes is nothing.
B Well ...
J We can't even get back here in ten minutes.
R You can't even get out of your seat in ten minutes.
J No, that's right.
Ju And not to be consulted ...
J Oh, this is ridiculous. I want to speak to someone about this.
B Well, I think you're getting a bit worked up about it ... ,

Conversation 2

J ... and he's making me so angry ...
B Just calm down, it's not as bad as all that ...
J Oh, it is, it really irritates me ...
S Yeah, take it easy. What he actually ... What actually happens?
J Well, he's a radio ham and he sets up his radio and he's got a huge aerial in the garden and you can hear him trying to contact other people in other countries like Australia where it's daytime, but of course it's night time at our place, so all we hear through the walls is him calling and, and, and talking to people in other countries where it's daytime
 6.9 and he's making me so cross.
B Have you spoken to him? Have you tried to reason with him?
J Well I've tried, yes. I've tried, and he says, 'Oh yes, hmm, hmm, hmm,' and then the next night it's the same thing.
B Well, I can understand your point of view, but I mean, I don't think, I mean, there are worse things.
J No, there aren't – it's making me lose nights and nights of sleep and I'm really, it's really getting me down. I don't know what to do any more, I really don't know what to do. I have tried talking to him.

S Well, neighbours can be pretty awful. I mean, we've, we got, the people next door to us, erm. We went ... I went out one morning and they, they, were in the process of building a wall between our house and theirs – they hadn't even asked us whether they could or not.
J Oh, you see, that's what's so irritating – people don't care.
S It's just so infuriating.
B Yeah, but I mean, you've got to, got to live with each other, you know, I mean ...
J Well, not at night time ...

· Check answers.

Possible answers

	Conversation 1	Conversation 2
a	Colleagues in some kind of workplace.	Not specified, but probably friends.
b	Their coffee break is being reduced from twenty to ten minutes.	Inconsiderate neighbours.

2 · **6.9** Play the recording, while students follow the extracts in their books on p.62, marking the functional language used by the speakers.
· Students add the expressions to their list.
· Check through the lists of functional language students have compiled from the conversations.

Answers
(This includes expressions from *Listening 1* and *2*.)
Expressing annoyance
6.7
I'm really fed up with ...   It's really getting me down.
It really annoys me.   It really irritates me.
How can you say that? (an expression of disbelief)
6.9 Extract 1
You're joking!   That makes me really angry.   Oh, that's outrageous.   I can't believe it! (an expression of disbelief)
That's ridiculous.   Oh, that's so infuriating.
(**From full conversation**
What?)
6.9 Extract 2
... he's making me so cross.   ... it's really getting me down.
It's just so infuriating.
(**From full conversation**
... he's making me so angry.   ... it really irritates me.)
Calming someone down
6.7
Don't let it worry you.   Relax.   Calm down.
6.9 Extract 1
... don't get so worked up about it.
6.9 Extract 2
Well, I can understand your point of view, ...
(**From full conversation**
Just calm down.   ... it's not as bad as all that ...   Take it easy.)

Note Notice the frequent use of *really* in the expressions of annoyance. It is used for emphasis.

© Oxford University Press **PHOTOCOPIABLE**

■ Features of natural conversation ■■■ p. 62 ■

This section focuses on the use of the phrase *I mean*
in conversation.

- You could elicit ideas on why speakers use *I mean* before
  students find examples in the extracts.
- Students find all the examples of *I mean* in the two
  extracts on p.62.
- They then discuss in pairs why the expression is used and
  what it means.
- Check their ideas.

Answers
Sometimes *I mean* is used when a speaker is trying to explain
something more clearly. It can also be used to correct a mistake.
More often, *I mean* has little meaning on its own, but is used as
a filler, one of several expressions used frequently in everyday
speech. Others include *you know, sort of, kind of*.

Extract 1
Barbara *I mean* (1), *don't get so worked up about it.* *I mean* (2),
you know, *I mean* (3), *we've got to be a bit more flexible,
perhaps.* *I mean* (4)

1 the speaker is signalling to the others that she is going to
  say something
2, 3, 4 here the phrase is simply a nervous filler

Extract 2
Barbara *Well, I can understand your point of view, but* **I mean**
(5), *I don't think,* **I mean** (6), *there are worse things.*

5 here the speaker is probably trying to clarify what she is
  trying to say
6 filler

Simon **I mean** (7), *neighbours can be pretty awful.* **I mean** (8),
we've, we got, the people next door to us ...

7 the speaker is signalling that he is going to say something
8 this is clarification, the introduction of an example

Barbara *Yeah, but* **I mean** (9), *you've got to got to live with
each other, you know,* **I mean** (10) ...

9, 10 fillers.

■ Practice ■■■■■■■■■■■■■■■■■■■■■■■■

1 a If your students are familiar with sentence stress they
      could work in pairs. Alternatively, elicit ideas from the
      whole class.

   Note There is often more than one possible answer as the context and
   speaker's viewpoint will vary.

   b **6.10** Students listen and check their answers.
   - Play the recording again and drill chorally and individually.

   6.10

   1 That's ridiculous.
   2 That really irritates me.
   3 It's really getting me down.
   4 That's really annoying.
   5 That makes me really cross.
   6 It really gets me.

Answers
See tapescript **6.10** for stress.

■ Exploitation ■■■■■■■■■■■■■■■■■■■■

- Students form groups and choose a topic to discuss.
- Explain that the discussions are about expressing
  annoyance. One student should be very annoyed and at
  least one other should try to calm them down.
- Monitor their discussions, listening for use of the
  functional and conversational language. Do not interrupt
  unless the language is incorrect or inappropriate.
- You could finish the activity by listing all the things that
  annoy people.

■ Writing ■■■■■■■■■■■■■■■■■■■■■ p. 63 ■

1a–c Allow students time to read the examples and think about
      or discuss their ideas in pairs.
- Elicit their ideas.

Suggested answers
a The conversation is very informal, someone is expressing
   their anger spontaneously. The letter is a formal complaint,
   written in serious, well-thought-out language.
- The letter is carefully structured and includes the expression
  of annoyance, examples of the cause of the annoyance, and
  a demand for action, backed up by a threat.
- The sentences or ideas are longer and more complex in
  the writing.
b *I find it quite appalling ...*
   On numerous occasions ...
   This is a completely unacceptable situation ...
   ... which I am not prepared to tolerate.
   ... I shall consult my solicitor.
   The writer uses formal language to impress upon the reader
   the seriousness of the complaint.
c *quite* appalling / **completely** unacceptable are used in the
   letter. You could also use: *absolutely, utterly,* and *totally.*

2 - Students should choose one of the two formal letters of
     complaint, then follow the paragraph plan suggested.
     They should aim to write 100–120 words.
   - Remind students to refer to the **Writing guidelines** on
     p.155 of their books.
   - They should use the letter on p.63 as a model.
   - Allow students time to plan their first drafts.
   - If the writing is too long to do in class, get students to plan
     and prepare in class, then write the letter for homework.

3 a Students exchange paragraphs and decide whether what
      their partner has written is formal enough and whether
      the feeling of annoyance comes through clearly.
   - Students discuss possible improvements.
   b Again, the writing of the final draft of these paragraphs
      may be done in class or as homework.

■ Summary ■■■■■■■■■■■■■■■■■■■■■■

- Encourage students to use the tick boxes to help them
  keep a record of their learning.

7 Survival

Theme

The theme of the unit is *Survival*.

Preview Australian Aborigines
Listening Personal survival stories
Reading The Brazilian city of Curitiba surviving pressures of the modern world

Grammar

- *can, could, be able to* (LC p.130)
- Ability and inability: *could, couldn't, manage to, succeed in* (LC p.131)
- Articles (LC p.131)

Vocabulary

- Connotations
- Distinctions between verbs

Functional language

- Persuading / advising someone not to do something

Conversation strategies

- Making generalizations

Features of natural conversation

- The use of *you know*
- Unfinished statements

Pronunciation

- *can / can't*
- Articles

Writing

- Radio scripts (WG p.157)

Workbook

- A popular science article about the weather
- Topic vocabulary: weather; Topic vocabulary: ways of walking; *come* + particle; Word-building: *-ness* noun endings
- *can, could, be able to* review; Ability and inability; Articles
- Cohesion; Writing a short preface for a tourist book

Preview

The first theme of the unit is the situation of the Aborigines in Australia. The reading texts also contextualize examples of the modal verb *can / could*.

■ Your thoughts ━━━━━━━━━━━━━━━ p. 64 ■

1–2 Before reading the texts, students think about and discuss the questions about indigenous populations in modern societies.

Note *Gypsies* are the subject of a later unit, so do not encourage too much discussion of them at this stage.

- Elicit ideas.
- You could allow this to develop into a class discussion.

Possible answers

1 North American (Red) Indians (Native Americans) / Indian populations of South American countries – e.g. the Guarani Indians of Brazil; the Jivaro of Ecuador / the Inuit (Eskimos of Greenland), Canada, etc./ the Lapps of Northern Norway and Finland.

2 Students' own personal answers.

■ Reading ■

1 • Students pool any knowledge they already have about the Aborigines.
- If they know very little about the subject, ask them to look at the photographs for some ideas. Set a time limit of two to three minutes for this.
- Elicit 'facts' and guesses from the students and write two lists on the board.
  - facts: *Aborigines live in Australia.*
  - guesses: *There are only a few hundred Aborigines left.*
- You may wish to teach these words and phrases before students read the texts: *poverty* (a state of being poor), *state benefits* (money from the government to help the poor), *bush (knowledge)* knowledge from traditional rural ways of life (*the bush* is the name given to areas of wild uncultivated land in Australia and Africa), *holy* (of religious significance), *eco-tourism* (tourism to places of environmental interest, for example, to see animals or plants in their natural environment).

2 • Students read the short texts and find out if any of the facts are mentioned or guesses confirmed.
- Go through the lists on the board, checking the facts and guesses.

3 • Students read the texts again and write lists of positive and negative features of present-day Aborigine life.
  • Pairs of students could share this task. Student A looks for positive features and B for negative features.
  • Students compare lists.
  • Check answers.

Answers (the text numbers are in brackets)
Positive features
Old people live with families, so do not have to live alone. (1) / Family members can look after each other's children. (1) / They have the right to vote. (2) / Can get state benefits. (2) / Some have their own councils and run their own business affairs. (2) / Many Aborigines have retained traditions, cultural identity and therefore dignity. (3) / Some communities are improving – tree-farming and eco-tourism. (4)

Negative features
They are poor. (1) / Houses are often overcrowded. (1) / Bad living conditions. (3), Widespread alcohol and drug problems. (3) / Health problems and unemployment. (4)

▩ Person to person ▩▩▩▩▩▩▩▩▩▩▩▩ p. 65 ▩

1–2 Students exchange opinions and experiences in pairs or small groups.
  • Monitor their discussions but do not interrupt.
  • To finish, elicit a few ideas from the class, and if time develop this into a class discussion.

— Grammar — *can, could, be able to* review —

The main focus here is on ways of talking about ability, but question 1 looks at other meanings of the verb *can*.

1–2 Students work through the questions individually or with a partner.
  • Remind students that they can refer to the **Language Commentary** on p.130.
  • Monitor, giving help where necessary.
  • Check answers.

Answers

Note Sometimes two answers are possible, as the uses of *can* overlap.

1 a possibility (or ability) **d** possibility
  b ability   **e** permission (or possibility)
  c ability

Note This section reminds students that *to be able to* has to be used where forms of *can* do not exist.

2 a *He **can** swim ...*   **d** No Present perfect form of *can*.
  b No future form of *can*.   **e** No infinitive form of *can*.
  c *he **could** run*   **f** *I **couldn't** play chess.*

▩ Pronunciation ▩▩▩▩▩▩▩▩▩▩▩▩▩▩▩▩

3 a Students can work in pairs, or you could elicit ideas from the whole class.
  • You could tell students that there are three different ways of pronouncing *can* / *can't*.
  b **7.1** Students listen and check their ideas.

  • You could write the answers on the board in phonetic script.

7.1

1 Can /kæn/ you swim?
   Yes, I can. /kæn/
   No, I can't. /kɑːnt/
2 How far can /kən/ you swim?
3 I can /kən/ play the piano, but I can't /kɑːnt/ sing very well.

Answers

a See tapescript **7.1** .
b **Rules of pronunciation**
1 The strong form of *can* /kæn/ is used in short answers and usually when the first word of a sentence. (Sentence 1).
2 The weak form of *can* /kən/ is used after *Wh-* words (sentence 2) and when it is embedded in the sentence. (Sentence 3)
3 *can't* is pronounced /kɑːnt/. In the United States and in some parts of the UK it is pronounced /kænt/.

Note If students have difficulty distinguishing between *can* and *can't* get them to listen for the short vowel sound /æ/ or /ə/ for the affirmative, and the long vowel sound /ɑː/ for the negative. In places where *can't* is pronounced /kænt/, the final *t* is usually pronounced more.

▩ Check ▩▩▩▩▩▩▩▩▩▩▩▩▩▩▩▩▩▩▩▩▩▩

  • Students work through the exercise individually, then compare answers with a partner. Point out that, if more than one form is possible, students should give them all.
  • Check answers.

Answers

a *could / was able to*   **d** *will (I'll) be able to*
b *couldn't / wouldn't be able to* **e** *to be able to*
c *been able to*   **f** *can / are able to*

—————————————— p. 66 —

Listening

1 • Before they listen, students use the headlines and photographs to predict what the stories are about.

Note The headlines refer to the incidents described in **7.2** , but the photographs are not accurate. Students are asked to identify the mistakes in question **3**.
  • Check that students know the words *inferno* and *fail* from the headlines.
  • Students compare ideas in pairs or groups.
  • Elicit, but do not confirm students' ideas.

2 This activity has two purposes: to pre-teach some of the phrases from the recordings, and to help students to make more accurate predictions about the stories.
  • Check that students understand the meanings of the words and phrases.
  • Students work individually or in pairs to decide which stories the words appear in.
  • You could elicit their ideas, but do not confirm or deny them at this stage.

3 • **7.2** Play the recording.

Speaker 1

It was so bright I really thought they'd switched on floodlights outside the hotel. Luckily I was still awake. As soon as I pulled back the curtains the heat hit me; all I could see was a wall of flames just a few centimetres from the window. I didn't realize until later that the floor below me was on fire. I moved back into the room. I'm sure there'd been no alarm but I could hear banging noises and people shouting. Someone knocked on my door – I opened it and a man grabbed my hand but I pushed him away and went back into my room – panic isn't logical – I can't believe it now, but I left with my shoes, a toothbrush, and a straw hat of all things.

The corridor was full of people hammering on doors and screaming. Someone yelled at me, 'Drop your things and run!' So I ran with the others to the end of the corridor away from the smoke to a staircase – I had to stop there to pick up my hat.

Anyway, at the bottom of the staircase there was a door. The man in front of me pushed and pulled at it but it wouldn't open. He turned back – you could see the blind panic on his face. We couldn't move, there were so many people. He tried again and finally succeeded in opening the door. We ran barefoot across the car park and scrambled over a two–metre-high fence. Eventually we were able to make it round to the front of the hotel. It was an amazing sight – windows were being smashed, people were jumping from the first two floors, others higher up managed to climb down on knotted sheets. One girl escaped by smashing the window with her shoe and jumping out; another had her life saved by a man breaking her window with a hammer from outside.

Fire engines kept arriving. One of them raised its ladder and moved towards a room on the top floor where there was someone sitting on a window sill.

Then the ambulance came and six of us were taken to hospital.

Speaker 2

We were flying along quite normally when I decided to roll the plane – it was an old two-seater air-force jet. It's a fantastic feeling flying upside down at 400 kilometres an hour. The next second, my brother's ejector seat had broken away from the plane and shot through the cockpit, and he was falling from 1,000 metres. The air was rushing in and for a moment I couldn't breathe. It was a few seconds before I managed to regain control. I looked down and watched my brother pulling at the rip-cord of his parachute but for some reason it didn't open. I just watched him fall – I was sure I'd never see him alive again. I circled round for six or seven minutes, looking for the parachute, but there was nothing. Finally I headed back to the airfield. The return flight was horrific – I was convinced that I'd lost my brother. When I landed and found out he was alive – it was incredible. I went straight to the hospital and there he was, sitting in an armchair with a brace round his neck, joking with the nurses. His first words were, 'Where have you been?'

Later he told me that the torn parachute had slowed him down just enough and he'd had a soft landing on a grassy bank. Amazingly, he could still walk, and was already on his feet when the rescuers arrived.

- Students check their predictions and look for mistakes in the photographs.
- Play the recording again if necessary.
- Check answers.

Answers

2 Terrifying journey through hotel inferno

banging noises

knotted sheets – bed sheets tied together with knots, which are traditionally used by people escape from bedroom windows, prisons, etc.

blind panic – *blind* here means *irrational*

ladder

the floor below – here *floor* means *storey*

wall of flames – related to *inferno*

Parachute fails at 1000 m

ejector seat – seat which automatically catapults a pilot out of a damaged plane

soft landing – gentle coming down to earth of plane, parachutist, etc.

torn parachute

upside down

roll the plane – make the plane go over and over sideways in mid-air

two-seater – plane (or other vehicle) with two seats, i.e. for two people

3 Hotel photograph

Fire in photograph is not an inferno. / It is daytime, not night. / Smoke is coming from top floors, not first or second.

Parachute accident

three men, not one / plane is not a two-seater.

4 • Ask students to read through the list checking they understand the phrases.
- Students now listen to the recording again and make a note of the significance of these phrases to the story.
- Check answers.

Answers

a	*bedroom curtains*	when the speaker opened the curtains she was hit by the heat
b	*toothbrush and straw hat*	in her panic the speaker took these things with her when she left her bedroom
c	*door at bottom of staircase*	at first the people trying to escape could not open this door
d	*hotel car park and fence*	the people escaping had to run across the car park and climb (scramble) over the fence
e	*shoe and hammer*	these were things that two people used to break the hotel windows

Vocabulary

- Students work individually or in pairs, guessing the differences in meaning between the verbs, then checking in a dictionary.
- Elicit ideas.
- Check answers.

Answers

a	*bang*	hit something hard, often making a noise and causing damage
	knock	hit, not usually violently, sometimes to attract attention
	hammer	hit hard repeatedly
b	*grab*	take or hold something suddenly and quickly, especially when you are in hurry
	push	move something away from you
	pull	move something towards you

c *shout* say something very loudly
  scream a loud, high-pitched shout especially when you are excited, frightened, etc.
  yell shout extremely loudly
d *smash* break completely into many pieces
  break separate into pieces or damage (not as strong as smash)

■ Role play

This role play is related to the second recording.

- Allocate roles and check that students understand the task.
- Play the recording again. Students make a note of any important points.
- Allow time for students to prepare, and then for their role. ask and answer questions in role.
- Monitor the conversations, but do not interrupt.
- Finish by eliciting any interesting questions or answers.

■ Speaking personally

- Students talk about their experiences in pairs or groups.
- Monitor, but do not interrupt.
- Finish the activity by eliciting one or two of the most interesting stories from the class.

Additional activity

- You could ask students to write a brief description of one of the stories they have heard. Suggest a past tense narrative of 80–100 words. You could refer students to the **Writing guidelines** on p.157 of their books.

— Grammar – Ability and inability

■ Exploring concepts ■ p. 67 ■

1–4 Students work through this section in the usual way.

- Remind them that they can refer to the **Language Commentary** on p.130.
- Monitor, giving help where necessary.
- Check answers.

Answers

1 a *I could see* **d** *others managed to climb down*
  b *we couldn't move* **e** *I couldn't breathe*
  c *we were able to make it* **f** *he could still walk*

2 Note This question highlights a crucial point which it is essential for students to understand – the fact that *could* can only be used to refer to general, not specific, past abilities. (The negative form *couldn't*, however, can refer to both specific and general past inabilities.)

Sentence b is incorrect because opening the door is a specific ability. Sentences a and c refer to general past abilities.

3 a *manage to* + verb (infinitive) and *succeed in* + *-ing* are both used to refer to specific past abilities and are used instead of *could* to refer to specific past abilities.

Note They could both be replaced by *was able to*.

b • *He tried once more and managed to open the door.*
  • *He tried once more and succeeded in opening the door.*

4 Note Make sure students realize that verbs of perception are frequently used with *can* or *could*: *hear, feel, smell, remember, sense, taste, understand*

■ Exploitation ■

1 a Tell students to quickly read the story for gist. Allow one or two minutes for this.
- You could ask students to give a one-sentence summary of the text to check they have understood the main points.
- You could also pre-teach these words and phrases: *dirttrack* (unmade road), *bumpy* (with an uneven surface), *hedge* (row of bushes or small trees planted close together to form a boundary), *reverse* (drive backwards), *to-ing and fro-ing* (going backwards and forwards).
- Students read the story again and fill the gaps with one of the ability verbs. Remind them that, depending on which of the ability verbs they choose, they may need to change the form of the verbs which follow.
- Give them time to compare answers with a partner.

b **7.3** Play the recording so that students can check their answers.

7.3

I turned off the main road on to a dirt track – it was narrow and bumpy with hedges on both sides. I drove quite slowly – then I noticed I was coming to a bridge over a stream. I could see that the road went steeply up to the bridge and dropped steeply again after the bridge. My car is very long and the bottom is close to the ground, which means that if you go over a bump it's easy to scrape the bottom. I knew by looking at the bridge that I couldn't get over it without damaging the car. I'd have to go back. The problem was, because the road was so narrow I couldn't turn the car round. The only option was to reverse the way I'd come. I remembered that about 500 metres back there was a farm entrance where I'd be able to turn. I started reversing but by then there was another car behind me – of course he couldn't overtake me so he had to reverse too. It was just as narrow and bumpy going backwards and there was an added problem: because of my bad neck I couldn't reverse quickly. Eventually I managed to reverse into the farm entrance and after a lot of to-ing and fro-ing I succeeded in turning the car round and driving forwards again. What a nightmare!

- Check answers.

Answers

1 *could see*
2 *couldn't / wouldn't be able to get*
3 *couldn't / wasn't able to turn*
4 *be able to turn*
5 *couldn't / wasn't able to overtake*
6 *couldn't / wasn't able to reverse*
7 *managed to reverse / succeeded in reversing / was able to reverse*
8 *managed to turn / was able to turn / succeeded in turning*

2 This exercise provides personalized controlled practice of *can, could,* and *be able to.*
- Elicit a few more examples of the three different types of ability from students to check they understand the task.
- Set a time limit for them to compile their lists.

- Students work individually, then compare lists with a partner.
- Monitor all stages of this activity, giving help and correcting.
- At the end of the activity, you could ask students to tell the class about some of the more unusual abilities they have talked about.

3 • This exercise practises *manage to*, *succeed in* and verb + *-ing*. It can be done individually in writing, or orally, in groups or as a whole-class activity.
- Elicit an example for **3a**, then let students do **b–d**.
- Monitor, giving help where necessary.
- Check answers.

Possible answers
a *Eventually ...*
I managed to start it by pushing it.
b *In the end ...*
she succeeded in getting a highly-paid job as a travel guide.
c *In the end...*
I managed to persuade them to get me a dog for my birthday.
d *Eventually ...*
I succeeded in putting it out with my neighbour's fire extinguisher.

4 This a personalized controlled practice of *could* with perception verbs.
- Elicit one or two examples, then let students continue in groups. If necessary, provide further prompts on the board.
A visit to your favourite restaurant.
The day you moved to a new home.
- Monitor conversations, correcting errors.
- To finish the activity, elicit a few memories from each group.

■ Free speech

5 This is mainly a fluency activity, so don't force the use of expressions of ability.
a–b Students think of one or two things they can do well, then discuss these abilities with a partner making notes about their partner's abilities.
- Monitor the conversations, but do not interrupt.
c Students use their notes to write briefly (100 words) about their partner's abilities or, if you have time, give students the opportunity to put their notes together and then tell the rest of the class about their partner. Alternatively, you could set this task for homework.

Note This activity often works best if students describe something they have taught themselves to do, rather than something they have learned in school or in a more formal situation.

▶ Photocopiable activity 9 p.166

Reading

This article outlines ways in which the Brazilian city of Curitiba has attempted to solve some of the typical problems that affect modern cities.

1 • Students discuss the photographs, trying to decide where the places are.
- Elicit their ideas and the clues that helped them to make their guesses.
- You could have a brief class discussion on the problems of life in large modern cities.

Answers
- top left picture: Bangkok, Thailand
- top right picture: Paris, France
- bottom picture: Curitiba, Brazil

2 This activity helps students to predict the content of the text at the same time as introducing some of the important vocabulary from it.
- Check that students understand the words and phrases in the list. They could use dictionaries to help with difficult words.
- Students now predict aspects of city life included in the article by grouping the words and phrases into topics. Ask students to read the title of the article to give them ideas.
- Elicit students' ideas and write word groups on the board. (There are several ways of grouping the words.)

Possible answers

Transport	*bus lanes, vandalism, fuel consumption, jams*
Poor people's lives	*better diet, fruit and vegetables, rural exodus, recyclable waste*

Other possible groups

The environment	*fuel consumption, recyclable waste*
Population problems	*better diet, rural exodus*
Housing problems	*vandalism, rural exodus,*
Food	*better diet, fruit and vegetables*

3 • Ask students to read the three questions.
- Students now read the text quickly to find the answers to the questions. They can read in more detail when they answer the Comprehension questions on p.69.
- Check answers.

Answers
a transport, poverty, waste, large population
b better – there are many references to improvements
c bottom picture

■ Close up

- Students work through the questions individually or in pairs.
- Check answers.

Answers

- l.2 *greenest* could mean:
  with the most trees and grassy areas (parks, etc.) / the most environmentally friendly.
- l.11 mushrooms grow large very quickly (overnight). This is how the city has grown.
- l.17 *purr* is a smooth, low, regular or continuous sound. Engines in good condition make this noise. Cats *purr*.
- l.30 Verbs like this are formed by adding the suffix *-en* to adjectives:
  shorten, flatten, weaken, sweeten, blacken, broaden, etc. or nouns: *lengthen, strengthen*.

■ Comprehension ━━━━━━━━ p. 69 ■

- Allow students time to think about possible answers to questions 1–4.
- Students read the article again.
- Check answers.

Answers

1 The population of Curitiba was growing very quickly. Fifty different bus companies were competing in the city, causing traffic jams.
2 It would have cost too much and taken too long to build. They wanted a quicker, cheaper solution.
3 People like and respect the transport system.
4 Widening the streets would have meant destroying the city's identity and people's memories. (It has been found that widening roads or building more roads does not solve traffic problems – it encourages more traffic to use roads and so potentially makes the problem worse.)

■ Speaking personally ━━━━━━━━

1–2 Students discuss these questions in pairs or groups.
- Elicit their ideas and, if time, broaden this out into a class discussion.

Possible answers

1 **Pros** often more direct than public transport, quicker except at peak traffic times, cheaper if several people travel in one car, more comfortable
  Cons environmentally unfriendly – causes pollution, slow at peak times, leads to traffic jams, risk of accidents, can cause stress, road rage, etc.

2 Personal answers.

— Grammar – Articles ━━━━━━━━

■ Exploring concepts ━━━━━━━━

1–4 Students work through questions 1–4 in the usual way.
- Monitor and help.
- Remind students that they can refer to the **Language Commentary** on p.131.
- Check answers.

Note It will be very time-consuming to elicit explanations for all the uses of articles. Once you are satisfied that students understand the concepts, move on to the next part of the task.

Answers

1 a–b • **bold text** = definite articles, (reasons 1, 2, 3 in brackets)
*They came from **the** (3) poorest areas of **the** (1/3) city and it was **the** (3) first time they had been to a̲ (5/6) theatre. And 35,000 low-income families exchange **X** recyclable waste for **X** food once a̲ (6) fortnight. At **the** (3) Parque Mane Garrincha, I saw **X** people pushing **X** wheelbarrows and carrying **X** bags with **X** tins, **X** old toys, **X** paper, **X** plastic, and **X** bottles. A̲ (4 or 5) young woman brought a̲ (4 or 5) broken window, another a̲n (4 or 5) old gas cooker. **X** Council workers weighed **the** (2) waste and loaded it in a̲ (4 or 5) lorry. **The** (2/3) women then both received **X** free food. Each four kilos meant a̲ (6) kilo of **X** fruit and **X** vegetables from another lorry.*

2 a–b u̲n̲d̲e̲r̲l̲i̲n̲e̲d̲ = indefinite articles (reasons 4, 5, 6 in brackets – see above). **X** = nouns without articles

3 • Uncountable nouns   *recyclable waste, food, paper, plastic, free food, fruit, vegetables*
  • Plural countable nouns *people, wheelbarrows, bags, tins, (old) toys, bottles, Council workers*

Note Here the nouns are referred to in general.

4 a 1 *The* + (comparative) adjective (*poorer*) / adjective (*more important*)
      The + noun phrase (*less importance*) / adjective (*better*)
    2 Personal answers.

Note Try to encourage students to think of a range of different grammatical ways of continuing this sentence.

■ Pronunciation ━━━━━━━━

5 a Students work in pairs or elicit ideas from the whole class. You could tell students that *the* has two different pronunciations and *a* and *an* have only one.
  b **7.4** Students listen and check their ideas and work out the rules of pronunciation.
  - To help students do this you could write the answers in phonetic script on the board.
  - To help students work out the rules of grammar, ask them to look at the first letters of the words that follow the indefinite articles 1–6 in their books.

7.4

1 the end /ðɪ/	4 an hour /ən/
2 the film /ðə/	5 a university /ə/
3 an umbrella /ən/	6 a holiday /ə/

Answers

a See tapescript **7.4** .
b **Rules of pronunciation**
  - The definite article is pronounced *the* /ðə/ when the next word begins with a consonant. It is pronounced /ði/ or /ðɪ/ when the next word begins with a vowel.
  - The strong form of *the* /ði:/ is only used when we want to emphasize something.
    The Julia Roberts? (the famous actress)?
  - The indefinite articles *a* and *an* are pronounced *a* /ə/ and *an* /ən/.

Rules of grammar
  - The indefinite article *a* is used when the next word begins with a consonant (*a book*), and the indefinite article *an* is used when the next word begins with a vowel sound (*an egg*).

- If you ask them to look at the words in phonetic script, they will be able to see that the above rule for the indefinite article is true, but that it refers to sounds, not spellings.
  an umbrella /ʌmbrelə/ (begins with a vowel)
  a university /juːnɪvɜːsəti/ (begins with a consonant)
  an hour /aʊə/ (begins with a vowel as the *h* is silent)
  a holiday /hɒlɪdeɪ/ (begins with a consonant)

Exploitation

1 • Students fill the gaps in the text; they can then check their ideas in the *Exploring concepts* section and / or the **Language Commentary** on p.131.
  • Check answers.

Answers
There is (1) *a* large crowd of (2) *X* people standing by (3) *the* side of (4) *a* busy London road. In (5) *the* middle of (6) *the* road (7) *a* bus driver is shouting and hitting (8) *the* front window of (9) *a* black London taxi. (10) *The* driver of (11) *the* taxi has decided to lock his doors and wait for (12) *the* bus driver to calm down and return to his bus and (13) *the* passengers waiting there.
(14) *X* Scenes like this are becoming more and more common and increasingly they are ending in (15) *X* violence and (16) *X* criminal charges.
In (17) *The* United Kingdom, as in (18) *X* other countries there seems to be (19) *an* epidemic of (20) *X* incidents like this.

2 • In groups of four or five, students each choose one of the subjects listed.
  • Give them time to prepare their short talk.
  • Monitor the talks, note any errors in the use of articles, and either feedback to the class after the activity or refer them again to the **Language Commentary** on p.131.

Note All the subjects suggested are uncountable nouns. If you make students aware of this, they are more likely to do it as a controlled practice activity. If you decide not to point this out, it will be more like a fluency activity, in which students are not thinking consciously about articles. This will give you a better idea of how well they have mastered and absorbed the grammar of articles.

Writing

3 • Students choose a topic, and should write about 75 words on it. This could be a class or homework activity.
  • If they do this in class, monitor, giving help if necessary.
  • Students exchange writing and check their partner's use of articles.
  • Students could write a final draft in class or as homework.

Connotations

Positive or negative? p. 70

  • Read through the introductory definition and go through the examples in the book (*skinny*, *slim*, *thin*) to check students understand the idea of connotations.

Note Connotations was first mentioned in the vocabulary section on p.10 in Unit 1.

1 • Students work individually or in pairs through the ten sentences. They should decide on their answers before checking in a dictionary.
  • Check answers.

Answers
a **eccentric** – positive or neutral. *Eccentric* behaviour or lifestyle may be chosen by independent-minded people. It is also associated with intelligence.
  mad – negative. It can mean *insane*. *Madness* is regarded as a mental illness.
b **chubby** – positive. It is often used to describe attractively fat babies. It is associated with being healthy and well-fed.
  fat – negative. It means overweight, unattractive, unhealthy, related to over-eating.
c **serious** – positive or neutral. It means thoughtful, not stupid or trivial-minded.
  stuffy – negative. If a person is *stuffy* they are too serious or lacking in fun, so dull and boring.
d **ambitious** – positive. It suggests the idea of wanting to become better by effort and hard work.
  pushy – negative. A *pushy* person is so ambitious that they disregard other people or use them to get what they want.
e **stubborn** – generally negative. Refusing to change your mind even if it would be logical or reasonable to do so.
  determined – positive. Serious about carrying through an intention or a decision.
f **keen on** – positive or neutral. Interested, but not fanatical.
  obsessed with – negative. Too keen or interested, unable to stop thinking about something to the extent of being unbalanced.
g **famous** – positive or neutral. *Famous* describes someone who is known to many people, often for something heroic or praiseworthy.
  notorious – negative. It means well-known for something bad.
h **confident** – positive or neutral. Believing in one's ability.
  big-headed – negative. Having too high an opinion of your own ability or personality.
i **cheap** – negative. Costing little money probably because it is poor quality.
  inexpensive – positive or neutral. Not costing a lot money; suggests good value for money.
j **proud** – positive in this sentence. Feeling of satisfaction or happiness due to having done something well.
  arrogant – negative. It means *proud* in the sense of superior to others.

Note *proud* can also mean *having* **too** *high an opinion of oneself or one's achievements* and so in some contexts has negative connotations.

2 • Students could continue working independently, or you could do this as a whole-class activity.
  • Elicit ideas and allow students to check in dictionaries before they write sentences.
  • Monitor and check answers.
  • Ask students to suggest some sentences to demonstrate the differences.

Answers
2 a *childish* – negative
  I was always embarrassed by my parents' **childish** *behaviour at parties.*
  childlike – positive or neutral
  My sister has a **childlike** *belief in people's honesty.*

b *effeminate* – negative – used to describe a man with unmasculine behaviour or appearance
*Many people think that men with long hair are **effeminate**.*
feminine – positive
*That long silky dress makes her look very **feminine**, doesn't it?*

c *macho* /mætʃəʊ/ – negative – used to describe unacceptably aggressive behaviour thought to be typical of a man:
*He thinks it's **macho** to drink a lot and get into fights.*
masculine – positive or neutral
*He looks very **masculine** since he's started body-building.*

Other associations

1
- Ask students to read the explanation.
- You could elicit examples from their own language to check they understand the idea of associations.
- Students can work individually or in pairs through the list of words.

Note As this exercise may be quite time-consuming, students could work on three or four words in class and then do the rest as homework. Or you could allocate a two or three words to each student and ask them compare answers in groups.

- Check answers.

Answers

Associations	Associated words	
belief	political	principle
	religious	(in God)
campaign	military	service – system in some countries in which young men train to be soldiers for a limited period of time
	legal	
class	social	working – middle – upper class
	political	class system
climber	social	a social climber, someone who tries to move upwards socially
	sporting	e.g. rock climber
confession	religious	admitting sins to a priest
	legal	a guilty person's confession
creation	artistic	
	religious	the making of the world by God
	musical	like *artistic* creation
defence	military	the defence of a country is military matter
	legal	opposite in court to *prosecution*
	sporting	opposite to *attack* in games like football
harmony	artistic	
	social	people of different types, backgrounds, races etc. living at ease with each other
	musical	way in which musical notes and sounds combine together
march	military	way in which soldiers walk
	political	political march is another name for a demonstration
	musical	music which accompanies soldiers walking
minister	political	important politician responsible for particular aspect of government, e.g. *minister for agriculture*
	religious	priest

score	musical	written form of music, e.g. for orchestra
	sporting	number of points, goals, etc. in a sport. *France beat Korea – the score was 3–0.*
service	religious	church ceremony *When I was a child, I went to a special children's **service** at my local church.*
power	military	military strength
	political	*multi-national companies often have political power*
freedom	artistic	*Censorship is an attempt to limit artistic freedom*
	political	if people have *political freedom*, it means they can express political ideas freely
	religious	being free to hold any religious beliefs you wish
	legal	the opposite of *imprisonment*

2
- Work through one example with the class, then let students work individually through the rest of the colours.
- Students can then work with a partner and compare and explain their associations.
- Elicit answers and explanations from the class.
- You could finish by asking what different associations colours have in different countries.

Answers (based on British associations)
- **red** – anger (*red rag to a bull*) / danger / stop (*traffic lights*) / socialist (*red flag*) / in debt (*to be in the red*)
- **blue** – upper-class (*blue blood*) / conservative / unhappy (*to feel blue / have the blues*)
- **green** – jealousy, envy (*green with envy*) / immature, inexperienced / good at gardening (*to have green fingers*) / environmentally friendly (*the Green Party*)
- **white** – purity, goodness, virginity (*white wedding*) / peace (dove)
- **black** – evil (*black magic*) / death (clothes at a funeral) / musical styles (e.g. soul) / financial credit (*to be in the black*)
- **yellow** – cowardice
- **pink** – liberal (slightly socialist or left-wing)

Language in action

Eavesdrop! p. 71

- The questions could be done as a class activity or as pairwork.
- Ask students to look at the picture and read the questions.
- Remind students that they are speculating and should try to come up with a variety of answers.
- You could elicit possible answers now, or move on to *Listening 1*.

Listening 1

1
- Draw attention to the extra question.
- **7.5** Students listen to the recording, check their *Eavesdrop!* ideas, and listen for the answers to **b**.

Father	Are you sure you're doing the right thing, Martin?
Martin	No, I'm not sure, but I want to give it a go. I've always been attracted to Africa.
Father	We don't think you should do it till you've finished university. That's what most people do.
Martin	I know that – but these people need help now; they may not be here in two years' time. Anyway, on the whole, I think it's better to do these things when you're young. You tend to get set in your ways when you're older.
Father	I don't call twenty-one old, Martin.
Mother	We're only thinking of what's best for you, Martin.
Martin	I know you are, but you don't know what's best for me. That's the whole point.
Mother	I mean, have you really thought this through? How are you going to cope with the heat – and apparently it gets very cold at night. And what about eating? Where will you get food?
Martin	Stop worrying, Mum. I'll survive. I mean, it's not as if I'm going to some remote village in the jungle.
Father	And what about wild animals? There are still quite dangerous animals in some parts of Africa, and terrorists.
Martin	What do you mean, terrorists?
Father	Well, you hear cases of foreigners being kidnapped and held hostage by terrorists, don't you? Surely it would be more sensible to go somewhere nearer home.
Martin	Look, I know what the dangers and the difficulties are going to be, but these people need help now and I'm going to do what I can to help.

• Check answers.

Possible answers
Eavesdrop!
• Mother, father, and their son, a young man in his early twenties (21).
• Young man's room / bedroom.
• Preparing to go away somewhere, having packed bags / reading a guidebook.
• They are worried and concerned about their son, not angry. They don't want him to go away.
Listening 1
b He is going to work for a charity or volunteer organization in Africa, helping people in difficulty, perhaps to do with famine relief or the results of war or a natural disaster.

Additional activity

You could follow up this topic by discussing these questions:
• *Would you like to do the kind of thing the young man is planning?*
• *How would your parents react / have reacted in the same position?*

2 • Students listen again and work in pairs. They note down the functional language used by the speakers.
• Check students know what to do by eliciting a few examples of each type of language they are listening for.
• Allocate tasks and play the recording again if necessary.
• Students note down the expressions and then compile lists. They help and correct each other at this stage.

Note Students add to these lists during the next listening task.

Answers
See full list of expressions after *Listening 2*, question 2.

Listening 2

1 • **7.6** Give students time to read the questions and then play the recording.

7.6 including **7.7**
Conversation 1

S	How much are you trying to lose?
B	About seven kilos.
K	In, in a couple of weeks?
B	Well, I hope so, yes.
J	Oh, I don't think you should do that. That'd be really bad for you.
B	Well, I mean, if I can't lose seven in a couple of weeks. I've got three weeks before I go on holiday. You know, I've, I've just, just got, I can't, … I look awful in my swim … swimming costume, I mean, I can't, … I wouldn't dream of getting into a bikini.
K	The trouble is if you lose weight that quickly, you, you, you're bound to put it back on again.
J	That's right. And I don't think you should eat just eggs, I mean, that's not a balanced diet.
B	But that's only today. Tomorrow I can have bananas and then the next day it's carrots and then the day after that it's grapefruit, so I mean it is a mixture.
S	**7.7** Oh, come, just think about it. Bananas for a whole day of bananas. Are you going to be able to stand that?
B	Yeah, I can put up with that for …
K	Shouldn't you be thinking about, doing things like exercise, not just about diet?
J	That's a good idea.
B	Well, you know, I mean, I haven't really got much time for that, you know. I'm just too busy. What time have I got to exercise?
K	Oh, I don't know, it just seems much more sensible to just, be … just eating …
J	That's all the good advice you always do read about, isn't it? You know, exercise as well as diet.
S	Yeah. Most peo … most people who are thin, or reasonably slim, are like that because they take exercise, I think, as a rule, anyway.
K	Or I think what you were saying about balance, I think that's generally right. You've got to have a balance of everything.
J	I mean, just think about it for a minute, you know. If you, if you're just stuffing yourself with eggs one day and grapefruits the next, your body's going to react in very strange ways.

Conversation 2

R	It's not going to be, any, any really any more expensive than, than a normal car.
J	**7.7** Oh, I wouldn't if I were you, you know – I'd really think again and perhaps buy a new car, I mean …
R	No, that's the whole point of a classic car is that it's not new, that, it's, it's something, something they … you can't get any more …
J	Well, you know …
R	It's like buying a piece of history …
J	Yeah, but I think you're making a big mistake, because if you're going to use it for travelling to and from work, I mean, is it really suitable for that sort of thing?
R	Well, I'm not going to use it to and from work every, every day perhaps, maybe during the summer, but erm, I'm not going to sort of …
J	I wouldn't if I were you, you know, it could be very difficult on the roads in traffic jams and all that sort of thing.
R	Yeah, but it's a car, it goes, that's what it was made for.
J	Mmm, mmm, I mean, what can I say to persuade you? I mean what, what, have you really thought it through? Have you thought about where you're going to park it, for inst … You can't park it on a street.

R I've got a … I've got a garage.
I've got all that lined up … , it's, it's, it's OK.
J And what about during the daytime when you're sort of parking near work for instance?
R That's fine. You have to … Life's a risk. You have to take a risk. If somebody hits it they hit it. But I mean you can't, you can't not do something …

- Check answers.

Possible answers

	Conversation 1	Conversation 2
a	Friends	Friends or colleagues
b	Losing weight / dieting	Buying a car
c	Friends are persuading Barbara not to diet.	Woman is persuading man not to buy an old, classic car.
d	They say she should do exercise.	She tries to persuade him to buy a new car.

2 • **7.7** Play the recording, while students follow the extracts in their books on p.72, marking the functional language used by the speakers.
- Students add the expressions to their lists.
- Check through the lists of functional language students have compiled from the conversations.
- You may need to clarify the functional language:
  –to think something through – to think about all the implications
  –to tend to – to be likely to behave in a certain way
  –most people – there are many phrases like this which are used to make generalizations (e.g. *the majority of people / almost everyone*, etc.).

Answers
(This includes expressions from **Listening 1** and **2**.)
Persuading someone not to do something
7.5
Are you sure you're doing the right thing …?   We don't think you should …   I mean, have you really thought this through?   Surely it would be more sensible to …
7.6 **Extract 1**
Shouldn't you (be thinking about) …?   It (just) seems much more sensible to …
(From full conversation
Oh, I don't think you should do that …)
7.7 **Extract 2**
I wouldn't if I were you, …   I'd really think again …   (I think) you're making a big mistake.   … what can I say to persuade you?   … have you really thought it through?   Have you thought …?
Making generalizations
7.5
On the whole, I think …   You tend to (get set in your ways) … Well, you hear cases of …
7.6 **Extract 1**
Most people …   … (I think) as a rule …   … (I think) that's generally right.
7.7 **Extract 2**
None used

■ **Features of natural conversation** ■■■■■■■■■■ **p. 72** ■

This section focuses on two features of natural conversation: the use of the phrase *you know* in conversation, and the meaning of unfinished statements. (This was first brought up in the equivalent section of Unit 4.)

1 • Students find all the examples of *you know* in the two extracts on p.72.
- Play the recording again, encouraging them to listen to the way *you know* is said.
a They then discuss in pairs why the expression is used and what it means.
- Elicit their ideas.

Suggested answers
7.7 **Extract 1**
B *Well, **you know**, (1) I mean, I haven't really got much time for that, **you know** (2). I'm just too busy. What time have I got to exercise?*
J *That's all the good advice you always do read about, isn't it? **You know** (3), exercise as well as diet.*
1 as a filler
2 used to remind the listener about something
3 here *you know* is used to introduce an example or illustration
7.7 **Extract 2**
J *Oh I wouldn't if I were you, **you know** (4) – I'd really think again and perhaps buy a new car, I mean…*
R *No, that's the whole point of a classic car … get any more*
J *Well, **you know** (5)…*
4 to make the advice sound friendly
5 a conversation filler

b Elicit ideas from students. Prompt by suggesting categories.

Answer
b Fillers   *mmm. er, erm, well, anyway, so*
Examples   *for example, like, such as*

c Students work in pairs and add *you know* to the extract. They could read the conversation aloud to each other.

Answer
c There are no right or wrong places to add *you know* to the conversation. One of the features of *you know* is that people can use it anywhere.

2 • Students work in pairs to complete the sentences.
- Elicit ideas.

Possible answers
a *… one day. / … a short time. / … a few hours.*
b *… use it like an ordinary car. / … drive it very often.*

■ **Practice** ■■■■■■■■■■■■■■■■■■■■■■■

1 • **7.8** Play the recording. Pause after each sentence and drill chorally and individually, paying particular attention to stress and intonation.
- Alternatively, you could ask students to predict which syllables they think will be stressed, before they listen.

7.8

a   I wouldn't do that if I were you.
b   I think you're making a big mistake.
c   Have you really thought it through?
d   Surely it would be more sensible to wait a bit longer.
e   What can I say to persuade you not to?

Answers

See tapescript **7.8** for stress.

2 Students work in pairs to make short conversations.
- Encourage them to use as many of the expressions as possible.

▨ Exploitation ▨▨▨▨▨▨▨▨▨▨▨▨▨ p. 73 ▨

▨ Role play ▨▨▨▨▨▨▨▨▨▨▨▨▨▨▨▨

- Ask students to read instructions and form small groups.
- Allocate roles. Students should take turns to be Student A.

Note If time is short, suggest that students choose only two situations.

- Stress that once Students A have said what they intend to do, the others should try to persuade them not to do it, using the functional language they have listed.
- Monitor their conversations, listening for use of the functional language. Do not interrupt conversations unless the language is completely incorrect or inappropriate.

▨ Writing ▨▨▨▨▨▨▨▨▨▨▨▨▨▨▨▨▨▨▨▨

1 • Ask students to think about different types of announcements broadcast on radio in their country. (Examples: flood or storm warnings; traffic reports; health warnings, etc.)
- Elicit a few ideas.
- Ask how, in general terms, the language of these announcements is different from normal conversation.

a–b Allow students time to read through the two examples, and think about or discuss their ideas.
- Elicit their ideas.

Suggested answers

a   The most obvious difference is that the conversation is a spontaneous, two-way dialogue between two people, while the script is a carefully structured monologue, written in language which is deliberately made to sound informal.
- The script has some of the characteristics of conversational language: it is personal; short forms of verbs are used; questions are asked, etc.
  But in this one-sided conversation, no answers are expected to the questions. (These are rhetorical questions.)
- The script is packed with factual information; there is little redundant language.

b   The writer asks the listener direct questions. Examples:
Have you really considered the effects on your family, your children?
So, how can we persuade you to give up?

2 • Check that students understand the writing task. They should choose one of the suggested scripts.

- Remind students to refer to the **Writing guidelines** on p.157 of their books.
- Elicit a few ideas about the subjects of the two suggested scripts before they begin to help prepare the writing.

Ideas
Script 1
- Dangers of driving too fast: accidents / serious injuries (physical and mental) involving children and old people; possibility of legal action.
- Benefits of driving more slowly: less stress for drivers; safer and quieter for people living in the area.
- Instructions to drivers: slow down especially at certain times of the day; think about how your life would be affected if you caused a serious accident.

Script 2
- Pleasures associated with hot sunny weather: holidays, relaxation, sport, carefree, open-air life-style.
- Dangers of exposure to sun: painful sunburn; illness (sun-stroke); skin cancer.
- Measures that can be taken: sun-cream; wear clothes; keep in shade; limit length of time you expose yourself.

- The first-draft writing could be done in class, rather than for homework. If necessary, limit the amount of time you allow, for example, to fifteen minutes.

3 • Students now work in pairs and read their finished scripts aloud to each other. They should then comment on the effectiveness of the script and discuss possible improvements.
- The final version of the script could be written in class, or for homework.

▨ Summary ▨▨▨▨▨▨▨▨▨▨▨▨▨▨▨▨▨▨▨

- Encourage students to use the tick boxes to help them keep a record of their learning.

8 In the family

Theme

The theme of this unit is *the family*.

Preview The Fonda and the Kennedy families
Reading The Benetton family business
Listening Children's position within families

Grammar

- Relative clauses (LC p.132)
- Relative words (LC p.133)
- Emphasizing words and structures (LC p.133)

Vocabulary

- Informal words, *nice* and *get*

Functional language

- Making and responding to requests

Features of natural conversation

- Preparing the listener for a difficult request
- The use of *OK*, *The thing is, …*

Pronunciation

- Relative clauses
- Sentence stress
- Sounding polite

Writing

- A letter of request (WG p.155)

Workbook

- An article about the work of a therapist
- Topic vocabulary: music and musicians; *make* + particle; Word-building: *-ness* noun endings
- Relative clauses review; Relative clauses; Emphasizing words and structures
- Connecting ideas (2); Writing a short biography

Preview

The first theme of the unit is American family dynasties (the Fondas and the Kennedys). It raises questions of parents' ambitions and expectations of their children.

Your thoughts p. 74

1–2 Students think about and discuss the questions.

- You could discuss question 1 as a whole-class activity, then get students to discuss question 2 in pairs.
- Elicit a few answers from students. Is there a consensus of opinion?

Reading

1
- Working in pairs, students answer questions **a** and **b** in as much detail as they can. They will, of course, get some information from the photographs and captions.
- Elicit students' ideas.
- You could write the ideas on the board, known facts and guesses about both families. Students can then refer back to this list after they have read the texts.

Pictured clockwise starting top left: Jane Fonda in *Cat Ballou*, Bridget Fonda in *The Assassin*, Peter Fonda in *Easy Rider*, J. F. Kennedy, Robert Kennedy, Rose Kennedy and Edward Kennedy, The Kennedy family, Henry Fonda in *On Golden Pond*.

Background information

a The Fonda family has been in films for three generations: Henry, his children Peter and Jane, and Peter's daughter Bridget. Jane has been an actress and has produced her own keep-fit books and videos.

b The Kennedys are probably the most famous political family in America.
John F. Kennedy – American president 1960–1963
Robert Kennedy – Senator and presidential candidate
Edward Kennedy – Senator
John and Robert were assassinated.

- You could pre-teach these words and phrases before students read the articles: *outspoken* (openly expressed / honest / candid / frank), *cult* (popular or fashionable for a short time, often among a particular group or type of people), *to achieve prominence* (to gain importance or fame), *clan* (group of families all related to the same ancestor (especially used about Scottish families)).

2
- Students now read the texts and check for ideas they mentioned.

3
- Elicit any recent information students may have about either family.

- If students do not know much about either of these families move on to *Person to person*.

▌ Person to person ▌▬▬▬▬▬▬▬▬ p. 75 ▌

1 • This question could be discussed briefly by the whole class. Students could think about what happens in most 'normal' families. What different kinds of ambition do parents have for their children?

2 • Students could discuss this second question in pairs or small groups.
- Monitor their discussions but do not interrupt.
- To finish, elicit a few ideas from the class.

— Grammar – Relative clauses review —

This grammar review revises relative pronouns and the difference between defining and non-defining relative clauses. If this is a difficult area for students, be prepared to spend a little longer on this section than on the other Preview grammar sections.
- Remind students that they can refer to the **Language Commentary** on p.132.

1 • Read the introductory rubric with the class, then elicit answers for **1a**.
- If necessary, continue working as a class or ask students to work through the questions individually or with a partner.
- Check answers.
- When they have identified the relative pronouns, ask students to think about the kind of information each relative clause contains. You could use **1a** as an example to check students understand.

Answers

relative pronouns	relative clause contains information about
a *where*	Dallas
b *who*	Lee Harvey Oswald
c *whose*	Joseph Kennedy
d *which*	the prominence of the Kennedy family
e *when*	the day he was killed
f *why*	a reason for something

2 • Students decide if **a–f** have defining or non-defining clauses.
- You could write these two sentences on the board to show the difference between the two kinds of clauses.
My brother who lives in France is an English teacher.
– a defining relative clause – it tells us which brother. We know that she has more than one brother.
My brother, who lives in France, is an English teacher.
– a non-defining relative clause – it tells us more about the brother. It also tells us that she only has one brother. Point out that the clause must be separated from the rest of the sentence by commas and that in spoken language the speaker would pause at these places.

Answers

a	non-defining	d	defining
b	defining	e	defining
c	non-defining	f	defining

▌ Pronunciation ▌▬▬▬▬▬▬▬▬▬▬▬▬

3 • **8.1** Play the recording as many times as necessary pausing, after each sentence to give students enough time to write it down. Help with spelling where needed.

8.1

1 Henry Fonda, who was Jane's father, had a long and distinguished film career.
2 The film which won him an Academy Award was *On Golden Pond*.

Answers
a See tapescript **8.1** .
b 1 non-defining relative clause

Note Non-defining relative clauses can be identified by:
– a pause before and after the clause (use of comma)
– a lower pitch than the rest of the sentence
– being spoken faster, as the clause is less important.

2 defining relative clause

Note In defining relative clauses the intonation rises until the end of the clause, when there is a brief pause before the intonation drops.

▌ Check ▌▬▬▬▬▬▬▬▬▬▬▬▬▬▬▬▬

4 • Students work through the exercise individually, then compare answers with a partner.
- Check answers.

Answers
a *Bridget Fonda, **whose** aunt is Jane Fonda, was born in 1964.* (non-def.)
b *She spent four years at the Lee Strasburg Theatre Institute, **where** she studied method acting.* (non-def.)
c *Scandal was the film **which** brought her to the attention of the public in 1989.* (def.)
d *It was the year **when** Single White Female and Singles were released.* (def.)
e *That's the reason **why** she went into films.* (def.)
f *Henry Fonda, **who** was Bridget's grandfather, won an Oscar for his part in On Golden Pond.* (non-def).

— p. 76 —

Reading

This article describes the origins and growth of the Italian company, Benetton.

1 a Working in pairs, students work in pairs and tell each other what they know about Benetton.
- You could have a brief class discussion of their ideas.

b Ask students to think of three questions they would like to ask about the company, e.g. *How did the company start?*
- Elicit a few questions and write a selection on the board.

- You may wish to pre-teach these words and phrases before students read the article: *founder* (person who starts / establishes something), *pillar* (person who actively supports an organization, business, etc. (e.g. *He's a pillar of society.*)).

2 • Students now read the text, checking their ideas and looking for the answers to their questions.
  • When they have finished reading, go through the questions on the board, checking if they were answered.
  • Ask students to say the most interesting fact or piece of information they read about.

Close up

- Students work through the questions individually or in pairs.
- Check answers.

Answers
- l.1 1950–1953 is called *the early 1950s / the early fifties*
  1957–1959 is called *the late 1950s / the late fifties*

Note Expressions like these are also used about people's age: *He's in his early / mid / late thirties* (notice the word *his*).
- l.17 *vice* here means 'next in rank'. Other examples: *vice-principal of a college / vice-chairman.*
- l.30 *once* here means *when, as soon as, after.*
- l.37 *five-star* is normally used to describe the standard of hotels, travel, and other public services. *A five-star lifestyle* might mean having enough money to do anything you want.
- l.39 *chatting into the night* means talking until very late.

Interpretation   p. 77

1–3 Allow students time to read the questions and think about possible answers. They could work in pairs.
  • Elicit their ideas.

Possible answers
1 Financial reasons / diversification from just one product / advertising opportunities.
2 The structure of the family has changed / more opportunities for young people / not all family members may be good at business.
3 mutual trust / loyalty / honesty / reliability / experience / commitment / enthusiasm / ambition.

Speaking personally

1–2 Students discuss these questions in pairs or groups.
  • Monitor but do not interrupt.
  • Elicit their ideas, then finish with a brief class discussion.

Grammar — Relative clauses

Exploring concepts

1–4 Students work through questions 1–4 in the usual way.
  • Remind students that they can refer to the **Language Commentary** on p.133.
  • Monitor and help.
  • Check answers.

Answers
1 a *the pullover*
  b *the bright, vibrant colours*
  c *the fact that Luciano has also come to include friends and colleagues in the business once they have demonstrated a solid commitment to the firm*
  d *One of the things (he does with his friends)*
2 a *that* cannot replace *which* in a non-defining relative clause as in **1c** or **1f** *which* follows a preposition as in **1b**.
  b In **1d** *which* is the object of a defining relative clause and so it is not necessary and can be omitted.
    In **1a** *which* is the subject of the relative clause and so it cannot be omitted.
3a–b Sentence 3 is the most formal and is written in a very formal style. The relative pronoun *which* is not omitted and the preposition *in* is placed in front of *which*. Sentence 1 is less formal than 3. The relative pronoun *which* is used but the preposition *in* is placed at the end of the relative clause. Sentence 2 is the least formal, the language of everyday speech. The relative pronoun *which* is omitted and the preposition *in* is placed at the end of the relative clause.
4 This final section focuses on *what* and *whatever* which are not relative pronouns, but have a similar purpose.
  a *what*   the things that   c *whatever* anything that
  b *Whatever* anything that   d *What*   the thing that

Exploitation

1 a Read the rubric and go through the example to check that students understand the task.
  • Remind them to refer back to the *Exploring concepts* section or to the **Language Commentary** on p.133 to check their answers.

Note These sentences are in very formal language. In **b** students will 'translate' these sentences into more everyday language.
  • Check answers.

Answers
1 *The song **for which** Bob Dylan ...*
2 *Woodie Guthrie is the musician **by whom** ...*
3 *... are the musical instruments **with which** ...*
4 *The style **in which** his son sings is reminiscent of his father's.*

b Students now work through 1–4 a second time, making the sentences informal. They could do this either in writing or orally.
  • Check answers.

Note Remind students that it is possible to leave out a relative pronoun *which* if it is the object of a defining clause.

Answers
1 *The song **(which)** Bob Dylan is most well-known **for** is 'Blowin' in the Wind'.*
2 *Woodie Guthrie is the musician **(who/m)** Bob Dylan was most influenced **by**.*
3 *The guitar and the harmonica are the musical instruments **(which)** he is most closely associated **with**.*
4 *The style **(which)** his son sings **in**, is reminiscent of his father's.*

Additional activity

- Students could make up sentences similar to those about Bob Dylan in formal and informal language about other famous people: musicians, writers, actors, etc. If students use a pronoun (*he* or *she*) instead of a name they could exchange their sentences for other students to guess who they are talking about.

–*The book (which) he is most well known for is 'War and Peace'.*

–*The book for which he is most well known is 'War and Peace'. (Tolstoy)*

Free speech

2 a Students work in pairs, taking turns to interview each other and collect biographical information. They write this information down in note form. For example, birthdate, birthplace, schools attended.

b Students then use their notes to write a brief profile of their partner. Suggest a limit of 100 words.

• They could write a first draft and then add extra or clarifying information to practise relative clauses.

• Students can then exchange their profile and correct any facts before giving it back to the writer to do a final version.

• Finished profiles could be displayed in the classroom.

— p. 78 —

Listening

Students now discuss families, personalities, and their position within their family.

1 • Students think of answers to these questions, then exchange information and ideas with a partner.

• If the class is not too large, this might make an interesting whole-class discussion.

2 • You may want to pre-teach the following words before students read: *siblings* (brothers or sisters), *goody-goody* (well behaved to impress others), *outdo* (do better than).

• Students now read the short text to see if it confirms any of their ideas.

Note This text is included as pre-listening information only. There is no need to exploit it any more fully than this.

3 • Finally, students work with a partner who is in the same position in the family as they are. They should discuss how accurate they think the text is and add any other ideas they have to the descriptions.

• Ask students for their ideas on different positions within the family.

Note If you don't have students for each position within the family, it may be better to do this as a whole-class activity.

Listening 1

1 • Ask students to read questions a–c.

• You may want to pre-teach the following words before students listen: *intolerant*, *rivalry*.

• **8.2** Play the recording. Students should make brief notes of the answers.

8.2

1 I'm twenty-six. I live with my mother and father. There's just me. They tried to have another child but my mother miscarried and she couldn't have any more children. I think being an only child does make you very spoiled and intolerant. But you do become more of an independent person when you're an only child. You tend not to follow the crowd or rely on what other people think, and you make up your own mind about things and take your own decisions. That's probably because there's no one there to say 'Why on earth do you want to do that?' or 'Maybe you should, you know, do something else'. It might have been nice to have had a brother or sister when I was young. Someone to play with.

2 I'm the middle sister. I've got an elder sister, she's eighteen months older than me – and a younger sister – she's three years younger than me. We're all very different indeed but we get on really well. My elder sister's got a very forceful personality and she does everything at a hundred miles an hour. She really knows what she wants and she goes for it, whereas my little sister is really laid back. She's a bit like a hippy – she's into environmental issues, and is a vegetarian and all that sort of thing. And I'm a bit … em … a bit of a loner, I suppose. I keep my feelings to myself really. And even though I'm really close to my elder sister, I don't confide in her. I'm just reserved, I suppose.

3 There are just the two of us. Just my sister and I – Michelle – she's two years younger than me. We get on well but there's always been a certain amount of rivalry between us – on my sister's side, anyway. When we were young, she always wanted to do better than me, so if I got second prize at something she wanted to get first. She was very competitive.

I think myself that when you're the elder child you always feel in some way responsible for the other person. Well, I certainly did. My sister was perfectly capable of looking after herself but just because I was the elder child I felt I had to look after her.

Chelle didn't really care about what my Mum and Dad thought – if she decided she wanted to do something, basically she went ahead and did it and she got into trouble quite often. I always tended to do the right thing.

• Play the recording again if necessary.

• Check answers.

Answers

	Jo	Emma	Clare
a	only child	middle (second of three)	first (one younger sister)
b	She is spoiled and intolerant, independent. (She sounds lonely.)	She's a loner / but doesn't express feelings.	She feels responsible for younger sister. She always did the right thing.
c	Yes – the text says only children are precocious and self-sufficient. This is close to Jo's description.	Uncertain. She describes her two sisters clearly, but is rather vague about herself. This could be no clear status.	Yes. She says she felt responsible for younger sister. Also *I tended to do the right thing*.

Listening 2

2 • Students are now going to hear about a brother-sister relationship.

• You may wish to teach this phrase before students listen: *to make a sacrifice*.

• Students discuss questions **a** and **b**.

- Elicit their ideas, but do not confirm whether they are right at this stage.

3 • **8.3** Play the first part of the recording. Students listen to find out if their answers to **a** were correct.
- Play the first part again if necessary.
- Check answers.

Answers

a – He felt he was a failure in comparison with his sister who was always a success. He often gave up without even trying.
 – He is still afraid of taking risks in case he fails.
 – He felt overshadowed by his sister and her achievements.

- Play the second part of the recording. Students listen to find out if their answers to **b** were correct.
- Check answers.

Answers

b – Other people in the family missed out on her father's attention: he didn't go out with his wife (Jenny's mother); he didn't do fatherly things with his son (Ben).
 – The whole family was forced to make sacrifices because the father was determined that Jenny was going to win.

8.3

Part 1

Jenny was always successful and did well. Mum and Dad were always so proud of her, especially Dad, and I wanted them to be proud of me too. When I was younger I always seemed to fail at things. And my father would sort of say, 'I might have known it, Ben's in trouble again', and that sort of stuff. So later on, the main thing for me was not to be a failure. If I thought I might fail at something, I wouldn't even try it – I'd leave it alone. Even now, you know, I'm still afraid to take risks sometimes in case I fail, because then it's like, 'Oh, Ben's messed up again'. I've tried loads of things and I've had lots of different experiences. In fact, I'd say I've actually done more than a lot of people I know and I'm sort of beginning to feel more confident, you know – I can say like, 'Well, actually, I've done that, I've done that, I've done that'. I may not go to the top in it, but compared with a lot of other people, I've been incredibly successful. But then, when I've got to that point, I've thought, 'Oh the next stage is quite a big step, I might fail', so I've said to myself, 'Right, I'll give that up and I'll try something else instead'.
In the end, I suppose there was only enough money and time in our family for one, and that was it, so rather than try and compete I'd just give up. It wasn't necessarily the right thing to do but I could never have beaten Jenny, so I didn't even try. In comparison with a lot of people, you know, we're pretty competitive in our family, believe me, but you don't go and try and beat someone if you know you can't win. That's how I felt anyway.

Part 2

It's easy enough now to look back and see how it affected the family, but it was different at the time – I just couldn't see it, 'cos when you're in the middle of it, I mean, you're young. I suppose you tend to be quite selfish. I think a lot of athletes are very selfish. They have to be, because they always have to do what they need to get the best performance. And Dad was always there for me, 'cos he was so determined that I was going to win and do the right things and compete at the very highest level. He used to make sacrifices without even realizing they were sacrifices. Mum and Dad hardly ever used to, you know, go out for a meal together or do any of the normal family things. Ben didn't have Dad there to take him to football practice or do any of the things fathers do with their sons. The thing is, all those sacrifices were for me and most of the time I wasn't even aware of them – you know – life was going on as usual and Mum was making

sure that I'd a clean kit and that dinner was on the table and I was in bed at the right time. She was brilliant, my Mum. I mean she was always my best friend, my Mum.

Interpretation

1–3 Get students to read through the three questions, then play the second part of the recording again.
- Students note down their ideas, then compare with a partner.
- Elicit their ideas.

Possible answers

Note The questions are very open and there is a wide range of possible answers.

1 Selfish behaviour of athletes.
Because theirs is an individual sport not a team game, they must train themselves to be single-minded in their determination to win. This is bound to affect others.
–Their practices and schedules dominate family life.
–They may need a special diet and sleep regime.
–Their involvement in athletics costs money.
–They may need to be taken to competitions, etc.
–They may need constant psychological support.

2 Normal family things could include:
going shopping, going away for holidays and weekends (other than to athletics meetings), sitting at home and relaxing, going places as a family.

3 Things fathers do with their sons could include:
playing sports, watching sports, helping with school work, teaching them practical things, giving them advice about growing up.

Speaking personally

- Students exchange ideas and experiences in pairs or groups.
- Monitor, but do not interrupt.
- Finish with a brief feedback of ideas from the class.

▶ **Photocopiable activity 10 p.167**

Grammar – Emphasizing words and structures

Exploring concepts ▬▬▬▬▬▬▬▬▬ p. 79 ▬

This section focuses on some of the grammatical and lexical ways of emphasizing information in English.
- Remind students that they can refer to the **Language Commentary** on p.133.
- Students work through 1–2 in the usual way.
- Monitor, giving help where necessary.
- Check answers.

Answers

1 a strong feelings | The speaker is confirming the popular idea that only children are spoiled and intolerant.

 b contrasting information | James isn't normally good at keeping in touch but (surprisingly and in spite of this reputation) he phoned last week.

c	strong feelings OR contrast	The speaker is trying to persuade someone that he cares about the children, even though he gets home late.
d	strong feelings	The speaker is adamant that what she is saying is true and the listener must believe this.

2 • Students identify other emphasizing words and phrases and work out how they are used.
   • Monitor, giving help where necessary.
   • Check answers.

Answers

2 a 1 on earth ...?   3 myself
     2 really   4 Whatever

Note The addition of on earth puts emphasis on the Wh- question word. It is also possible to say:
Where on earth have you been? / **Who on earth** was that? / **What on earth** are you doing?

Note The addition of the suffix ever puts emphasis on the Wh-question word. It is possible to say:
Wherever have you been? / **Whoever** was that? / **Whatever** are you doing?

     5 very and indeed

Note Very comes before the word it emphasizes. Indeed is normally used for emphasis after a word already qualified by very.
You cannot say: He was tall indeed.

b 1 really (2) and very (5)
   2 indeed (5)
   3 1 (Why on earth ...?) and 4 (Whatever)
   4 2 (really) and 5 (very – without the word indeed)
   5 myself (3)

Note Other personal pronouns can be used in this way: himself, herself, ourselves, yourself, themself, themselves.

Pronunciation

3 a Students identify main and other stressed syllables.
   • You could ask students to predict which words they think will be stressed before they listen.
   • **8.4** Students listen and check.

Note Point out that stressed syllables normally occur in nouns, adjectives, verbs, and adverbs, and not in prepositions, pronouns, or articles.

8.4

a I think being an only child / does make you very spoiled and intolerant.
b James isn't very good at keeping in touch / – he did phone last week, though.
c I get home late, / but I do always spend time with my children at the weekends.
d I know you don't believe me, / but I did try to contact you. / Honestly.

Answers

3 a See tapescript **8.4** for stress.

b Students have to decide which words to stress and which words carry the main stress. Students can either work in pairs or, if time is short, elicit ideas from the whole class.
   • **8.5** Students listen to possible answers and check their ideas.

8.5

1 Why on earth do you want to do that?
2 We get on really well.
3 I think myself / that when you're the elder child ...
4 Whatever does Karen see in him?
5 We're all very different indeed.

Possible answers

3 b See tapescript **8.5** for stress.

Exploitation

1 a Go through the example to check that students understand the task. Point out that they should use as many ways of emphasizing as possible.
   • Students work individually, then compare answers in pairs.
   • Check answers.

Possible answers

Jackie was **really** young (or **very young indeed**) when she got married – just seventeen. Now, **she herself** admits it was a mistake. 'I **really thought** (or I **did think**) it would work. My parents **did warn** me that I was too young but I didn't listen.' So **whatever** (or what on earth) went wrong? 'I **do love Dave**,' said Jackie, 'but we've changed. We both want **very different things** (indeed) (or **really** different things) from life now.'

b Students work out which words would be stressed in their version of the text if it was spoken.
   • Students read their texts aloud to a partner and compare ideas.
c **8.6** Students listen and compare their version with the recording.
   • You could play the recording again, pausing to allow students to repeat each phrase.

8.6

Jackie was very young indeed when she got married / – just seventeen. Now, / she herself admits it was a mistake. / 'I really did think it would work. My parents did warn me that I was too young / but I didn't listen.' So whatever went wrong? 'I do love Dave,' / said Jackie, / 'but we've changed. / We both want very different things from life now.'

Possible answers

See tapescript **8.6** for stress.

Role play

2 • Ask students to read through the two situations to ensure they understand the task.
   • Students could use magazine pictures as prompts for this activity. Find pictures of houses, rooms, or people. Students could imagine that the rooms are theirs or that they are the people in the pictures.

- You could suggest that the students whose role it is to be complimentary or reassuring should try to use emphasizing language.
- Monitor conversations, but do not interrupt.
- If you hear any interesting or entertaining conversations, you could finish by asking pairs of students to re-enact their conversations for the rest of the class.

Informal words

The focus here is on the adjective *nice* and the verb *get* and their various meanings.

Note Because both words have so many meanings, they can be overused. It is sometimes said that people use them because they cannot be bothered to think of more precise words. For this reason, you could suggest that students should try to use alternative words with more specific meanings, especially when writing.

- Read through the introduction with the whole class.

▣ *nice* ▬▬▬▬▬▬▬▬▬▬▬▬ p. 80 ▣

1 • Start by asking the class what *nice* means. When it becomes clear that it can have several different meanings, ask students to work through the matching exercise individually or in pairs.
- Check answers.

Answers

a	kind	d	enjoyable
b	complimentary	e	likeable / kind
c	smart		

2 • Students make up their own sentences showing the five meanings of *nice*. Suggest that they describe people, things, places, and activities.
- Elicit a few sentences for each meaning.

3 • Ask students to read through the introduction.
- Students match the nouns and adjectives and then make up their own sentences.
- Monitor, making sure students use both possible constructions.
- Check answers.

Possible answers

cold	bed	(glass of) orange juice	legs	room
	weather			
comfortable	bed	room	weather	
easy	exam			
large	bed	(glass of) orange juice	room	
long	exam	legs	room	
sunny	room	weather		

▣ *get* ▬▬▬▬▬▬▬▬▬▬▬▬▬▬▬▬▬▬▬▬▬

1 • Students match the uses of *get* with different meanings.
- You could pre-teach *fetch* and go through question **b** as an example to check students understand.
- Check answers.

Answers

a	*become*	f	*earn(s)*
b	*fetch (go and bring)*	g	*obtain*
c	*receive(d)*	h	*understand(s)*
d	*arrive at*	i	*take (or catch)*
e	*bought (buy)*	j	*annoy(s)*

2 • Students make up their own sentences showing some of the meanings of *get*.
- Elicit a few sentences for each meaning.

Language in action

▣ Eavesdrop! ▬▬▬▬▬▬▬▬▬▬▬▬ p. 81 ▣

The questions could be done as a class activity or as pairwork.

- Direct students' attention to the picture and the four questions.
- Remind students that they are speculating about what they see and should try to come up with a variety of different answers.
- You could elicit possible answers now, or move on to *Listening 1*.

▣ Listening 1 ▬▬▬▬▬▬▬▬▬▬▬▬▬▬▬▬▬▬▬

1 • **8.7** Students listen to the recording and check their *Eavesdrop!* ideas.

8.7

BM Now, how can I help you, Mr Bennett? I don't normally deal with these matters myself you know.
C No, I realize that. I'm very grateful. Thank you for seeing me.
BM Yes?
C Well, actually I was … It's a bit awkward. You see I borrowed some money from you last year and I … well, I was wondering … do you think you could extend the repayment period?
BM Are you trying to tell me that you are unable to keep up with the interest payments, Mr Bennett?
C No! No! Well, not exactly. It's just that one of our machines has broken and we really need to replace it, otherwise we'll get behind with the orders.
BM What sort of business do you run, exactly?
C It's a family business. Bags, purses, belts, that sort of thing – leather goods.
BM I see. And the original loan was for £10,000?
C That's right.
BM I'm afraid that's not possible, Mr Bennett. It's quite out of the question.
C Well, could you possibly increase my loan?
BM How much would you need?
C £2,000 would be enough.
BM Oh, certainly. No problem, provided you can keep up with the payments.
C That won't be a problem.
BM Excellent. Well, I can authorize that now if you'll just step into the bank, Mr Bennett. Mr Smith will give you the relevant forms to fill in.

- Check answers.

Eavesdrop!
- Bank manager and a customer who has his own business.
- Bank manager's office.
- The customer is asking for a longer time in which to repay a £10,000 loan, or an extra loan of £2,000.
- He is anxious at the beginning, but relieved in the end when the bank manager agrees to his second request.

2 · Students work in pairs and listen again, noting down the functional language used by the speakers.
  · Allocate tasks and play the recording a second or third time if necessary.
  · Students then tell each other the expressions and compile lists. They help and correct each other at this stage.

Note Students add to these lists during the next listening task.

Answers
See full list of expressions after *Listening 2*, question 2.

■ Listening 2

1 · Ask students to read questions **a–d** before listening.
  · **8.8** Play the recording.

8.8 including **8.9**

Conversation 1
H **8.9** Might be possible, Tony. It depends how long you would want me to work for, though.
T Well, is there any chance of working, er, a couple of evenings and maybe Saturday, or some time at the weekend, perhaps?
H I'm not sure if I can do that.
T Er … Are you sure? 'Cos really we need to get it now. We need to get it finished by Monday and it's going to be very difficult to get it done, you know, just in the normal working hours.
H I would if I could, Tony, but it very much depends on when you would want me to work.
T Well, how about, erm … How about tomorrow evening? Say till about six or six-thirty, something like that, and maybe Saturday morning? Is that any good?
H I'm afraid I can't do the weekend. No. I can do tomorrow evening, but not the weekend.
T Would it be possible to do a couple of evenings then? Say tomorrow evening and Thursday evening?
H I'm afraid not. One evening would be all right.
T Erm … Hmm. Any chance of working through till say about seven then?

Conversation 2
H Hello.
K Hi! Is that Heather?
H Yes, it is.
K Hi there. It's, er, Karen here. How are you?
H Oh, fine, Karen.
K **8.9** Erm … Heather, I know this is really short notice … erm … Would it be possible … em … to borrow your car this evening?
H Oh, Karen, I'm sorry. I'd lend it to you if I could, but I've really got to go to a meeting tonight.
K Oh, right. Erm … Oh, OK. Well, thanks anyway.
H All right …
K Thanks. Speak to you soon.
H Yes, OK …

K OK, bye.
H Bye.

Conversation 3
T 722342.
K Oh hi! Er … Tony?
T Oh, hello Karen, hi.
K How … How are you?
T Well, thank you. You?
K Oh, that's … yeah, I'm fine actually … yeah. How's work?
T Oh, you know. It's not so bad but … We get by …
K Oh great, great. Em, Tony, I've got a bit of a problem … em … I really need to get hold of, em, a car this evening and, em, I was wondering, er … Is there any chance of, em, possibly bor …
T Oh, Karen, I'm sorry. It's in the garage at the moment. I took it in for an MoT this morning and there's some work to be done on it.
K Oh, that's bad timing.
T Sorry. Er … no good tomorrow night?
K No. It's, it's tonight … Oh, well …
T OK. Yeah, I'm sorry I can't.
K OK, well, thanks anyway …
T OK …
K OK.
T Bye now.
K Bye.
T Take care.
K I will. Bye.

MoT (Ministry of Transport Test) – this is an annual safety test for all British cars over three years old.

Conversation 4
S Hello?
K Hi, Simon. It … It, it's Karen here.
S Oh, Karen, hi.
K How … how are you?
S Oh, not so bad … you know … long day, busy day.
K Er, oh, right. Em?
S Tired.
K **8.9** Em. Em … Simon? Is it …? em, I really, I've got a bit of a problem. I need to, em, I need to get hold of a car this evening. Em … I need to give a friend of mine a lift and I was wondering, would it be possible to borrow your car at all?
S To, to borrow mine?
K Yeah …
S Em … I'm not sure, really. When do you want it?
K Well … about seven, really, this evening.
S This evening? That's about in an hour and a half's time.
K Well, yeah, I know it's short notice. Em …
S I've got to … the thing is, I've got to go and pick up …
K Right.
S … my daughter from the station …
K Right. What, what? Would, would, would, er …
S I know, I mean it's, it's possible, em …
K Yeah? I mean, I could, I could come round. I mean it, it, maybe I could make it a bit later. Seven-thirty?
S … That might be OK actually, seven-thirty …
K Yeah?
S I'm picking her up about twenty-past seven.
K Right.
S It takes about another fifteen …
K Right.
S I could … It's possible …
K Yeah, I mean, I'd have the car back to you by at least ten …
S This evening?
K Yeah, oh yes, yeah …
S OK, em, all right.
K Yeah? Oh, that's brilliant.
S Yeah, fine, OK …
K Oh, thanks ever so much!

- Check answers.

Possible answers

	1	2	3	4
a	Someone is being asked to work overtime (evenings and weekends).	Someone wants to borrow a car.	(see 2)	(see 2)
b	Manager / boss and employee / secretary.	Friends		
c	No	No	No	Yes
d	No excuse is given – the employee simply says she can't work at the times requested.	She has to use her car to go to a meeting.	The car is at the garage being repaired.	

2 · **8.9** Play the recording. Students follow extracts from **three** of the conversations in their books on p.82, marking the functional language used by the speakers.
   · Students add the expressions to their lists.
   · Check through the lists.

Answers
(This includes expressions from *Listening 1* and *2*.)
Making requests
   8.7
I was wondering ... Do you think you could ...? – This is an alternative to: *I was wondering if you could ...*
Well, could you possibly ...?
(... if you'll just (step into the bank). – This is a different kind of request, so it need not be included in the list.
   8.9 Extract 1
Is there any chance of ...?
   8.9 Extract 2
Would it be possible to ...?
   8.9 Extract 3
I was wondering, would it be possible to ...? – This is an alternative to: *I was wondering if it would be possible to ...*
Responding to requests
   8.7
I'm afraid that's not possible. Negative / *It's quite out of the question.* Negative / *Certainly.* Positive / *No problem, ...* Positive
   8.9 Extract 1
Might be possible, ... Uncertain (short for *It might be possible.*)
I'm not sure if I can do that? Uncertain
I would if I could ... but ... (+ an excuse) Negative
I'm afraid I can't ... Negative
   8.9 Extract 2
I'm sorry. I'd ... if I could, but ... (+ an excuse) Negative
   8.9 Extract 3
Em, I'm not sure, really. Uncertain / *It's possible ...* Uncertain / *That might be OK, actually ...* Uncertain
(From full conversation
OK, em all right ... / Yeah, fine, OK ...)

© Oxford University Press **PHOTOCOPIABLE**

Features of natural conversation ▬▬▬▬ p. 82 ▬

This section focuses on ways of preparing a listener to consider a potentially difficult request, the use of *OK*, and the phrase *The thing is ...*

1 · Ask students to read the introduction to check they understand the task.
   a Students underline all the examples of *preparatory phrases* in Extracts 2 and 3.
   · They then discuss, in pairs, the purpose of the preparatory language in each example.
   b Students consider in particular why Karen spends so long preparing the listener in Extract 3.
   · Elicit their ideas.

Suggested answers

Preparatory language	Purpose
a **8.9** Extract 2 *I know this is really short notice ... em ...*	The speaker wants the listener to know that she realizes her request is unreasonable. It allows the listener to refuse the request without feeling awkward.
8.9 Extract 3 *I've got a bit of a problem. I need to, em, I need to get hold of a car this evening. Em ... I need to give a friend of mine a lift and I was wondering ...*	The speaker signals that she needs help. She then states her need in general terms (this is not the request) and gives a reason. By the time she says *I was wondering ...* the listener has guessed what the request will be and has had time to think of a response.

   b The point of spending so long preparing the listener is to give him the opportunity to offer his car and so relieve her of the need to make a difficult request.

Note This is typical of polite, indirect spoken English. To some nationalities it may seem unnecessarily indirect.

2 · **8.10** Ask students what the word *OK* means. When it becomes clear that there are several possible meanings, ask them to listen to the recording and try to work out the exact meaning of *OK* in each case.
   · Elicit ideas.

8.10

a H I've really got to go to a meeting tonight.
   K Oh, right, Em ... Oh, OK. Well, thanks anyway.
   H All right ...
b K Thanks. Speak to you soon.
   H Yes, OK ...
   K OK, bye.
c K Maybe I could make it a bit later. Seven-thirty? ...
   S ... That might be OK, actually ...

Suggested answers

a *I understand and accept what you have just said.*
b 1 *Yes, I expect we will speak again soon.*
  2 *I'm glad we agree.*
c *possible, practical, all right*

3 · Elicit students' ideas about the meaning of *The thing is, ...*

Answer

The thing is ... Is commonly used in spoken English to introduce an explanation, a contrasting idea, an excuse, an objection, or an opinion about something that has just been said.

Practice

1 These exercises give students practice in identifying and reproducing intonation patterns for sounding polite.

- **8.11** Play the recording. Pause after each expression and drill chorally and / or individually
- Ask students to identify the main stressed syllable in each sentence.

Note To sound polite students should start HIGH and fall on the main stressed syllable.

8.11

a Do you think I could use your phone?
b Could you possibly give me a lift?
c Would it be possible to bring a friend?
d Is there any chance of lending me that video?

Answers

See tapescript **8.11** for stress.

2 · **8.12** Play the recording. Pause after each expression and drill chorally and / or individually.

8.12

a	Certainly.	f	I would if I could.
b	No problem.	g	I'm afraid not.
c	Yes, OK.	h	I'm sorry.
d	I'm afraid that's not possible.	i	I can't.
e	It's quite out of the question.		

3 · **8.13** Play the recording. Students should decide which speaker in each sentence refuses politely and how they would describe the other speaker.

8.13

1 I'm afraid that's not possible. (polite)
  I'm afraid that's not possible. (impolite)
2 It's quite out of the question. (impolite)
  It's quite out of the question. (polite)
3 I would if I could. (polite)
  I would if I could. (impolite)
4 I'm afraid not. (impolite)
  I'm afraid not. (polite)
5 I'm sorry. (polite)
  I'm sorry. (impolite)
6 I can't. (impolite)
  I can't. (polite)

Answers

3 See tapescript **8.13**.

4 · Allow all students time to think, and note down four requests to ask their partner.
- Students then work in pairs, making their requests and giving appropriate answers.
- Monitor, checking that the language and intonation is appropriate.

Exploitation Role play

- Students work in new pairs. They make requests or refuse and give excuses.

Note If time is short, suggest that students choose only two situations.

- Monitor their conversations, listening for use of the functional language. Do not interrupt as this is primarily a fluency activity.
- If necessary, feed back to the class any errors you heard while monitoring.

Writing p. 83

1 a Get students to think about the differences between spoken and written requests and give students time to read the two examples.
- Elicit their ideas.

Suggested answers

a In the conversation the person making the request gets immediate feedback from the other person. This means they can judge the person's response and adjust their request accordingly. Speakers can also rephrase and request again in different ways. They may know the other person, and this will affect their language.
- In writing, the writer must prepare the reader more carefully and lead up to the request gradually, as they can make the request only once. When the requests are made, they are less direct. The writer may not know the person they are writing to and so may have to use more formal language.

b · *I was wondering if you could **possibly** give me some information …*
- *I was hoping you **might** be able to let me know …*
- ***Would it be** all right for me to phone you …*

c What makes these requests polite is their indirectness. Notice particularly the words and phrases marked in bold type above (the use of the Past continuous verb forms, and modal verbs).

2 · Ask students to read both of the suggested letters, choose one and follow the paragraph plan.
- You could divide the class into two groups according to the letter they are going to write.
- Groups could then brainstorm the contents of the second paragraphs.
- Monitor, and help as necessary.
- Remind students of the **Writing guidelines** in their books on p.155.

Note The second letter is to an acquaintance rather than a friend, so the style should be quite polite or formal.

- You could ask students to write notes and do the first draft of the letters for homework.

3a–b Students now work in pairs in the usual way, writing and then re-writing the final versions of their letters.

Summary

- Encourage students to use the tick boxes to help them keep a record of their learning.

9 On the move

Themes

The theme of this unit is *movement*.
Preview The phenomenon of New-Age Travellers in Britain
Reading Population changes affecting Europe's capital cities in the summer
Listening Young car drivers

Grammar

- Time and reason clauses (LC p.134)
- Participle clauses (LC p.134)
- Cause and effect (LC p.135)

Vocabulary

- Synonyms

Functional language

- Making, accepting, and rejecting suggestions

Conversation strategies

- Ending conversations

Features of natural conversation

- The use of *Just*, *Actually*

Pronunciation

- Sounding enthusiastic and unenthusiastic

Writing

- Letters of suggestion (WG p.156)

Workbook

- A transatlantic race
- Topic vocabulary: travel; Collocations; *put off*, *pull out*
- Time and reason clauses review; Participle clauses; Cause and effect
- Connecting ideas (3); Describing a journey

Preview

The first theme of the unit is Britain's New-Age Travellers. Students are asked to think about the pros and cons of a nomadic lifestyle and to consider the place of travellers in modern society.

Your thoughts p. 84

1 · You could start by getting students to describe what they can see in the photographs and to talk about the probable lifestyle of the three groups of people. Matching the names and the photographs may emerge from this.
 · Students match the photographs with the names of the groups.

Answers

top and main picture: Bedouins
middle picture: New-Age Travellers
bottom picture: Gypsies

2 · Allow students a few minutes to exchange any information they have about the three groups.
 · Elicit a few 'facts' from the class and note them on the board.

Background information
Bedouins
The Bedouin are Arabic-speaking nomads in the Middle East and North Africa. They are mainly associated with camel-herding in desert areas, although many Bedouin also tend sheep, goats, or cattle. In the cooler, rainy season, Bedouin typically migrate in small groups into the desert with their animals. In the hot, dry season they congregate in larger groups around water sources on the desert margins. Some groups make annual migrations of as far as 1,000 km (620 miles).

Gypsies
Although mingled with other populations, the Gypsies are a distinct ethnic group that originated in India. They were of a low caste and earned their living by singing and dancing. Their language, Romany, is a mixture of Sanskrit and loan-words from various countries in which they have lived. All Gypsies speak Romany. Today there are an estimated eight to ten million Gypsies in more than 40 countries, an estimated one million of them in North America.

---

3 · Allow students a few minutes to discuss the advantages and disadvantages of a nomadic way of life.
 · Elicit their ideas and note them on the board.

Possible answers

Advantages
- not dependent on the state
- freedom to go where they want, when they want
- live a life that is close to nature
- can go to where there is work
- interesting, exciting way of life – not stuck in a routine
- can live according to their own ideals and beliefs
- strong family and racial communities

Disadvantages
- insecure lifestyle
- outsiders in 'normal' society and therefore may be victimized and discriminated against
- may disadvantage children from an educational point of view
- increasingly difficult these days to find places for Gypsies to camp

▆ Reading ▆▆▆▆▆▆▆▆▆▆▆▆▆▆▆▆▆▆▆▆

- You may wish to teach these words and phrases before students read the article: *itinerant, settle down.*

1–2 Students read the questions, then read the text to find the answers. Compare the answers from the text with those you noted on the board earlier.

Answers

1 New-Age Travellers and Gypsies.

2 • Difficult to settle down after a nomadic life
 • Children's education suffers

Vocabulary in the text	
wagon	old-fashioned, horse-drawn carriage once used by Gypsies
municipal caravan site	a local council site where caravans can stop – like a *camp-site*
anti-consumerist	adjective describing people who do not believe that the focus of life should be on material possessions
to have your home repossessed	people who cannot repay home loans have them repossessed by the lenders and they have to leave their homes
to fall on hard times	to become poor

▆ Person to person ▆▆▆▆▆▆▆▆▆▆ p. 85 ▆

1–2 These questions could be discussed briefly in pairs or groups before being opened up to the whole class.

— Grammar – Time and reason clauses review —

In preparation for the introduction of Participle clauses in the next grammar section this grammar section revises these time and reason clauses:

– Time clauses – *when / as soon as / after / before / until / while*
– Reason clauses – *because / as.*
- Remind students that they can refer to the **Language Commentary** on p.134.

1 • Go through question **1** as a class to check students understand the meaning of *clause.*

- Check their answers.

Answers

a–b 1 *when* introduces a time clause
 2 *because* introduces a reason clause

2–4 Students could now work through tasks 2–4 individually or in pairs.
- Monitor and give help.
- Check quickly through the answers.

Answers

2 a *as* (reason) **c** *Because* (reason)
 b *When* (time) **d** *as soon as* (time)

3 a–b 1 Present simple – a present situation
 2 Past simple or Past perfect – a past situation

Note The Past perfect is used where we need to emphasize that one action was completed before another. In most contexts this is not necessary and the Past simple is more commonly used.

 3 Present simple – a future situation

Note Remind students if necessary that it is incorrect to say:
*After Guiseppe **will leave** school, he'll go to work for his father.*

 c In the sentences in **3a**, *when* or *as soon as* can replace *after*, and *then* can replace *before*.

4 a He made the decision when he became seventeen.
 He made the decision before he was seventeen to leave at seventeen.
 b The speaker has time now, so she will take the person out for a driving lesson. (*As* = because)
 She hasn't got time now, but promises to give the person a driving lesson at some time in the future.
 c These sentences have similar meanings. In both cases he became a *New-Age Traveller* **after** he left university. In the first sentence we do not know exactly when; in the second we know he became a New-Age Traveller **immediately** after leaving university.
 d There is no difference in meaning between these two sentences.

▆ Check ▆▆▆▆▆▆▆▆▆▆▆▆▆▆▆▆▆▆▆▆▆

5 • Do an example with the whole class.
- Students then work through the exercise individually, then compare answers with a partner.
- Check answers.

Answers

a 4 People are suspicious of Gypsies *because / as* they have a strange lifestyle.
b 6 The farmer phoned the police *after / when* the travellers started to cross his field.
c 5 The travellers moved off the land *when / as soon as* the police arrived.
d 3 They set up camp by the roadside *when / after / as soon as* it got dark.
e 1 They didn't sleep well *as / because* there was a violent thunderstorm.
f 2 The convoy set off again *as soon as / when* it was light.

Reading

This article describes three European capital cities in the summer, when the locals go away on holiday and the tourists arrive.

1 This activity helps students to get a general idea of the text before they read.
   - Ask students to say where the cities are and to describe what they can see in the photographs in as much detail as possible. Students can compare their ideas in pairs. Don't spend more than five minutes on this activity.
   - Ask students to read the headline and elicit the meaning of: *locals* (the people who live in a place), *flee* (escape from / get away from as quickly as possible), *the big heat* (very hot weather).
   - Now elicit their ideas about the content of the article.

   Note You do not need to pre-teach any of the words from this text as most of the difficult words are either non-essential to students' understanding of the text as a whole or are 'guessable'.

2 - Allow students five to six minutes to read the text quickly and check their ideas.
   - As they read you could also ask them to think about whether there is a city in their country where something like this happens.

■ Close up

   - Students work through the questions individually or in pairs.
   - Check answers.

   Answers
   - l.8 *Break up* here means to finish and is used about schools and school-children. *Our school / My sister breaks up in two days.*
     Other common meanings:
     – break into small pieces / disintegrate
       The satellite broke up as it entered the earth's atmosphere.
     – come to an end (a relationship)
       They're breaking up after being married for three years.
     – disappear (communication signal)
       You're breaking up. I'll phone you again later.
   - l.16 *Shine* here means to do well at something.
     Other meanings:
     – radiate light *The sun is shining.*
     – look bright *He polished his shoes until they shone.*
     – point a light *She couldn't see anything so she shone a light all round the room.*
   - l.17 – cram means to try and learn a lot of information quickly just before an exam.
     – retakes means exams you take again because you failed them the first time. It is from the verb *to retake (an exam).*
   - l.25 *via* means by way of / through. *We went home via the town centre.*
   - l.30 You would feel under close scrutiny. Eagles have very keen eyesight – nothing escapes their attention, not even the smallest movement.
   - l.37 *en route* means travelling / on the way to.

■ Interpretation

1–2 Give students time to read the questions, look back at the text, and think about possible answers.
   - Elicit their ideas.

   Possible answers
   1 They can't wait to get away from the city and go on holiday. During the summer the city will be hot and full of tourists.
   2 Life is not straightforward because businesses and shops close down for the summer.

■ Speaking personally

1–2 Students discuss the questions in pairs or groups.
   - Monitor but do not interrupt.
   - Elicit their ideas in the answer to 2 and, possibly, finish with a class discussion.

Additional activities

1 The class could conduct a survey to find out how students and their families spend the summer holidays.

2 Students could write an account of a typical summer in their town or city. They could include pictures or photographs.

— Grammar – Participle clauses

■ Exploring concepts

   - You could start by reminding students of the time and reason clauses in the Preview. Ask them to finish these two sentences.
     a *In the summer Parisians leave the city because …*
     b *They leave when …*

1 - Ask students to read the question.
   - Go through the examples and elicit ideas from the whole class to check students understand.

   Note Point out that participle clauses are used in formal writing, and are uncommon in everyday speech.
   - Remind students that they can refer to the **Language Commentary** on p.134.

   Answers
   1 *Present participles* are the same as the continuous or *-ing* form of verbs.
     Perfect participles are formed with *having* + past participle.

2–4 To check students understand, ask them to rephrase the examples in question 1.
   a *In July Parisians go on holiday and leave the city to foreign tourists.* (*and* or *but*)
   b *Being impatient to get away, they often drive all night long.*
     Because they are impatient to get away, they often drive all night long. (reason)
   c *Having spent two or three days in Madrid, foreign tourists go on to other places.*
     When / Once / After they have spent two or three days in Madrid, foreign tourists go on to other places. (time)

- Now let students work individually or in pairs through questions 2–4, monitoring and giving help where necessary.
- Elicit their answers.

Answers

2 a The participle clause replaces a *relative clause*:
*Major roads out of the city become clogged with motorists **who are heading for the countryside.***

Note Participle clauses can only replace *defining* relative clauses.

b The participle clause replaces a main clause joined by *and*:
*Parisians avoid city location for their holidays **and head instead to the mountain retreats.***

c The participle clause replaces a relative or a result clause:
*Some food shops close **which makes day-to-day life more complicated.** (relative)*
*Some food shops close **and so day-to-day life is (made) more complicated.** (result)*

d The participle clause replaces a time clause:
***As / When / While I was travelling around Paris in August,** I couldn't help noticing how quiet it was.*

e The participle clause replaces a reason clause:
***Because / as they do not need to explain their every move to their parents,** young Madrileños stay out till all hours.*

f The participle clause replaces a reason clause:
***Because they have done well in end-of-year exams,** lucky children are sent to holiday camps.*

Note This could also be replaced by a conditional clause:
If they have done well in end-of-year exams, lucky children are sent to holiday camps.

3 e • *Young Madrileños, **not needing to explain their every move to their parents,** stay out till all hours.* or
• *Young Madrileños stay out till all hours, **not needing to explain their every move to their parents.***

f • *Lucky children, **having done well in end-of-year exams,** are sent to holiday camps.* or
• *Lucky children are sent to holiday camps, **having done well in end-of-year exams.***

Note
• The first alternative in each case is a rather formal literary style.
• The second alternative sounds strange because the participle clauses are a long way from their subjects: *Young Madrileños* in **e**, and *Lucky children* in **f**. It is better to position the participle clause close to its subject.

4 In **d**, which contains a present participle clause, the two actions *travelling* and *noticing* take place simultaneously.

In **f**, which contains a perfect participle clause, one action (*doing well in exams*) takes place before the other (*children are sent to holiday camps*).

■ Exploitation ■

1 • Tell students they must think of an appropriate verb and then choose the correct participle form to fill the gaps in **a–f**.
• Do **a** as an example with the whole class to check they understand.
• Point out that they may need to use perfect participles and the negative form.
• Suggest they compare and discuss answers in pairs.
• Check answers.

Answers

a *Not being able / Not knowing how*
b *Not having tasted / eaten / tried*
c *buying / looking for / choosing*
d *leaving*
e *Having seen / visited*
f *Having spent / got through*

2 • You could start by getting students to look at the illustration and suggest what is happening. This would give you an opportunity to introduce or elicit some of the vocabulary.
• Go through one or two answers with the whole class, then let students continue working individually or in pairs.
• Check answers.

Answers

1	*believing*	5	*causing*	9	*knocking over*
2	*riding*	6	*hitting*	10	*trapping*
3	*helping*	7	*carrying*		
4	*Staring*	8	*hearing*		

Additional activity

Students could make up a story of their own, using participle clauses where possible.

• You could provide an opening sentence.
I woke at three in the morning. The telephone was ringing …
All the passengers were on board. The plane was ready to take off …
• Students continue in pairs, writing simple sentences.
• Set a length or a time limit – for example ten sentences or ten minutes.
• Pairs of students now rewrite the stories linking the simple sentences together with participle clauses where possible.
• Monitor and help where necessary.
• Finally, they hand stories back to the original writers, who could be asked to make final corrections and other improvements.

▶ Photocopiable activity 11 p.169

— p. 88 —

Listening

1 • To prepare for the listening, students discuss the two statements about driving and drivers.
• Allow pairs a few minutes to discuss, then elicit their ideas.
• This may turn naturally into a class discussion but this should be kept brief, as there are other discussion opportunities later in the section.
• You could take a quick vote to see how many people agree or disagree with the statements.

2 • Students listen to **part 1** of a radio programme which gives factual information about young drivers.
a They should listen for information related to the statements that support **1a–b**.

- You may wish to teach these words and phrases before students listen: *attitude, to impress someone, to overestimate, immortal.*
- **9.1** Play **part 1** of the recording. Students make a note of any information relevant to the statements. They then compare their ideas in pairs.
- Play the recording again if necessary.

9.1

Part 1

Good afternoon. In today's programme we'll be looking at the subject of cars and young people and considering just how safe a combination they are.

First, some statistics. According to recent research, young people – that is people between the ages of seventeen and twenty-five – are involved in nearly a fifth of motoring accidents. What is significant about this figure is that only one in ten of all drivers are in this age group. This means that a young man aged, say, twenty, is nine times more likely to die in a road accident than his father.

Researchers have also looked into exactly what makes someone a safe or an unsafe driver. They tested young people's skills as well as their attitudes to driving. The results are disturbing to say the least.

Apparently between 30 per cent and 40 per cent of young drivers were found to be potentially dangerous. In many cases, it is not because they lack the necessary driving skills but because they choose not to use them. In what is a fairly common situation where a teenager is in a car with a group of friends, it is more likely that they will be driving to impress their friends, rather than to be safe. This, of course, means that they often end up taking unnecessary risks, which can lead to accidents. Andrew Graham, a driving instructor, says:

In my experience, and colleagues of mine say the same thing, both the young and the old overestimate their ability behind the wheel. Erm, actually their ability to judge situations is not as good as they like to think, though I should add, how good a driver you are has more to do with attitude than your age. Older drivers on the whole are more careful and take fewer risks. They are more aware that the car is potentially a lethal weapon. Young people, on the other hand, tend to think of themselves as being in some way immortal.

- Check answers.

Answers

The research information in the programme shows that young drivers are more dangerous than older drivers. The key sentences are:

- *… young people – that is people between the ages of 17 and 25 – are involved in nearly a fifth of motoring accidents.*
- *… a young man aged say 20 is nine times more likely to die in a road accident than his father.*
- *Apparently between 30% and 40% of young drivers were found to be potentially dangerous.*
- *… they often end up taking unnecessary risks, which can lead to accidents.*
- *Older drivers on the whole are more careful and take fewer risks.*

b Students listen to **part 2** of the recording and listen for information which contradicts statements **1a–b.**

- You may wish to teach these words and phrases before students listen: *aggressive, maniac, overtake.*
- **9.1** Play the recording once or twice if necessary, then allow students time to compare answers in pairs.
- Play the recording again if necessary.

9.1

Part 2

Here are some views on driving which you phoned in to us. First, Jane Haycock, aged nineteen, from Croydon.

JH

I'm really glad I've got a car. I passed my test second time round and I've been driving for two years now. Driving has made me more independent and it's really necessary for going out and socializing. I wouldn't feel safe out on my own at night waiting for buses, and taxis are quite expensive here.

I've been very lucky really. I've never had a bad accident – thank goodness – but I find it quite difficult to concentrate for a long time when I'm driving. If I'm not careful, I find myself looking around and not watching the road. I think my bad habits probably all come from being a passenger in other people's cars.

I'm probably a more aggressive driver then my parents – I mean, I try not to drive too fast and I never, never drink and drive, but I'm not as patient a driver as my Mum. The way I see it, safe driving is about your attitude as much as your ability to handle a car. I mean, you can't do without the skills, because you've got to be able to react instinctively in any situation you find yourself in – but it's attitude that makes some people drive like maniacs and overtake every car in sight. I know quite a few boys like that. They drive dangerously just to impress their friends. I don't usually drive so fast if there are other people in my car.

Now let's hear what Dan Masters, aged twenty-two, from Philadelphia has to say.

Everyone, but absolutely everyone, has a car in the States. It's really important. Unless you live in a big city like New York or San Francisco there isn't really much in the way of public transport. So you need a car to get around. In LA, you're likely to get picked up by the police if they see you on foot.

I think people of my age are much more aware of the dangers than people of my parents' generation. For example, me and most of my friends stick to soft drinks if we're driving, whereas my dad and lots of older drivers I know think it's OK to drink a bit if they're driving. I think that's fairly typical.

Young drivers always seem to get the blame for causing accidents. That's not fair. Sure, young people drive fast but driving slowly causes just as many accidents as driving fast – and elderly drivers, boy can they go slow! They sometimes seem completely unaware of what's going on around them. One nearly drove into the back of me when I was stopped at a junction the other day! Amazing.

And finally Gabrielle Richards from Doncaster.

I have a Citroen 2 CV. It's twenty years old! I've had it for a year. My parents bought it for me when I passed my test. I've had the odd accident – nothing big – when I've driven too close to parked cars but apart from that nothing – touch wood*! I'm very safety-conscious and I always feel responsible for my passengers especially as there are no safety belts in the back. I never drink alcohol if I'm driving and I wouldn't get in a car with anyone that had been drinking. And I'd never speed. Someone I know was injured in an accident involving two young drivers who were racing each other. I don't usually have problems with other drivers. They never act aggressively towards me when I'm in the Citroen but I have noticed a more negative attitude when I've borrowed my father's Golf GTI. Some men, particularly older men, don't like to see a woman overtake them. Some of them get very aggressive. They drive up really close behind you and flash their lights. It makes me furious. I'm sure they wouldn't do it if I was a man.

Note *touch wood is an expression we use to avoid bad luck.

- Check answers.

Answers

- The first speaker, Jane, thinks older people are a danger on the road:
  As far as older people are concerned, I think everyone over sixty should have to take a special driving test just to check that they can cope with modern conditions.
- The second speaker, from the USA, believes his generation is safer than his parents' generation:
  I think people of my age are much more aware of the dangers than people of my parents' generation. For example, me and most of my friends stick to soft drinks if we're driving, whereas my dad and lots of older drivers I know think it's OK to drink a bit if they're driving.
  ...young people drive fast but driving slowly causes just as many accidents as driving fast – and elderly drivers, boy can they go slow! They sometimes seem completely unaware of what's going on around them. One nearly drove into the back of me recently when I was stopped at a junction the other day!
- The third speaker believes that attitude rather than age is what is important:
  I always feel responsible for my passengers especially as there are no safety belts in the back.
  I never drink alcohol if I'm driving and I wouldn't get in a car with anyone that had been drinking.
  And I'd never speed.

Interpretation

There is no need to play the recording again. It contains no specific answers to the question.

1 • Students think of simple questions that the researchers might have asked young drivers.
Examples
What is your attitude to driving?
They could take a more indirect approach like this:
What makes a good driver?
Or they could think up multiple choice questions, like this:
When do you drive fast?
A *Whenever I can.* B *When it is safe.* C *Never.*
• Set a time limit of five minutes or a limit of five questions.
• Elicit ideas.

2 • You could elicit ideas about bad driving habits from the whole class in a short brainstorm or ask students to work in pairs.

Possible answers

- not paying enough attention
- driving too close to the car in front
- taking hands off the steering wheel
- using a mobile phone while driving
- not using indicators, etc.
- not wearing a seat-belt
- not using mirrors
- speeding
- lack of consideration

Vocabulary

1 • Students work through these vocabulary items individually or in pairs. They could refer to tapescript **9.1** at the back of their books.
• Check their answers.

Answers

a	*it has less to do with*	has less connection with, or relation to
b	*in sight*	that you can see / that is visible
c	*in the way*	of that could be called / defined as

Note This expression has very little meaning and could actually be left out of this sentence.

d	*stick to*	continue to (drink)
e	*the odd*	an occasional

2 • Students now consider other meanings of the same expressions. Point out that the meanings here are different.
• Follow the same procedure as for **1**.

Answers

a	*I could do with*	I would like / I need
b	*in sight*	in the near future
c	*in the way*	blocking my path / standing where I want to walk / go
d	*stick to (rules)*	obey
e	*odd*	different In *odd* socks wearing socks of different colours / not a matching pair.

Speaking personally

Note For this activity it is preferable for drivers and non-drivers to work separately.

1–4 Start by getting students into groups of drivers and non-drivers.
• Students discuss their two questions.
• The drivers and the non-drivers have one question in common: *What makes a good driver?* Groups could be asked to write a list of five qualities that make a good driver.
• Monitor, but do not interrupt.
• Finally, mix students from the two groups and get them to compare their lists of qualities that make a good driver alternatively get feedback from the whole class.

Additional activities

1 If students are of the same nationality, get them to think of advice they would give to foreign visitors who wanted to drive a car in their country.

2 If students are of different nationalities, they could tell each other what the driving test consists of in their country.

Grammar – Cause and effect

Exploring concepts p. 89

This section focuses on some grammatical and lexical ways of expressing cause and effect.
• Remind students that they can refer to the **Language Commentary** on p.135.

1–2 Read the introduction and go through the first question as an example to check that students understand the idea of cause and effect.

Note It might be helpful to get them to think about how this idea can be expressed in their own language.

- Elicit from students the causes and effects. (The structures themselves are in bold.)
- Students work individually or in pairs through the remaining questions.
- Check their answers.

Answers

1

	Cause	Effect
a	attitude	they drive like maniacs
b	people drive up really close and flash their lights	I become furious
c	desire to impress friends	some drivers take unnecessary risks
d	driving slowly	as many accidents as driving fast
e	the taking of unnecessary risks	accidents
f	Advertising campaigns	a change in public opinion
g	High accident rates for young drivers	higher insurance charges

2
a	*makes*	object + infinitive without *to*
b	*makes*	object + adjective
c	*causes*	object + infinitive with *to*
d	*causes*	object (noun phrase)
e	*lead to*	object (noun)
f	*brought about*	object (noun phrase)
g	*resulted in*	object (noun phrase)

Exploitation

1
- Go through one example with the class. Point out that they should use all the cause and effect constructions that they have just worked on in Exploring concepts.
- Students work individually, then compare answers in pairs.
- Check answers, pointing out possible alternatives.

Answers

a 4 Being able to drive *makes* you more independent.
b 7 Cars *cause* a lot of pollution.
c 1 Poor air quality *leads to* / *causes* / *brings about* / *results in* an increase in diseases like asthma and bronchitis.
d 5 Sitting in traffic jams *makes* people irritable.
e 2 Talking on a mobile phone while driving can *result in* / *lead to* a heavy fine.
f 8 Selfish driving can *make* me lose my temper.
g 3 The wet road surface *caused* the car to skid.
h 6 New tougher driving laws have *brought about* / *led to* / *resulted in* a decrease in serious accidents.

2 This is a freer activity in which students practise cause and effect structures.
- Elicit a few endings to sentence a, then get students to continue in pairs. They should think of their own sentences using *result in* and *cause*.
- Check answers.

Possible answers

a ... *be impatient, fed up, miserable, angry.*
b ... *an increase in traffic.*
c ... *an improvement in driving standards.*
d–e Students' own ideas.

3 This is a free discussion activity which could involve cause and effect language.
- Students read the instructions. Elicit a few suggestions to check they understand.
- Working in groups, students discuss the situation and how it would affect their country. If students are from different countries, they will be talking about the likely *general* effects. If they are from the same country, they can be more specific.
- Monitor discussions but do not interrupt.
- You could extend the group work into a full class discussion.

— p. 90 —

Synonyms

- First, ask students if they know what *synonyms* are. Elicit some examples / suggestions that students know.

1a–b Let students work through these two tasks individually or in pairs.
- Check answers.

Answers

a
1	d	5	f	8	c
2	e	6	i	9	j
3	g	7	a	10	b
4	h				

b 1 take, test
2 proposes, carry out
3 as soon as / when, collected
4 terrible / dreadful / horrible / shocking
5 difficult / tiring / exhausting
top, amazing / impressive / marvellous / sensational

2
- Students read the introductory rubric and examples which explain the idea that pairs of words are sometimes but not always synonyms.
a Students then work individually or in pairs through 1–4, checking their ideas in a dictionary.
- Check answers to this exercise before moving on to b.

Answers

1 normal / complicated   3 discovered
2 take part in   4 obvious

b Students now make up sentences to show the meaning of the other words from a1–4. Again, they could check their ideas in a dictionary.
- Check answers.

Possible answers

1	usual	*In the end I found my keys in their **usual** place.*
	uncooperative	***Uncooperative** children can make life hard for teachers.*
2	appreciate	*I've always **appreciated** good food and wine.*
3	picked up	*I **picked up** Spanish by living in Spain for a year.*
4	definite	*I need a **definite** answer to my question by the weekend.*

3 This section distinguishes between words with the same meaning but with a different register.

- Go through the example to check that students understand and then let them work through **a–e** individually or in pairs.
- Check answers.

Suggested answers

a *get you down / upset you* **d** *rich / well-off*
b *hand out / give out* **e** *spare time / free time*
c *I'm sorry*

4 • Check that students understand this vocabulary practice exercise.
- Students ask and answer in pairs questions **a–c**. Encourage short conversations rather than simple questions and answers.
- Monitor, checking their use of the informal synonyms.

Language in action

■ Eavesdrop! p. 91 ■

The questions could be done as a class activity or as pairwork.

- Direct attention to the picture and the three questions.
- Remind students that they are speculating about what they see and should try to come up with a variety of different answers.
- Elicit students' ideas, but do not confirm or deny them at this stage. Alternatively, move on to *Listening 1*.

■ Listening 1 ■

1 • Draw attention to the extra question **b**.
- **9.2** Students listen to check their *Eavesdrop!* ideas and to think about an answer to **b**.

9.2

A How far is it?
C From here?
A Of course. Where else?
C Well, I don't know.
N Erm, it, it's about 400 miles, I think.
D Surely it must be more than that, Nick. It's about 400 miles from London to Glasgow to start with.
C Well, anyway, it's a long way.
A That's a big help, Chris.
D Oh, stop being so stupid, you two. We'll never get anything sorted out at this rate.
A OK. Point taken. Any ideas on the best route, Nick?

N Oh, erm, have we actually decided to drive up?
A Haven't we? I just assumed that we were.
N Well, I mean, once we get to – what's the name of the place?
D Ullapool.
N Ullapool.
C Where is Ullapool?
D It's on the north-west coast of Scotland.
N …Once we get there, we've still got to get a ferry across to Stornoway.
C Couldn't we just fly to Stornoway? From London?
D There aren't any direct flights. And, anyway, I'm sure it's bound to be mega expensive.
A And we'd still need a car once we were there. I don't imagine the bus service would be very good.
N Would it be an idea to fly up to Glasgow and hire a car there?
D Yeah, that's a good idea, Nick. I'm pretty sure there are cheap flights so long as you book in advance.
A I still think driving up in my car would be a better option. If we flew up we'd have to go into London, and that isn't cheap. How much is a return fare to London?
N Don't you think it'd be a better idea to actually sit down and do some sums before we start?
D Definitely.
N We need to find out the cost of driving up in Andy's car, which uses leaded petrol, and compare that with the price of flying up to Glasgow and hiring a car for ten days.
D We'd also need to add the cost of a night's accommodation.
A We could always sleep in the car.
C Sleep in the car? No way. It'll be bad enough sitting in the car all that time.
D Yeah, I'm not keen on that idea either.
A Are you sure you want to come, Chris? I mean you don't have to you know. It is supposed to be a holiday.
D Is that the time? I'm going to be late. Sorry, but I've got to go …
N Well, look, since Diana's got to go, erm, shall I make a few enquiries, find out a few prices and then we can get together next month and decide.
C Great idea, Nick!
D Mm. I'm not sure we should leave it till next month, especially if we do decide to fly.
A OK. Next Friday?
N Yeah.
D Yeah, that'll be fine. Look, I really must go or I'll be late.

- Check answers.

Possible answers
Eavesdrop!
- **They are friends. Diana could be in a relationship with either Chris or Andy. It is also possible that two of the people are related, brother / sister or two brothers.**
- **They are in one of their houses, a living room / lounge.**
- **They are planning a trip to Scotland.**

Listening 1
b Nick is not sure where the place they are going is, he thinks they haven't planned or thought enough about what they are doing, he thinks they should get more information before making a decision. It's possible he doesn't know the others as well as they know each other and so is afraid of being assertive.

2 • Students listen again and note down the functional language used by the speakers.
- Allocate tasks to students and play the recording again if necessary.
- Students note down the expressions they hear and then compile lists. They help and correct each other at this stage.

Note Students add to these lists during the next listening task.

Answers
See full list of expressions after *Listening 2*, question 2.

Listening 2

1 • **9.3** Let students read the three questions, then play the recording.

9.3 including **9.4**
Conversation 1
J I think we could make it a mixture of both, couldn't we?
R Possibly.
R Yeah.
J I mean, would they like to … you know…for instance have a trip into Birmingham, don't you think that would be nice? We could see the galleries and er… the theatre.
K Well, but the best galleries are … it's got to be London, really.
R Well, that is true, yeah. I mean London's got the … well, I
K But don't …
R wouldn't say best… biggest.
K Yeah…
R Anyway…
J Well, there must there must be another way of doing it really because I mean they're going to be studying in London anyway …
R Yeah.
J … so, it's not sort of not like having a holiday or a break, is it?
R **9.4** Well, look, I've em, … you know, got to go, so, er… well, what do you think?
J Oh, right, erm …
R What do you think?
K Well, what about we try and combine both? I mean …
J Yeah, I think that's a good idea.
K Is it a nice idea to try and do a bit of both?
R Yes … mmm …
J Mmm, mmm, mmm…
K Some place in London and a bit of, sort of natural…
J And some countryside or something, er… yes, the Welsh hills. Would that suit you?
R Well, yeah, I'd go along with that, yes.
J Yeah, all right then.
R So, I mean, we could …
J Just a few days in each, sort of thing. Would that be a good idea?
K Might be a good idea …
R Yes. So, I mean, we can continue this maybe …
K Well, it'd be nice to make a …
J Yeah …
K … you know, a sort of decision today really …
J Yeah, I think it would be a good idea to do that …
K What would you … what do you want to do? Where would you take them?
R Well, I think outside of London. I think they see enough of London, anyway …
J Mmm, I'd agree with that.
K So where? Where would you go?
R York, as I said, Edinburgh, somewhere like that. Anyway, look … erm… you know… can we carry on with this maybe …?
J Yeah, yeah we'll have to have to think about the cost you know. And if it's going up as far as Edinburgh, I think …
K But there's also time as well …
J Mmm.
K I think Edinburgh's just too far.
J Mmm.

Conversation 2
J Oh, no!
S What?
J Well, it's stopped.
R Oh, no.
J Em, oh, dear.
R Try the buttons. Try the buttons.
J Yeah, press that …
R Try the buttons.
J Press the red one.
S What? This one?
J Yeah. Oh.
R Well, that's the alarm, well we saw it…
B Well, there's a telephone there. Why don't you try that?
J Oh, yes. See if you can…er…
S No, I can't. The, the, the little door seems to be stuck.
R Oh, no!
J **9.4** Wouldn't it be a good idea to try and get that little door open? Has anybody anything we could …?
S Mmm … we could try. Have you got something?
B Oh, I wouldn't do that!
K No. Don't fiddle with it.
B I wouldn't, I wouldn't do that …
S Why?
B Well, you don't know, I mean …
R Just, just, play, play with the buttons.
S Well, wouldn't that be a way of letting anybody know …?
K Yeah, they'll know… Why don't we just, just wait? I mean it's only just …you know …
B We could, em, bang on the door? Sing and shout?
J Actually, this has happened before so, hmm it's, nothing new.
S Is it?
J So perhaps if we just wait …
S … How long have you been in here before?
J Well, it's happened once or twice, you know. Oh, a few minutes … a few minutes.
S Oh, it's not too long.
K It'll go in a minute. We'll be all right.
S What about that? There's that little hatch thing up there.
J Oh, no.
S I mean, we could go … I mean … how long have we got in here before the air runs out?
B Oh, well, not, not yet. I mean we could always, erm, just sit, sit down?
K Yes, yes that's …
S A bit like giving up!
J A bit dirty on the floor, though, em…
S Fag ends.
J What about the buttons for opening the doors? If you, if you push that one…
R Well, that's what I said. Play with the buttons.
J Yeah, yeah, good idea.
S Perhaps, perhaps we should try and pull the doors apart.
R No, don't do that. You might see something up there.
B Well, I mean, I think we should just wait a few minutes.

• Check answers.

Possible answers

Conversation 1	**Conversation 2**
a organizing excursions for a group of students	how to get out of a lift that has stopped between floors
b Birmingham art galleries and theatres. London / Welsh hills / York / Edinburgh	press buttons / press red button use telephone / open the little door / wait / sing and shout / wait for a few minutes / sit down / pull the doors apart

2 • **9.4** Play the recording, while students follow the extracts in their books on p.92, marking the functional language used by the speakers.

 • Students add the expressions to their lists.

 • Check through the lists with students.

Answers

(This includes expressions from *Listening 1* and *2*.)

Making suggestions

9.2

Couldn't we …? Would it be an idea to…? Don't you think it would be a better idea to…? We could always …

9.4 Extract 1

Well, what about we …?

Note This is an alternative to *What about trying …?*

So, I mean we could …

(From full conversation

I think we could …)

9.4 Extract 2

Wouldn't it be a good idea to …? Why don't we …? We could … Perhaps if we …

(From full conversation

We could … What about …?)

Accepting suggestions

9.2

Yeah, that's a good idea. Definitely. Great idea! OK. … that'll be fine.

9.4 Extract 1

I think that's a good idea. I'd go along with that, yes. Yeah, all right then. Might be a good idea … Mmm. I'd agree with that.

9.4 Extract 2

Rejecting suggestions

9.2

I still think (going up in my car) would be a better option. No way! I'm not keen on that idea … I'm not sure we should…

9.4 Extract 1

9.4 Extract 2

Oh, I wouldn't do that …

(From full conversation

No, don't do that.)

Ending a conversation

9.2

Is that the time? Sorry, but I've got to go … Sorry, but, I really must go …

9.4 Extract 1

Well, look, I've em, …you know, got to go, so er …

Anyway … can we carry on with this maybe …

9.4 Extract 2

© Oxford University Press **PHOTOCOPIABLE**

Features of natural conversation ▬▬▬▬ p. 92 ▬

This section focuses on the use of *just* and *actually* in conversational English. Both words are very commonly used – and often have no very precise meaning. It is important to make students aware of how common these words are and to

provide them with an opportunity to think about what they mean or add to a conversation.

1 • Start by reading the meanings of *just* 1–5, to check students understand them.

 a **9.5** Play the recording of sentences a–e and get students to match sentences with an appropriate meaning.

9.5

a *Just, just*, play, play with the buttons.

b Why don't we *just, just* wait?

c Hurry up! We're going to be late!

 I'm *just* coming. I'm *just* finishing this letter.

d Can I *just* borrow your pen a minute?

e I've *just* finished my course.

 • Check answers.

Answers

a 4 (3 is also possible)   **d** 1

b 3   **e** 2

c 5

2 • **9.6** Students match the sentences to meanings and then listen to check.

9.6

a *Actually*, this has happened before…

b A I imagine the weather was pretty awful.

 B *Actually*, it was quite good. It only rained once.

c We don't *actually* allow non-members into the club, I'm afraid.

d *Actually*, it might be better if we stop for a break now.

e A Did you know that Joe was thinking of leaving?

 B I'm not surprised, *actually*. He never really settled in, did he?

 • Check answers.

Answers

a 5   **d** 3 / 4

b 1 / 4   **e** 3

c 2 / 4

▬ **Practice** ▬▬▬▬▬▬▬▬▬▬

1 a **9.7** Play the recording.

 • Students listen and repeat the suggestions.

 b Ask students to say which speaker sounds more enthusiastic.

9.7

1 Would it be an idea to go by train? (not enthusiastic)

 Would it be an idea to go by train? (enthusiastic)

2 Don't you think it'd be a better idea to fly? (not enthusiastic)

 Don't you think it'd be a better idea to fly? (enthusiastic)

3 We could always hire a car. (not enthusiastic)

 We could always hire a car. (enthusiastic)

Answers

1b See tapescript **9.7** .

Note The second speaker sounds enthusiastic about their suggestion. They achieve this by starting HIGH.

2 • **9.8** Play the recording. Pause after each sentence and drill chorally and individually.

9.8

a That's a good idea. (enthusiastic)
b I'd agree with that. (enthusiastic)
c Great idea! (enthusiastic)
d Definitely! (enthusiastic)
e I'm not keen on that idea. (not enthusiastic)
f I'm not sure we should do that. (not enthusiastic)
g I wouldn't do that. (not enthusiastic)

Answers

2 See tapescript 9.8.

3 • 9.9 Play the recording sentence by sentence.
 • Students could work in pairs or small groups and tell each other their responses using the expressions from 9.8.
 • Finish by eliciting a few responses from individual students. Alternatively you could pause after each sentence and select an individual student to respond. They can choose to accept or reject the suggestion.

9.9

a Would it be an idea to invest the money?
b Don't you think it'd be a better idea to spend it all on a big party?
c We could always spend it on more lottery tickets.
d Don't you think it'd be a better idea to share it out and then everybody can decide to spend it how they like?
e We could always give it to a charity, like Save the Children, or something.

■ Exploitation   p. 93 ■

 • Ask students to read the instructions and the first situation.
 • Students form groups, then think up ideas for solving the problem.
 • Students take turns to make and respond to suggestions. You could also suggest that one student in each group tries to end the conversation.
 • Monitor the conversations, listening for correct use of the functional language. Do not interrupt conversations unless the language is completely incorrect or inappropriate.
 • Finish by checking on the most popular suggestions.
 • Repeat this procedure for the second situation.

■ Writing

1 a Allow students time to read through the two examples, and think about or discuss their ideas.
 • Elicit their ideas.

Suggested answers

a • **Similarities**
  Both the conversation and the letter use questions as well as statements to make suggestions.
  In both, the suggestions are tentative and polite.
 • **Differences**
  In the conversation the person who makes the suggestions gets an instant response from the listener.
  The letter is in more formal language than the conversation.
  The letter writer chooses a variety of different suggestion expressions to avoid repetition (listed in **b** below).

b Students underline suggestion expressions in the letter.

Answers

b *Have you considered discussing the problem...?*
 ...you could try inviting him for a drink...
 I suggest you make a formal complaint...

Note You could remind students of the ways of using the verb *suggest*:
I suggest (that) you make a formal complaint.
I suggest making a formal complaint.
It is not possible to use an infinitive construction. You cannot say:
I suggest ~~you to make~~ a formal complaint.

2 • Ask students to read both letter plans and choose one. The first letter is to a friend and so can be informal. The second, which is to a colleague, should be less informal.
 • Remind students to refer to the **Writing guidelines** on p.156 of their books.
 • If you think students may be short of ideas, have a short brainstorming session for students to make suggestions to be included in the letters.

Ideas
Letter 1
 • Before moving, the friend could visit the town for a few days and look up some old friends. They could visit some favourite old places to check if they still feel comfortable there.
 • They could make a list of the pros and cons of moving back before making a final decision.
 • The friend could ask for advice from other people whose opinions they value.
 • The friend could prepare for moving back by making a short visit.
 • Once they move, the friend could invite old friends round.
 • The friend could join clubs or organizations of various kinds.
Letter 2
 • The colleague could move to a more attractive part of their own country rather than abroad.
 • They could spend all future holidays in the holiday resort.
 • They could buy a flat in the holiday place and visit.
 • They could change their lifestyle completely – get a new job, etc.
 • They could put off making a decision until they had considered the matter properly, drawn up lists of pros and cons, and talked to other people who had gone to live there.

 • The letters should follow the suggested paragraph plans.

3 • Students exchange letters with a partner who has written a different letter.
 • They read each other's letters, make suggestions for improvement, and check that the letters are suitably formal or informal.
 • They discuss their suggested improvements before writing the final version of the letter. This could be set for homework.

■ Summary

 • Encourage students to use the tick boxes to help them keep a record of their learning.

Theme

Ways in which people play with or change reality.

Preview The story of a man who lied about his age to get into university
Reading Virtual reality pets
Listening Optical illusions

Grammar

- Passives (LC p.135)
- Passive constructions: *… is claimed to be / are said to be / It is believed that …* (LC p.135)
- The pronoun *it* (LC p.136)

Vocabulary

- Metaphorical language
- The verbs *look* and *see*

Functional language

- Announcing / confirming decisions
- Questioning decisions

Features of natural conversation

- Missing words: *(It) sounds a bit risky to me.*

Pronunciation

- *be*
- Sentences stress

Writing

- Announcing decisions in writing (WG p.155)

Workbook

- A magazine article about the art of lying
- Topic vocabulary: crime; Colour idioms; *work out, take in*
- Passives review; Passive constructions; The pronoun *it*
- Supporting statements; Presenting an argument

Preview

This tells the story of Brandon Lee (real name Brian McKinnon) who as an adult went back to his old school to 'try again'.

■ Your thoughts ■ ■ p. 94 ■

These questions establish students' views on lying about age or experience.

- This could be done in pairs or as a class brainstorm, but keep it brief.

■ Listening ■

1 • Students look at the photographs and think about questions **a** and **b**, then compare ideas in pairs.
- If anyone in the class actually knows or remembers this true story, ask them simply to make written notes of what they remember, rather than spoil the story for the rest of the class.
- If you elicit students' ideas, do not confirm or deny their answers yet.

2 • Students read questions **a** and **b** before they listen to the recording for the first time.
- You may wish to teach these words and phrases before students listen to the recording: *deception* (trick, hoax, lie), *nerve-racking* (causing great mental strain), *birth certificate* (official document giving details of date and place of a person's birth).
- **10.1** Play the recording once without stopping.

10.1

This is the story of an incredible deception which started out as a desire to help people. Brian McKinnon desperately wanted to become a doctor. In 1980 he was accepted at Glasgow University to study medicine, but a few months into this demanding course he caught a mystery illness and had to spend much of his time in bed. Subsequently he failed his exams and was asked to leave the university.

In 1984 he went back to Glasgow University as a librarian, hoping to be able to transfer back to medicine. When that failed, he began a degree in experimental pathology, still hoping to switch back. After four years, however, it became clear that he wasn't going to achieve his ambition, so he left without graduating. At the age of twenty-seven, as determined as ever, Brian McKinnon went to Canada and started a pre-medical course. However, that route too was blocked when he realized that his immigrant status would prevent him from completing his studies. So he came home from Canada to visit his sick father – an event that was to change his life.

During their last conversation McKinnon asked his father whether he thought he'd ever be able to do anything meaningful with his life. His father replied that he had never lost confidence in his son. That conversation convinced Brian that the only thing to do was to re-invent himself and go back to school.

His only real worry was whether he could pass for a seventeen- year-old boy. He believed he could. But this incredible plan became even more bizarre when Brian realized that the only school that would let him in with minimum documentation was in his old home area. He had to go back to the school he'd left thirteen years before.

He went along, with bogus documentation under the name of Brandon Lee, and enrolled. It was nothing very sophisticated – just a letter from his father who he said was a professor and another letter from a tutor in Canada. The headmaster of the school remembers a very articulate, friendly young man who arrived at the school for interview with excellent credentials. He said he had been touring the world with his mother who was an opera singer and because of this he had been educated by private tutors, not in normal schools.

Brian McKinnon later admitted that he had found walking through the school gates an intensely nerve-racking experience. He was acutely aware of the fact that at any moment a question could arise that he wouldn't be able to answer. He thought, for example, he might be asked for his birth certificate. He remembers meeting one of his original teachers. He says he simply kept his head down, and looked shy.

- Allow a minute or two after playing the recording for students to react to what they hear and compare ideas.
- Check answers.

Answers

a The person who deceived the school was the boy / man in the photograph, Brian McKinnon.
  He lied to get a second chance of going to medical school.
b Brandon Lee is Brian McKinnon.

3 • Students should read through the events in the life of Brian McKinnon before listening to the story again. They could try to remember the sequence of events before listening, then listen and check.
- Play the recording again.
- Allow students a few minutes to compare answers.
- Check answers. When students read their sentences out they should use the pronoun *He* and change them to *his*.

Note They is used in the original to hide the identity (gender) of the person.

Answers – correct sequence of events

1 He went to Glasgow University to study medicine.
2 He got an unknown illness.
3 He left university because he failed his exams.
4 He went back to the university as a librarian.
5 He followed a degree course in experimental pathology.
6 He went to Canada.
7 He began a pre-medical course of study.
8 He returned to Britain.
9 He had an important conversation with his father.
10 He enrolled at the school.

▓ Reading ▓▓▓▓▓▓▓▓▓▓▓▓▓▓▓▓▓▓▓▓▓▓ p. 95 ▓

1 a Before reading ask students to predict the ending of the story.
- Elicit a few ideas, but don't deny or confirm anything at this stage.
b Students now read the story and check their predictions.

2 • Students discuss these questions in pairs, groups, or as a whole class.

▓ Person to person ▓▓▓▓▓▓▓▓▓▓▓▓▓▓▓▓▓▓

1 • This question could be discussed briefly (two or three minutes) by the class.

2 • Students think of a person they would like to become if they were to change their identity.
- You could ask students to write the name of the person they'd like to become on a piece of paper. Collect all the papers in and read them out at random. The class has to guess whose new identity you are reading.

─Grammar – Passives review ─────────

The main focus of this section is on when or why the passive is used in preference to the active. It is assumed that students are familiar with the basic forms.

1–4 Students could work through these tasks and questions individually or in pairs.
- Remind students that they can refer to the **Language Commentary** on p.135.
- Monitor, helping when needed.
- Check answers.

Answers

1 a *was asked*   (past simple)
  b *was blocked*   (past simple)
  c *he had been educated*   (past perfect)
  d *(might) be asked*   (modal + infinitive)
  e *was informed*   (past simple)
  f *had been passed*   (past perfect)

2 • We use the passive when we want to focus attention on the person or thing affected by the action rather than on the person or thing who actually did the action.
  The passive is also used when we want language to sound more formal.
  a *Brandon Lee* is the key figure; he is the person we are interested in. The *private tutors* are unimportant in comparison.
  b The key detail here is that the headmaster found out the truth; the identity of the informant is unimportant.

3 a The agent of a passive verb is the person or thing responsible for the action.
  b c *private tutors*
  c It is often difficult to say for certain why the agent is not mentioned; there might be a mixture of reasons. Reason 1 could apply to all the examples.
  1a reasons 1 and 2 (The agent is obviously the university authorities because no one else has the authority to ask a student to leave.)
  1b reasons 1 and 4 (Nobody or nothing in particular *blocked* the *route* this was brought about by circumstances.)
  1d reason 4
  1e reasons 1 and 3 (The informer might not wish to be identified for passing on valuable information; or the headmaster might not have actually known who was giving the information.)
  1f reasons 1 and 3

4 1a *... he failed his exams and the university authorities asked him to leave.*

1c *... private tutors had educated him, not teachers in normal schools*

1d *He thought someone / people might ask him for his birth certificate.*

1e *Someone informed the headmaster that ... or*
An informant told the headmaster ...

1f *Someone / The informant had passed the information to the press.*

■ Pronunciation ▬▬▬▬▬▬▬▬▬▬

5 a Students read sentences 1a–f aloud to each other and decide how the passive verbs are pronounced.

b **10.2** Students listen and check their ideas.

10.2

a ... he failed his exams and was asked (/wəz ɑːskt/) to leave...

b ... that route too was blocked (/wəz blɒkt/) when he realized that his immigrant status would prevent him from completing his studies.

c ... he had been educated (/had bɪn (bin) edʒukeɪtɪd/) by private tutors, not in normal schools.

d He thought he might be asked (/maɪ(t) bɪ ɑːskt/) for his birth certificate.

e ... the headmaster was informed (/wəz infɔːmd/) that Brandon Lee and Brian McKinnon were the same person.

f ... the information had been passed (/had bɪn (bin) pɑːst/) to the Press.

• You could get students to repeat the sentences, focusing on the pronunciation of the weak forms of *be*.

• You could also write the weak forms of *be* on the board.

Answers

1 a See tapescript **10.2**.

b • Past passive *was* /wəz/; *were* /wə/
• Present perfect passive *have been* /(h)av bɪn (bin)/
   has been /(h)əz bɪn (bin)/
   Contracted forms *'ve been* /v bɪn (bin)/;
   's been /z bɪn (bin)/
• Past perfect passive *had been* /(h)əd bɪn/;
   'd been
• Modal passive *might* /maɪ(t) bɪ(i)/
   should be /ʃʊ(d) bɪ (i)/
• Future passive *'ll be* /l bɪ(i)/

Note In the negative there are no weak forms and been can be pronounced /bɪn/ or /bin/ but not /biːn/.

■ Check ▬▬▬▬▬▬▬▬▬▬

6 • Students work through the exercise individually, then compare answers with a partner. Point out that they need not always include the agent (the subject of the active sentences).

• Check answers.

Answers

(The agents are included where they are useful.)

a I have / I've been accepted on a course starting next week.

b The President was not recognized (by anyone) in his old jeans.

c Photographs have been sent to national newspapers by amateur photographers.

d The fraud was not discovered (by the police) for nearly two years.

e One of the directors might be sent to prison.

f I've just been told that I've got an interview.

— p. 96 —

Reading

This newspaper article reports the development of *norns*, which are virtual pets.

1 • Start by doing a class survey. If you have a small class, you could elicit responses and note the information on the board. If you have a big class, divide students into groups to answer the questions and make notes.

• Elicit each group's results and record these on the board.

2 • Ask students to read the headline, look at the illustration, and answer **a** and **b**.

• You may wish to teach these words and phrases before students read the article: *to breed* (to arrange or organize the reproduction of animals), *DNA* (abbreviation for the chemical in the cells of animals and plants which carries genetic information), *floppy disk* (name for disk used in a computer to record and store information), *neural patterns* (patterns in the nervous system).

• Check answers.

Answers

a *virtual* means *almost, nearly.*
In this headline *virtual* means *almost real.*

b *virtual reality* – a system in which images that look like real objects are created by computer and appear to surround a person wearing special equipment.

3 • Elicit a few ideas in answer to the two questions. Do not say whether they are right or not at this stage. Students will find out when they read.

4 • As they read, students should make a list of the advantages and disadvantages of norns as pets.

• Although the text is quite short, it contains quite a lot of information, so allow students plenty of time to read it.

• Check answers.

Answers

3 • Why is the pet (the norn) special?
It is not real – it 'lives' in computers.

• How does it 'live life to the full'?
It is born, develops, has illnesses, breeds, dies, etc.

4 Advantages of norns

• They are easy to care for.
• They cost nothing to feed.
• They don't make a mess or smell.
• They respond to stimuli (being tickled).
• Owners can have them cured of illnesses.
• Owners can exchange eggs over the Internet.
• They can be looked after while owners are on holiday.
• They can breed.
• They can learn.

Disadvantages

- Their behaviour is unpredictable.
- Norns can get drunk and sick and can die.
- If you send them away their new owners may teach them to swear.
- They are not real.

Close up

- Students work through the questions individually or in pairs.
- Check answers.

Answers

- l.6–9   This question draws attention to the use of speech marks to highlight a special or unusual use of words. These include: *virtual pets* (l.2) *pets* (l.6) / *virtual creatures* (l.6) / *virtual eggs* (l.8).
  If reading this passage aloud, a reader would pause just before the word or expression and then speak the words in a louder voice or with more stress.
- l.10   *slap* to hit with a flat hand – (similar to *smack*)
  tickle to touch lightly to cause a tingling sensation that makes people laugh and move
  The effect of *slapping* is pain / the effect of *tickling* is squirming and uncontrollable laughter.
- l.16   *a groan* – a low noise made by a person or animal experiencing pain, discomfort, or disappointment
  a cry – a louder, higher call or shout, caused by pain or sorrow

Interpretation

1–3 Allow students time to read the questions and think about possible answers.
- Elicit their ideas.

Possible answers

1   Scientists could have started a number of developments:
   - They may have invented computer systems which can think simple thoughts or live lives independent of humans.
   - Computer systems which can express feelings, opinions, etc.
   - A new craze among young people for computer pets.

2 a   Some animal lovers might appreciate having an 'animal' that costs nothing and makes no physical demands. On the other hand, norns are not living beings and cannot give affection.
   b   Someone interested in computer technology would probably want to find out how norns are programmed to develop over time. They would also be interested in the link between norns and thinking machines.
   c   Someone with a busy, stressful life might find it relaxing to 'play' with norns, animals they would not need to spend specific amounts of time on every day.
   d   Someone who is lonely or bored might become involved in the life of their norn and look after it as they might a real animal.

3   - As part of research into bio-chemistry, neurology, and DNA.
   - For their own amusement / entertainment.
   - As a by-product of more serious research into a new generation of computers.
   - For commercial reasons. Norns might become a fashion or craze which would bring in large amounts of money.
   - To make comparisons with how we live and learn.
   - To use in experiments.

Speaking personally

1–3 Students discuss these questions in pairs or groups.
- Monitor but do not interrupt.
- Elicit their ideas.
- You could take a quick class vote for the questions in 3.

Possible answers

1   because they are lonely / for company, for security, for particular practical purposes: e.g. blind people need guide dogs., because they want a living creature to look after

2   It is well known that people choose pets similar to themselves in character and sometimes appearance. Do students have any interesting examples of this phenomenon?

3   Personal answers.

Grammar – Passive constructions

Exploring concepts   p. 97

1 - Give students a few minutes to think about and discuss this first question, then check their answers.
- Remind students that they can refer to the **Language Commentary** on p.135.

Answers
In **a** 2, **b** 2, **c** 2 the speaker or writer states facts.
In **a** 1, **b** 1, **c** 1 the speaker or writer uses the passive to distance themselves from the facts and to cast doubt on the truth of the statements.
For example, in **a**1 the writer suggests, by the use of *are said to be,* that they think norns may not be easier to care for than hamsters.

2–5 Now let students work through the rest of the questions and tasks individually or in pairs.
- Monitor and help.
- Check answers.

Answers

2   **a** 1, **b** 1, **c** 1 – all B / C

3   *thought, reported, understood, assumed, considered, found, presumed, suggested*

4   This exercise gets students to practise different passive forms.
   a **a** 1 *It is said that the pets, furry cartoon-like virtual creatures called norns are no harder to …*
      b 1 *It is believed that scientists trying to develop thinking machines are interested in this feature.*
   b **c** 1 *Norns are claimed to respond to being slapped or tickled.*

5   **a** 1 *apparently,*
      2 *According to*
      3 *They say that*
      They are all used as distancing devices to cast doubt on the truthfulness of the information.
   b 1 *It is claimed that norns can also get drunk or sick.*
      2 *It is believed that people will be able to exchange eggs.*
      3 *It is said that more and more people are buying computer pets. / More and people are said to be buying computer pets.*

◼ Exploitation

1 a Allow students one or two minutes to skim read the KyttyKyts advertisement to find out the main purpose of the programme.

Answer

Its main purpose is as a screen saver for a computer, not a form of entertainment or a game.

b You could suggest that the sentences students write are the kind that could appear in a review.

- Elicit one or two ideas from the class before getting students to write their own sentences. Remind them to use a variety of 'reporting' verbs and passive constructions rather than repeating the same formula for every sentence.

Note This exercise should be done in writing, as these language forms are formal rather than conversational.

Sample answers

- It is claimed that you can watch KyttyKyts dreaming of mice and birds.
  KyttyKyts are said to dream of mice and birds.
- It is reported that KyttyKyts chase mice across your screen.
  KyttyKyts are said to chase mice across your screen.
- It is suggested that you can hear KyttyKyts purr when you stroke them.
  KyttyKyts are believed to purr when you stroke them.
- It is stated that different KyttyKyts have their own personality.
  KyttyKyts are said to have their own personality.

Additional activity

- You could get students to discuss well-known advertising claims that they find difficult to take seriously. Bring in (or ask students to bring in) magazine adverts, or television adverts on video.
- Let them discuss their ideas in groups or as a whole class. Encourage fluency, but listen out for the use of all constructions used to report facts they are not sure about, i.e. passive constructions and other key language, such as *apparently*, etc.

2 • Students work in pairs and they refer to p.159 at the back of the book.

- Explain that they are going to read some facts and probably will not know whether they are correct.
- Give an example to check they understand what to do.
  Example
  Fact: *People with blond hair have more hairs on their heads.*
  Reporting fact: *Apparently, people with blond hair have more hairs on their heads than people with dark hair.*
- Students take turns to report the facts to each other, using passive and other constructions.
- Monitor their conversations, correcting where necessary.
- Now, let students discuss which statements they think are true and which are false.

- After a minute of two, tell them that only one statement in each set of five is false. Allow another two or three minutes discussion before checking their ideas.

Answers

The two false statements are these:
In Student A's list:
The average person can tell the difference between 2,000 smells.
The correct answers is *4,000 smells.*
In Student B's list:
Forty-six countries in the world don't have a coastline.
The correct answers is *Twenty-six countries.*

◼ Free speech

3 a You could spend a few moments on the language of the newspaper headlines. Point out or elicit some of these grammatical and lexical features of the headlines:

Omission of articles:	*government /rock star* (instead of **the** *government* / **a** *rock star*)
Omission of auxiliary verbs:	*hit / cheating* (instead of *is hit* / **is** *cheating*)
Present simple instead of Present perfect:	*resigns / cheating* (instead of **has resigned** / **has been cheating**)
Short, punchy words:	*hit / top* (instead of **damaged, affected** / **important, famous**)

- Students now discuss in groups the probable stories behind these three headlines.
- Monitor their discussions, but don't interrupt or correct.

b Finally give the class a chance to discuss stories of current interest. They may be 'political' stories, or the more trivial affairs of singers, film stars, and other public figures.

Note In this activity, it is more natural to use these expressions: *apparently, … according to …* and *They say that …* than the passive constructions. These will more naturally occur in the writing exercise which follows.

◼ Writing

4 • Students write up one of the stories they have discussed. They can choose to write about one of the headlines in their books, or a story of current interest. You may set the writing for homework, but the word limit (sixty to seventy words) is short enough to allow the work to be done in class.

- Read through the rubric to check that students understand and remind them to use the more formal passive constructions.
- If this is done in class, monitor, giving help where necessary.

▶ **Photocopiable activity 12 p.170**

Listening

The theme of this part of the unit is optical illusions.

1 a Students discuss **a** and **b** in pairs or as a whole class.
 • Do a quick class survey. Do students find these illusions intriguing or irritating? Ask them to give reasons.
 • Discourage them from looking at p.159 until they have had a chance to make their own suggestions about how the Kennel of Confusion was constructed.

2 Students are going to hear two extracts from a science programme.
 • Students listen out for the names of the objects 1–5. One object is not described.
 • **10.3** Play the first part of the recording. Students match the names with the impossible objects.

10.3

Part 1

In today's programme we're going to look at ways in which the human brain processes visual information. But before we do that, let's look at some of the impossible objects artists have created by bending the rules.

For the next few minutes, you'll need to refer to the illustrations. We're all so used to two-dimensional drawings of solid objects that we don't give them a second glance, but look at these drawings.

First of all there's the blivit, so called because it asks you to believe it. This is a classic 'impossible object' from the early 1960s. The separate parts of the drawing make sense, but when the two ends are seen together things begin to fall apart. What is the middle prong of the fork attached to and how could the three nuts be made?

Then there are the baby blocks, which can be seen as a pile of boxes standing on the floor or hanging from the ceiling. If you can't see the two different images, try turning the page through forty-five degrees.

Thirdly, there's the staircase to nowhere. The eye sees the obvious fact that the steps must be coming out of the hole in the ground. But the first storey cannot be flat.

Then there's the mad spiral. Here it is the illusion that all the angles are right angles and all the lines are straight lines that gets you into trouble.

Last of all, and perhaps the most famous, is the tribar, which was invented in the 1950s. Each part is correct, but the whole triangle will get you in a twist.

 • Check answers.

Answers

1	baby blocks	**3**	staircase to nowhere
2	Object 2 is a Necker cube	**4**	mad spiral
	(not mentioned in part 1)	**5**	tribar

3 a Check that students understand the meanings of the words in the list before they discuss the question in pairs.

Note You could demonstrate some of these terms by looking at pictures of buildings in magazines, for example *perspective*, *shadow*, *three-dimensional*.

 • Ask them to make a list of their ideas. You could elicit some of them and write them on the board.
 b Play the second part of the recording once.

 • Play the recording again, pausing occasionally if you think this will help students to deal with the density of information.

10.3

Part 2

Why are our brains fooled by these impossible figures? When we look at any picture, the brain instantly processes the visual data and allows us to see the three-dimensional object on a flat surface, although we know it cannot actually be there. That illusion is commonplace – and is very useful to us. The art of painting depends on it for a start, as does any activity where we need to convey a sense of three dimensions on a piece of paper.

But our brains didn't evolve to appreciate paintings, or blueprints for that matter. They evolved to make life-saving judgements in a world where it was vital to interpret visual information very fast.

It is our brains, however, that sort out the information, not our eyes. Light from the outside world hits the retina, but the patterns of brightness mean nothing without the power of the brain to process these signals. That's quite a trick on the part of the brain. Scientists have made artificial retinas– for collecting information from light. But it seems that interpreting the patterns is much harder. Programmers have found it extremely difficult to 'teach' even super-computers to recognize quite simple images.

So it's not surprising that the human brain can be fooled. Where and how it is fooled is a subject that interests psychologists studying how perception works. But people have been playing around with ambiguous figures for far longer than psychologists have been explaining them. Designs incorporating baby blocks are found on the floors of churches dating from the 10th century. The first person to write about ambiguous figures was L.A. Necker, a Swiss professor, who described the Necker cube in 1832. This is simply a cube, drawn from an angle and without perspective, and it has the same effect on our perception as the baby blocks. The 'front corner' can become the 'back corner' and vice versa.

As 19th-century interest in perception grew, more ambiguous figures were developed. One major, if elementary, discovery was the effect of shadow – a picture of a sun-lit hill appears to be a hollow when turned over – and the crucial role light and shade play in art. In effect, visual clues are interpreted by the brain in a programmed way – which can be tricked remarkably easily.

It is a small step from the Necker cube to the truly impossible tribar. More subtle than the blivit, the tribar has three linked sections; any two of the links make perfect sense. It is only when the eye follows the loop all the way round to the third link that the inconsistency leaps out.

Put the Necker cube together with the tribar, add skilful photography, and you get the apparently three-dimensional dog kennel. Created by the American William Wick back in the early 1980s, it too is impossible. The clues the brain uses to reconstruct a solid image from a flat picture have been cleverly manipulated and added to real three-dimensional elements, until the mind cannot cope with all the contradictions it is being asked to accept.

 • Students check their pre-listening ideas from **a** and discuss them with a partner.

Answers

 • Brains have evolved to interpret visual information *quickly* (in order to make life-saving decisions).
 • The brain interprets clues, especially *light* and *shade*, in a programmed way. Clues can be manipulated and so trick the brain.

■ Interpretation ■

1–2 Students work through the questions in pairs or groups.

- Briefly check a few ideas with students as a whole class.
- Round off with a brief feedback of ideas.

Answers

1 – Many professions depend on this ability: architects, designers, planners, engineers, Artists: painters, etc.
– Everyday life: drawing sketch-maps of places / the layout of furniture in rooms, etc.

2 – escaping from enemies / attackers
– judging speed (e.g. crossing the road)
– judging distances, heights, etc.

■ Vocabulary

1 • Students can do **1** and **2** individually or in pairs.
• Check answers.

Answers

1 a *study, investigate, consider*   c *notice, perceive (with eyes)*
  b *see, examine with our eyes*

2 a *searching for / trying to find*   e *understand*
  b *direct your eyes towards me*   f *meet*
  c *resembles / takes after*   g *try to*
  d *appears that it is going to*

■ Speaking personally

- Students exchange ideas and experiences in pairs or groups.
- Monitor, but do not interrupt.
- Finish with a brief feedback of ideas from the class.

— Grammar – The pronoun *it*

■ Exploring concepts   p. 99 ■

This section focuses on the many different uses of the pronoun *it*.
• Remind students that they can refer to the **Language Commentary** on p.136.

1 • Start by reminding students that it can refer to things, animals, ideas, or situations, then elicit what it refers to in the two extracts from the recording.

Answers

- ...we know **it** cannot   the three-dimensional object
  possibly be there.
- The art of painting   the illusion that an object
  depends on **it**.   is a picture is three-dimensional

2 • Point out to students that *it* has further uses. (Make sure they understand the terms: *object, subject, clause.*)
• Ask students to read through and then match the five sentences with the five uses of *it*.
• You could do **a** as an example.
• Monitor, giving help where necessary.
• Check answers.

Answers

2 a 1 *It* is not necessary for meaning but it does provide emphasis. We could simply say: *Our brains sort out the information ...*
  b 2 It replaces the infinitive as the subject: *to interpret visual information very fast was vital.*
  c 5 *Seems* is a verb like *appears*.
  d 3 It replaces the long complex object which comes later in the sentence:
    ... teaching even super-computers to recognise quite simple images. Without this use of *it*, the sentence would be: *Programmers have found teaching (**not** to 'teach') even super-computers to recognize quite simple images quite difficult.*
  e 2 It replaces the clause *that the human brain can be fooled* as the subject.
  f 4 This sentence contains the time expression *until*.

Note Other examples of use 4:
  Weather **It**'s going to be wet and windy tomorrow.
  Time   **It**'s four o'clock. / **It** was late on Friday evening.
  Distances **It**'s ten kilometres to Madrid. / How far is **it** to Aberdeen?

■ Exploitation

1 • This task practises use 2 of *it*. Students need to be inventive to complete the endings in an appropriate way.
• Elicit a few sample answers to **a**. ... *it's important to relax.* / ... *it's not a good idea to spend too long in the sun if you aren't used to it.*
• Students do the exercise individually or in pairs.
• Monitor and correct where necessary.
• Elicit a few possible answers for each beginning.

2 This task practises use 3 of *it*.
• Point out that students should complete these beginnings in a personal way.
• Monitor and correct where necessary.
• Elicit a few answers for each beginning.

3 This task practises use 1 of *it*.
• Read the rubric and example to students to check they understand. If necessary, demonstrate the process by giving another example involving your students.
• Example
  X(wrong name of student) went to New York for his holidays, didn't he?
  If students contradict you, they may say:
  No, Y(correct student's name) went to New York, not X (wrong students' name).
  Give them the correct form for this exercise:
  *No, they didn't, **it was Y who** went to New York, not X.*
• Each student writes five sentences about people in the class.
• In pairs students take turns to read out their sentences to each other using the wrong name every time.
• Their partners correct them using an *It* construction.
• Monitor the conversations, correcting and helping.

4 This task practises use 4 of *it*.

- Elicit a few sample sentences from the class, then let students work in pairs or groups for a few minutes on each of the topics listed.
- Monitor and correct.

■ Free speech

5 This is a fluency activity which gets students to speculate about and discuss the picture. They may be able to use some of these expressions: *It appears that … / It seems to be … / It looks as if …*
- The discussion could be done in pairs, groups, or as a class.
- When students start running out of ideas, tell them the title of the painting 'Flying over the town at a speed of three hundred km an hour' and this may lead to further discussion.

▶ Photocopiable activity 13 p.171

— p. 100 —

Metaphorical language

This section looks at words which have literal and metaphorical meanings.

1 • Students read the opening rubric and the three examples to establish the difference between *literal* and *metaphorical*.
- Check that students understand the three words used literally, then elicit their metaphorical meanings.

Answers

	word / phrase	literal meaning	metaphorical
a	*to block a route*	to prevent cars / vehicles passing along a road, etc.	to prevent someone progressing in a particular direction
b	*to bend*	to change the shape, (often of metal)	bend the rules to interpret rules flexibly
c	*a step*	one pace (step here is short for footstep)	move / distance

2 • If you didn't study the features of newspaper language earlier in the unit (p.97) you could run through the general features now.
- Elicit students' ideas about why newspaper headlines often include metaphorical language.

Suggested answer
Metaphorical language is colourful and often creates interesting visual images. It can make abstract ideas come to life.

a Students read the headlines, identifying metaphorical language.
- Check that they have identified the correct words or phrases before getting them to think about the meanings.

Answers

1	*tumble*	fall quickly or suddenly
2	*takes off*	becomes quickly or suddenly successful
3	*closes the door on*	says 'no' to / gives a negative response to
4	*shot down in flames*	destroyed completely
5	*unlocks*	makes it possible to know or understand
6	*Frosty*	cold, unfriendly

b Students now fill the gaps with the literal meanings of the expressions used in 2. Do the first one as an example.
- Check answers.

Answers

1	*unlock*	4	*took off*
2	*frosty*	5	*tumbled*
3	*shot down in flames*	6	*closed the door*

3 The italicized words and phrases in 1–6 have a literal meaning when used as nouns, but can be used as verbs with a metaphorical meaning.
a Individually or in pairs, students read 1–6 and decide the literal meanings of the nouns.
b Students then work out the metaphorical meanings.
- You could do an example to check understanding.
- Check answers.

Answers

	word	literal noun/meaning	metaphorical verb
1	*to wolf down*	*wolf* – wild animal	to eat quickly and hungrily
2	*cloud*	*cloud* – misty patch in sky	to affect / make unclear
3	*to beaver away*	*beaver* – hard-working animal	to work hard, often for a long time
4	*stormed out*	*storm* – extreme weather with heavy rain and strong winds	to leave angrily
5	*toying with*	*toy* – thing a child plays with	to play with feelings or emotions / refuse to be serious about
6	*tower over*	*tower* – tall building (e.g. Eiffel Tower)	to be much taller than

c This is a short pairwork activity which practises three of the previous metaphorical verbs.
- Monitor, but do not correct.
- Elicit ideas from a few students.

Language in action

■ Eavesdrop! ▓▓▓▓▓▓▓▓▓▓▓▓▓▓▓▓▓▓ p. 101 ■

The questions could be done as a class activity or as pairwork.
- Direct attention to the picture and the three questions.
- Remind students that they are speculating and should come up with a variety of answers.
- You could elicit possible answers now, or move on to *Listening 1*.

Listening 1

1 • **10.4** Students listen to check their *Eavesdrop!* ideas and choose the best word to describe the conversation.

10.4

MD Natalie, come in, sit down, what can I do for you?
N No, I won't sit down, thank you, Mr Roberts. I've just come to give you this.
MD Oh, what is it?
N It's my resignation. Open it and read it now if you like.
MD Natalie, I'm sure we can work this out.
N No, no. I've decided. I've got a job in New Zealand. I'm starting next week.
MD New Zealand? But, but, what if you don't like New Zealand?
N I'm sure I will. Everyone says what a wonderful place it is.
MD If it's a question of money, …
N It's nothing to do with money, Mr Roberts.
MD Martin, please. Call me Martin. Is it the people you're working with, then? I'm sure we could work out …
N No, I get on fine with all my colleagues. I'm sorry, but it doesn't matter what you say, I'm not going to change my mind.
MD I was thinking of offering you promotion within the next month or so.
N Look, Mr Roberts, you won't change my mind.
MD But all your family's here. What would you do if you were in New Zealand and your mother or your father was ill?
N Martin, it's no use. My mind's made up. I'm going.
MD It's us, isn't it?
N I'm sorry, I have to go.

• Check answers.

Possible answers
Eavesdrop!
• Boss / manager and employee / secretary
• Colleagues / The man is the woman's boss. There is a suggestion of a past relationship between them.
• It's the woman's resignation.

Listening 1
b The man (Martin Roberts) wants the conversation to be casual and informal; the woman (Natalie) tries to keep it formal.

2 • Students listen again and note down the functional language used by the speakers to announce and confirm decisions, and to question decisions.
 • Allocate tasks and play the recording again if necessary.
 • Students note down the expressions and then compile lists. They help and correct each other at this stage.

Note Students add to these lists during the next listening task.

Answers
See full list of expressions after *Listening 2*, question 2.

Listening 2

1 • **10.5** Give students time to read through the questions a–d and then play the recording.

10.5 including **10.6**

Conversation 1
J Well, I was, you know, getting a bit bored and feeling a bit staid in the same work, so I thought – well, a complete change, so …
B Have you tried any teaching before? I mean, what …

J Well, they, they will give us … erm … a bit of training I think beforehand.
B Well, what happens if you decide you don't like it? I mean it seems a bit of a risk to take to give up a good job.
J Yes, I know, but I've, I've been doing this for, you know, a number of years now …
T What are you going to do about living there? I mean, what happens, …
J Well …
T … what happens if you can't find anywhere to live?
J Well, I think they're going to try and help us to find somewhere and erm, yes, so I'm really excited – it's going to be a great opportunity.
T What are you going to do about the language?
J Ah, yes, well, I shall …
T **10.6** You don't speak Czech.
J No – awful, I shall …
B It's quite a difficult language.
J Yeah, I think so, mmm, I'll have to get some lessons sorted out, won't I?
T Sounds a bit …
J Aren't you excited? Don't you think it's great?
B Well, I mean …
T Well …
Ju I just wish I had your confidence.
J Oh, but it's nothing. I mean, if you want to have a change in life, why not do it?
B Well, I mean, it just seems a big risk to me to take – I mean you've got a … I mean, I know it's not an exciting job, but it's a permanent job and …
J Well, yes …
B You know, it just seems an awful big risk, I mean, what, just what happens if it doesn't work out?
T And what do you do about friends? You're leaving all your friends here. Think about that.
J Well, I shall make new friends and, I mean, I'm outgoing and sociable and I shall meet an awful lot of new people in the school I'm going to.
T I'm not so sure. Sounds a bit risky to me.
J No, no, they're a very nice lot. I've, I've talked to them quite a lot and I've, I've talked to some other people who've been there and they're very enthusiastic about it so, you know, I've got to make a move, really I've, well, I've made my mind up – I have to have a change in life, I think.
B Well, I think you should really, you know, think twice before you take it – it's a big decision.
J Well, it is a big decision and I have been thinking about it for, well, to be honest …

Conversation 2
S What's so good about the country?
Ju The best thing is, is the lack of people really – the, the city's too full. It's not natural for people to live in the city.
R **10.6** Yes it is, it's, it's, it's exciting, there are things to do, I mean, the country – slow death.
Ju Yeah, but then you can choose, you can choose to go into the city to do the pastimes you want and then you just escape to the peace and quiet of the country.
S Yeah, what happens if it's, like the weekend and you think – what can I do at the weekend? There's nothing to do, is there? What do you do?
Ju Oh, you read and you go for walks and you listen to music and just listen to the, the countryside and it's all quiet.
R I mean, what would you do if you … suddenly had an emergency, you, you got ill or …
Ju Oh, well, it's not, it's not out in the outback, there are … we still get sort of … the emergency services …
R Sounds like it.
S You hear terrible stories of people getting stuck when they're …

R   Yeah, I mean in winter.
S   Yeah, cut off …
Ju   Well, yes, you can get cut off, yes, yes, I have heard stories of that, but that, that's just a small price to pay for, for just a life.

- Check answers.

Possible answers

	Conversation 1	Conversation 2
a	probably colleagues / maybe friends	probably friends / maybe colleagues
b	one speaker (Jill) has decided to give up her current job and take up a new job abroad	one speaker (Julie) has decided to move house from the city to the country
c	she's bored in her job (*staid*) and wants a change	the city is too crowded / full of people for her / city life is unnatural
d	• She hasn't taught before. • She is giving up a good job for one she knows almost nothing about. • She may not be able to find somewhere to live. • She doesn't speak the language of the country she's moving to – and this is a difficult language. (Czech) • The experiment may not work – it may be a failure. • She will miss her friends.	• Life in the country is boring – (*a slow death*). • Nothing to do in the country compared with the city. • What would happen if there was a sudden emergency? For example, illness? • Isolated – cut off in the winter.

2a–b ▐**10.6**▐ Play the recording while students follow the extracts on p.102 in their books, marking the functional language used by the speakers.

- Students add the expressions to their lists.
- Check through the lists.

Answers
(This includes expressions from *Listening 1* and *2*.)
Announcing or confirming decisions
▐**10.4**▐
I've decided. … it doesn't matter what you say, I'm not going to change my mind. … you won't change my mind. … it's no use. My mind's made up.
▐**10.6**▐ **Extract 1**
… I've made my mind up … … it is a big decision and I have been thinking about it for …
▐**10.6**▐ **Extract 2**
None

Questioning (arguing with) decisions
▐**10.4**▐
But what if …? What would you do if …?
▐**10.6**▐ **Extract 1**
I just wish I had your confidence. … it just seems a big risk to me to take … … it just seems an awful big risk … I'm not so sure … sounds a bit risky to me. …I think you should really, you know, think twice before you take it – it's a big decision.
(*From full conversation*
Well, what happens if you decide you don't like it? … what happens if …?)
▐**10.6**▐ **Extract 2**
… what happens if …? I mean, what would you do if …?

▨ **Features of natural conversation** ▰▰▰▰▰ p. 102 ▨

This section focuses on two features of natural conversation:
- Ellipsis – specifically the omission of words or phrases in conversation that would be necessary in more formal speech or writing.
- Negative questions. Example *Aren't you tired?*

1 • Ask students to read the example to check they understand the task.
  a Allow time for students to look at the other three examples in Extract 2, and work out which words are missing.
  • Check their ideas.

Suggested answers
- … the country • *slow death.*
  … the country, **that's like dying a** slow death. / … **it's a kind of** slow death.
- • *Sounds like it.*
  It sounds like it.
- *Yeah • cut off.*
  Yeah **when they are / get** cut off …

  b Get students to read through these conversations in pairs before trying to work out what is missing. Point out that this is perfectly correct natural language and that leaving out words does not make it wrong.
  • Check answers.

Suggested answers

1 A *Have you got the time?*
   B *Yes, it's just gone six o'clock.*
2 A *It's a nice day, isn't it?*
   B *Yes, it's not bad.*
3 A *Have you been here long?*
   B *About ten minutes.*
4 A *I'm sorry. I must dash.*
   B *OK. I'll see you later.*

2 • Ask students to compare the questions in **a** and **b** and work out the differences.
- Elicit students' explanations.

Answer
  a By asking *Aren't you excited?* the questioner is implying something like this: *I'm excited. You should be excited, too. Why isn't it obvious that you are excited? I shouldn't be having to ask you this question.*
Negative questions like this sometimes imply slight criticism.
  b The questioner wants to know the answer.

▨ **Practice** ▰▰▰▰▰▰▰▰▰▰▰▰▰▰▰▰

1 **a** Students work in pairs. Ask them to read the sentences aloud and decide which words and syllables are stressed.
  b ▐**10.7**▐ Students listen and check their ideas.

▐**10.7**▐

1 I've made up my mind – I'm leaving.
2 I'm leaving, and I'm not going to change my mind.
3 My mind's made up – I'm going.
4 I've decided to go – you won't change my mind.
5 I'm definitely leaving.

Answers

1b See tapescript **10.7**.

c Play the recording again and drill the sentences chorally and individually.

■ Exploitation Role play

- Ask students to read the three situations. Point out that Student A in Situation 3 has the authority to make a decision. (This should not stop the other two students questioning the decision!)
- Students form groups of 3 and allocate roles. They should take turns to be Student A.
- Give students time to prepare their announcements and objections.
- Student A starts by announcing their decision. The other students should question the decision, point out any disadvantages. A should be unconvinced, and should confirm their original decision by giving more reasons.
- Monitor the conversations, listening for use of the functional language. Do not interrupt unless the language is completely incorrect or inappropriate.

■ Writing p. 103 ■

1 • Point out that students are now going to announce decisions in writing, in either a letter or a prepared statement.

a–c You could let students work through the questions before checking ideas, or work through them one by one.
- Elicit their ideas.

Suggested answers

a • The spoken language is spontaneous. The person announcing the decision is reacting, as she speaks, to the people she is with. She's trying to counter their possible arguments.
  The speaker has to keep re-stating her decision.
  • The first sentence of the letter states the decision clearly and concisely and does this once. The writer gives some background information in preparation for possible objections.

b • *I have finally decided / my mind is made up*
  • The use of the present perfect verb in *I have accepted a place at Oxford University* – makes the decision sound irrevocable.

c • The writer assures people that the decision has not been hurried:
  After careful thought ... / I have been thinking about this move for a number of years ...
  • The writer anticipates and counters possible arguments that may be raised against the decision he has already thought about: *career / salary / other practical considerations.*

2 • Ask students to read both situations and choose one.
  • Remind students to refer to the **Writing guidelines** on p.155 of their books.

- Allow students time to read the situation again, work through the suggested plan, and ask for any clarification.

Note The style of the prepared statement can be as formal as that of the letter. It should not be conversational in tone. Both the letter and the statement can be based on the example of writing on p.103.

- The first draft of the writing may be done in class or for homework.

3 • Students exchange their pieces of writing, if possible with a partner who has chosen a different situation.
  • They suggest improvements to their partner's writing, paying particular attention to the firmness with which the decision is expressed, and the extent to which they have anticipated and answered any possible objections.
  • When suggested improvements have been discussed and agreed upon, students should write their final letter or prepared statement.

■ Summary

- Encourage students to use the tick boxes to help them keep a record of their learning.

11 Followers

Theme

The activities of fans (followers).
Preview The *paparazzi* and the effects on their 'victims'
Reading People who chase after tornadoes
Listening A devoted Elvis Presley fan

Grammar

- Causatives: *to get* or *have something done* (LC p.136)
- Causative verbs and the passive: non-causative use of *have something done* (LC p.137)
- Question tags (LC p.137)

Vocabulary

- American and British English (some words compared)
- Word-building: prefixes
  - negative prefixes *un- / im- / ir- / il- / dis-*
  - other prefixes *over- / anti- / multi- / auto- / re- / mis- / under-*

Functional language

- Expressing likes, dislikes, and preferences

Conversation strategies

- Giving examples

Features of natural conversation

- Uses of the pronoun *You*

Pronunciation

- Intonation on question tags
- Word stress

Writing

- A film or album review (WG p.158)

Workbook

- A couple obsessed by volcanoes
- Topic vocabulary: geographical features; Topic vocabulary: sounds people make; Word-building: *-able, fall* + particle
- Causatives review; Causative verbs; Question tags; Question tags and requests
- Connecting ideas (4); Presenting advantages and disadvantages

Preview

This focuses on the relationship between paparazzi, celebrities, and the general public.

▮ Your thoughts ▬▬▬▬▬▬▬▬▬▬▬▬▬▬▬▬▬ p. 104 ▮

- Use the opening question and the photographs as the basis for a class or group discussion. The discussion will probably move to the subject of the paparazzi and their victims. Don't spend too long on this discussion as students are asked for their opinions in *Person to person*. Pictured clockwise left to right Madonna, Sean Penn and Diana, Princess of Wales.
- Before they read, find out how many students are interested in reading articles about, and seeing photographs of celebrities.

▮ Reading ▬▬▬▬▬▬▬▬▬▬▬▬▬▬▬▬▬▬▬ p. 105 ▮

1 • Students discuss the two questions in pairs.
  • Elicit a few answers before students read the text.

  #### Answers

  a People who want to become famous need publicity – for this reason, they want the attention of the press. Once they are famous, this relationship can change and become irritating.

  b The paparazzi go to extreme lengths because of the huge amounts of money (*financial rewards*) they can get.

2 • Students now read the text and check whether their ideas are mentioned.

▮ Listening ▬▬▬▬▬▬▬▬▬▬▬▬▬▬▬▬▬▬▬▬▬▬

1 • Allow students a few minutes to predict how the paparazzi interviewed will answer the four questions.
  • Elicit some ideas and write the most common suggestions on the board as a check for when students listen.
  • You may wish to teach these words before students listen to the recording: *to get a buzz* (to experience great excitement), *exhilarating* (strong feeling of excitement), *to develop a photograph* (to make photographs from negatives), *to trespass* (to go on to someone else's land or enter a building without permission).

2 • **11.1** Play the recording and let students check their predictions.

I Why do you do this job?

A It's a question of money really. To make money. For one photo you can get 60,000, 70,000 if you take in all the worldwide sales.

B There's a definite buzz to it. The most exhilarating moment is quite literally the second that you stop taking the photos. At that precise moment, that's it. You've achieved what you set out to do. Obviously, there's a great sense of satisfaction when you see the results as well.

I Do you develop the photographs yourself?

B No, I have them developed. I'm not all that technically minded. A friend of mine does that. Obviously, it has to be someone you can trust.

I How do you get your photographs?

B You drive around. You look at various restaurants in certain areas of town that you know are frequented by celebrities. You go there and you have a look to see if there are any interesting cars, i.e. any chauffeurs that you know drive certain people about, any number plates that you recognize. And if there are, then you wait.

A Sometimes you get a tip-off from a chauffeur or a waiter. You slip them a few pounds and they tell you who's there, what time they're likely to leave, whether they'll be coming out the back door or the front door – that sort of thing.

I What kinds of things are you prepared to do to get a photograph? How far are you prepared to go?

A Well, the end result you are aiming for is a sellable picture so you'll go as far as you feel you need to go. If necessary, I'll climb up trees, hide behind bushes, whatever. Sometimes it means actually going into people's gardens, but that's usually quite difficult because of the security systems.

I So you trespass on private property?

A It isn't trespass to me. I'm only doing my job.

I Do you think that the general public supports what you do?

B If there wasn't such a great demand from the public, we wouldn't be supplying this type of picture, we'd all be doing something different.

A I go all over the world doing this job. I've asked people if I can use their gardens or their front rooms and I never ever remember anyone saying 'no'. I don't remember anybody looking at any pictures and saying, 'This is wrong'. All I remember everybody saying is, 'Can we have more?' The world wants to see the pictures. We're just doing what most photographers do all the time.

- Check answers.

Answers

a • For money – world wide sales of good photographs can bring in a lot of money – 60,000–70,000 are mentioned.
  • For excitement – *There's a buzz / exhilarating / sense of satisfaction, to get a buzz* – to experience great excitement.

b Go to the places celebrities go to / Try to get information (*tip-offs*) from chauffeurs or waiters.

c The photographer interviewed says he'll do whatever he has to to get photographs. This may include going into people's garden – *trespassing on private property.*

d One of the photographers says the fact that people want to see their photographs is evidence of support. The other says no one has ever refused permission to use their garden or room, or said that a particular photograph was wrong.

■ **Person to person** ■

1–2 Students discuss these questions in pairs, groups, or as a class.

- You could promote discussion by deliberately taking a different line of argument from the students.

Additional activity

Photocopy this section for pairs or groups of students. Would you make a good paparazzi?

If you suddenly found yourself in a situation where you could take a photograph of a celebrity, would you take the photograph or not? → **YES 1 or NO 1**

YES 1
If the celebrity was someone you had always admired, would you take the photograph?
→ YES 2 or NO 1

YES 2
If you knew that the photograph would damage the celebrity's reputation, would you take the photograph?
→ YES 3 or NO 2

YES 3
If there was a good chance that the celebrity would take you to court and win, would you still take the photograph?
→ YES 4 or NO 3

YES 4
You would make a ruthless paparazzi photographer. People will dislike you, but you may end up very rich.

NO 1
If you were sure that the photograph would not damage the celebrity, would you take the photograph?
→ YES 1 or NO 2

NO 2
If you knew you could get ten million dollars for the photograph, would you take it?
→ YES 3 or NO 3

NO 3
You will never make a paparazzi photographer – you are too kind. People will like you but you'll never have much money.

Grammar – Causatives review

This grammar section reviews the causative structures *have something done* and *get something done*, and clarifies when each form can be used.

- Remind students that they can refer to the **Language Commentary** on p.136.

1–2 Students work through 1 and 2, individually or in pairs.
- Elicit their ideas.

Answers

1 a 1 This means: *I arrange for the photographs to be developed by someone.* (The verb is Present simple.)

  2 This means: *I have developed the photographs myself.* (The verb is Present perfect.)

  3 This means: *I develop the photographs myself.* (The verb is Present Simple.) So, in sentences 2 and 3 the speaker does the developing themself, but in sentence 1, another person does the developing for the speaker.

b 1 This means: *Someone decorated my room for me before I went on holiday.* (The verb is Past simple.)

2 This means: *I had decorated the room myself a week before another event in the past.* (The verb is Past perfect.)

2 • **a**1 and **b**1.
• The causative structure is *have* + object + past participle.

3 • Read through the rubric, then let students do questions **a** and **b** individually or in pairs.
• Monitor, giving help where necessary.
• Check answers.

Answers

a *have* is more formal than *get*

b	Sentence	Use	Rule
1	*Get your hair cut!*	c Imperative	B *get* is used
2	*I had to get my car brakes fixed. They were dangerous.*	b an urgent action	A *have* possible but *get* more usual
3	*Have you had your windows cleaned recently?*	a Present perfect	C only *have* is possible

Check

4–5 Students work through the exercises individually, referring to the previous exercise or the **Language Commentary**.
• They could compare answers with a partner.
• Check answers.

Answers

4 **a** *You'd better get your cooker checked.*
b *Have you had your eyes tested recently?*
c *I am having some new bookshelves made.*
d *Get that tree cut down.*
e *We had our car resprayed after the accident.*

5 **a** *get the windows repaired*
b *Have you had your hair cut?*
c *are having / getting our house painted*
d *Get your computer checked!*
e *would have / get the locks changed.*

— p. 106 —

Reading

This article describes the activities of *twister chasers* – people in the USA who try to predict where tornadoes are likely to occur, then flock to those areas.

1 • Allow students a few minutes to think about the three statements and decide whether they are true or false.
• Elicit their ideas.
• You could note the number of 'trues' and 'falses' on the board for each statement.

Note This text contains some difficult technical and descriptive language, but students should be able to understand the main points.

• Don't pre-teach any of the words and encourage students to read without using a dictionary.

2 • Students read the text, checking the answers to 1a–c.
• Check their answers and refer back to the notes on the board to see how many students guessed correctly.

Answers

a True. (75% of the world's tornadoes occur in the area covered by Oklahoma, Kansas, and Texas.)
b False. (Scientists can predict where tornadoes *could* form, but they can't be sure whether they will form or not.)
c True. (Their forward progress is about thirty-two kilometres an hour.)

Close up

• Students work through the questions individually or in pairs.
• Check answers.

Answers

• l.3 *a mecca* – a place many people are attracted to. *Mecca* is in Saudi Arabia and is the holy city of Islam.
• l.6 *hard data* – factual or definite
• l.7 *flock* is the word used for a group of sheep or birds. The verb *to flock* means to gather or move in large numbers.
• l.25 The other two words with the same meaning as *twisting* are *spinning* (l.26) and *rotating* (l.27).

Interpretation p. 107

1–3 Allow students time to think about possible answers to the three questions. They could discuss their ideas in pairs.
• Elicit their ideas.

Possible answers

1 • *satellite scanners* – devices to contact satellites for weather reports, or images of the earth from space showing tornadoes which have already formed, or weather patterns likely to develop into tornadoes
• *video cameras* – to film tornadoes
• *maps* – to find tornado locations

2 The tornado is described as a *curiously exhilarating phenomenon* as it is thrilling and exciting and because it is dangerous and destructive. (*Curiously* here means *surprisingly*.)
Similar phenomena might include natural occurrences like erupting volcanoes, thunderstorms, hurricanes, forest fires, tidal waves, etc., as well as things people choose to do like mountaineering, white-water rafting, parachute jumping, etc.

3 • They never know where or when tornadoes will form. (l.16)
• Equipment used to measure the speed of tornadoes is destroyed when the tornado passes over it, so no one is quite sure how fast they travel. (l.33)

Speaking personally

1–2 Students discuss these questions in pairs or groups.
• Monitor but do not interrupt.
• Elicit ideas, allowing students time to tell any interesting personal experiences they may have had.

Grammar – Causative verbs and the passive; non-causative use of *have something done*

Exploring concepts

1–3 Students work through questions 1–3 in the usual way.
- Remind students that they can refer to the **Language Commentary** on p.137.
- Monitor and help.
- Check answers.

Answers

1 a focuses on the action (passive verb)

b tells us who was responsible for the action (causative verb)

Note The agent or subject, person who did the decorating, is missing in both sentences.

2 They all refer to negative events like accidents or disasters which are outside people's control. The sentences are examples of the *have something done* form being used 'non-causatively'. The subjects do not cause the action or arrange for it to take place.

3 The passive forms used in sentences **a–c** convey information about the same events, but in a more objective and less dramatic way.

Exploitation

1 • Elicit students' ideas about the effects of the flood on the lives of the farmers. There is no need to insist on the use of *have something done* or passive verbs.
- **a** Check that students understand the meaning of the words in the two lists, then get them to match the nouns (A) with the verbs (B).
- Check their ideas before moving on to the next task.

Answers
- *crops*   *destroy / uproot / ruin / damage*
- *livelihoods* *destroy / ruin*
- *trees*   *uproot / washed away*
- *walls*   *destroy / knock down / wash away / damage*
- *fences*   *destroy / knock down / wash away / damage*
- *furniture*   *ruin / damage*

b Students now write two sentences for each of the matches, using passive verbs and the *have something done* structure.
- Check answers.

Answers
- *Their livelihoods have been destroyed. / They have had their livelihoods destroyed.*
- *Their trees have been uprooted. / They have had their trees uprooted.*
- *Their walls have been washed away. / They've had their walls washed away.*
- *Their fences have been knocked down. / They have had their fences knocked down.*
- *Their furniture has been damaged. / They have had their furniture damaged.*

Role play

2 • Ask students to read the instructions and allocate roles.
- Monitor conversations, but do not interrupt. Make a note of any problem areas or common mistakes.
- Pairs who finish early could be asked to make a note of the key facts in their interviews.
- There is no need for a rounding-off activity, but you could spend a few minutes going over any problem areas you noted during the pairwork.

3 • Students work individually or in pairs on this news bulletin.
- Introduce the activity and set a time limit for the bulletin, for example thirty to sixty seconds.
- Monitor the activity, helping and correcting where necessary. Pay attention at this stage to the correct use of the passive and the *have something done* structure.

Additional activity

Get students to think about what would happen if their town was flooded. They could exchange ideas in pairs or groups, or they could write a letter to a friend, describing the damage to the town, their home, and their possessions.

— p. 108 —

Listening

As an introduction to the third theme of the unit, students think and talk about *fans* and their activities.

1 • Start by eliciting some ideas about the questions. Discourage students from talking about people they personally admire at this stage. They will have a chance to discuss this later in *Speaking personally*.

Possible answers
- A *fan* is a *fanatical* follower or supporter of someone famous, sports personalities (or teams), pop musicians (or groups), etc. Fans sometimes belong to a *fan club* and letters sent by fans to the people they admire is called *fan mail*.
- – Being a fan can brighten up ordinary people's lives.
  – The obsession can be a replacement for a normal, real-life relationship.
  – Some people need heroes to look up to.
- – They may follow them all over the world.
  – They may buy everything related to the person – e.g. books, records, pictures, memorabilia, etc.
  – They may give the celebrity's name to their children.
  – They may dress like them.
  – They may stalk their celebrity and sometimes attack them.

2 • Students now predict some of the activities of an Elvis Presley fan they are going to listen to.
- You could note a few suggestions on the board. Do not spend too long on this if students are having problems thinking of ideas.

3 • **11.2** Play the recording for students to check their predictions.

J That's very interesting. I didn't know that. How long have you been an Elvis fan, Mr McDonald?

C Just call me Chuck, will you? Mr McDonald sounds awful formal. Let me see now. Must be going on for forty years now.

J And you consider yourself his number one fan?

C Me and my boy both. This is Elvis Junior.

E Howdy.

J Pleased to meet you.

C Called him after the King – Elvis Aaron Presley McDonald. You know he was just a kid when the King passed on. Now, you know more about Elvis than anyone else in the world, don't you?

E Sure do.

C You got a question about Elvis? He knows the answer. His music, his movies, anything and everything.

J Amazing. When did you decide to open your house to the public?

C I decided to open up my home to the public few years ago. I had so much stuff it just seemed a shame not to let the other fans share it. My wife left me not long after that. It kind of got to her in the end I suppose. She told me she'd had enough, packed her bags and left.

J Do you regret that?

C My wife leaving me? Or opening up the house?

J Both.

C Hell, just one of those things. Anyway, let me show you round. That's what you're here for, isn't it? I put all my newspaper cuttings in these here files – not just articles – anything at all that even mentions his name goes in here. And at the last count I had 1,350 files.

J Wow.

C Well, that's not such a lot when you think I've been collecting stuff for the last thirty-six years. Over here I've got all his albums. These ones are the original ones I bought when they first came out but I've got tapes and CDs and all the cover versions too. On those shelves over there are videos of all his films, excerpts of his concerts. Now this, this is one of my most prized possessions. It's signed to me. See? I put it in a gold frame to go with the gold and blue satin drapes.

J Very striking.

C They were his favourite colours. Course I keep the drapes closed all the time just like he did. He hated sunlight – even went so far as to paste tin foil over his windows. I took this photograph at the last concert he gave – had it enlarged.

J It's come out really well, hasn't it?

C I'm pleased with it. These plastic bags here are full of ribbons and flowers from his funeral wreaths. Did you know it took 100 vans to transport the wreaths?

J Really?

C Yeah. More than when Kennedy died. Saddest day of my life that was, the day he passed on. We still can't believe he's gone, can we?

E Sure can't.

C Matter of fact I was at 'Graceland' day before he died. Who'd have thought? Now in here is the TV monitoring room. Elvis Jnr is in charge of this. As you can see there are four TV monitors, four VCRs. The TVs are on twenty-four hours a day. Elvis Jnr looks through the TV listings and we tape anything that makes any mention of the King. In that trunk there we got details of all the Elvis impersonators. Do you know there were 30,000 at the last count, including a parrot with a miniature jump suit and a microphone fixed to its feathers. Matter of fact we've got him on videotape doing 'Blue suede shoes'. He doesn't exactly sing it, though does he?

E It's kinda more like a squawk.

C Yeah. It's an absolute hoot!

J Did you ever meet Elvis?

C No. Greatest sorrow of my life is that I never actually met the King. I got real close to him eight times but there was always too many folks between us. Never did get to reach out and touch his hand. Never did. Real shame that. Real shame.

- Play again if necessary, then check answers.

Possible answers

- He has called his son *Elvis Aaron Presley McDonald*.
- He has opened his house to the public (with its collection of Elvis memorabilia).
- He collects any newspaper cuttings which mentions Elvis.
- He has collected all Elvis's albums, CDs, tapes, films, etc.
- He keeps the curtains (*drapes*) closed all the time like Elvis did.
- He has a collection of some of the wreaths and ribbons from Elvis's funeral.
- He video-records everything from TV which mentions Elvis.
- He has details of all Elvis impersonators.

Interpretation

This section is in two parts; the first asks questions about what students have just heard; the second draws attention to the way Chuck McDonald leaves out words when he speaks. Deal with the two parts separately.

1 • Students read through questions **a–d**. (If necessary you could play the recording again.)
   • Students note down their answers, then compare and discuss them with a partner.
   • Check their ideas.

Possible answers

a Chuck McDonald's wife got fed up with her husband's obsession. She left soon after he opened the house to the public. She was obviously less important to him than the dead singer.

b He probably followed his father's obsession.

c Elvis may have had weak eyes. (He often wore sunglasses.) He may have been used to performing at night and sleeping during the daylight hours.

d Other obsessed fans, or possibly bodyguards.

2 • Remind students that missing words was the focus of *Features of natural conversation* in Unit 10.
   • Use the example to check that students understand, then let them work through the exercise individually or in pairs.
   • Check answers.

Answers

a *Hell,* **it is / it was** *just one of those things …*

b *It's signed to me.* **Do you / Can you** *see?*

c **Of course,** *I keep the drapes closed all the time …*

d **As a** *matter of fact, I was at 'Graceland'* **(on) the** *day before he died.*

e *Who'd have thought* **it / that**?

f **The** *greatest sorrow of my life is that I never actually met the King.*

Vocabulary

This focuses on the differences between some British and American English words.

1 • Give students a few minutes to think about the British English equivalents of the five words from the recording. They could refer to tapescript **11.2** at the back of their books if necessary.
   • Check answers.

Answers

American English	British English
• *drapes*	*curtains*
• *folks*	*people*
• *howdy*	*Hi! / How are you? / Hello*
• *kid*	*young child*

Note *kid* is also commonly used in British English.

• *movies*	*films*

2 • The five sentences contain nine American English words. This time, students should be able to guess the meanings from the contexts.
- Students work individually or in pairs through the exercise, 'translating' the American English words into British English.
- Check answers.

Answers

	American English	British English
a	*elevator*	*lift*
b	*truck*	*lorry*
	sidewalk	*pavement* (*footpath* is also possible)
c	*baggage*	*luggage* (*baggage* can also be used in British English)
	trunk	*boot*
	vacation	*holiday*
d	*check*	*bill*
e	*candy*	*sweets*
	cookies	*biscuits*

Note *candy* is an uncountable noun, whereas *sweet(s)* is countable.

Additional activity

- Find out whether there are any more words students know that are different in British and American English.
- Put up a list in the classroom for students to add words to as they come across them in books, films, song lyrics, etc.

▉ Speaking personally ▉

1 • Students can now tell each other about the people they admire or have admired in the past.
- Monitor conversations, but do not interrupt.
- Elicit a few personal experiences from the class.

2 • This second question could be a class discussion.
- Elicit students' suggestions.
- Write up the most popular names mentioned, then get the class to vote for the two people they think may become as popular after their death as Elvis Presley.

Additional activity

- This could be a whole-class activity or pairwork.
- Do a class survey to find out if students collect anything (for example, football programmes, teddy bears, etc.).
- Find out why they started collecting, how many 'things' they have got, and what they do with them.

▶ Photocopiable activity 14 p.173

Grammar – Question tags

▉ Exploring concepts ▉ p. 109 ▉

- Since the meaning of question tags is dependent on intonation, this *Exploring concepts* begins with a pronunciation focus.
- Remind students that they can refer to the **Language Commentary** on p.137.

▉ Pronunciation ▉

1 a **11.3** Play the recording sentence by sentence. Ask students to decide if the tags are asking real questions or asking for agreement.
- Play the recording again and ask students to notice whether the intonation rises or falls on the question tags.

b Students could work in pairs or you could elicit the rules of pronunciation from the whole class.

11.3

1 Now, you know more about Elvis than anyone else in the world, don't you?
2 That's what you're here for, isn't it?
3 It's come out really well, hasn't it?
4 We still can't believe he's gone, can we?
5 He doesn't exactly sing it, though, does he?

- If students have difficulty in distinguishing between rising and falling intonation, it may help to isolate the tag from the rest of the sentence and 'hum' or say it with both intonation patterns to demonstrate the difference.

Answers

a All the sentences are asking for agreement (falling intonation) except 2, (which has rising intonation).
b Rules
- We use rising intonation on question tags when we are asking a real question.
- We use falling intonation on question tags when we are expecting agreement.

2 This focuses on the rules for forming question tags. The box presents the rules for twelve different patterns of tags, which students match with the sentences a–j.
- Ask students to read the rules. Point out that several rules apply to some of the sentences.
- Students then match **a–j** with the correct rules **1–12**.
- Check answers.

Answers

Sentence	Rule	Notes
a	3	*never apologises* is a negative verb – the question tag is affirmative: *does*
	7	There is no auxiliary in the first part of the sentence – the tag has *does*
b	4	*left* is an affirmative verb – the question tag is negative: *didn't*
c	9	*Don't forget* is a negative imperative – question tag is *will*
	3	Negative – positive tag

d	6	*Let's* is followed by the question tag *shall*
e	1 / 4	Auxiliary *she's (has) got* – tag *hasn't*
f	5 / 4	Non auxiliary use of *has* – question tag – auxiliary verb *doesn't*
g	10 / 3	*Nobody* – pronoun in question tag *they*
h	11 / 3	*Nothing* – pronoun *it*
i	12 / 3	Modal verb – *can't* – same modal verb *can*
j	8	Affirmative imperative – question tag *would*

3 • **11.4** Students listen to pairs of sentences and decide which is less formal.

11.4

a Can you lend me ten pounds?
b You can't lend me ten pounds, can you?
c Could you give me a hand?
d You couldn't give me a hand, could you?
e Do you mind if I smoke?
f You don't mind if I smoke, do you?

• Check answers.

Answer
The second sentence in each pair is less formal.

Note It is harder for the listener to refuse a request which is phrased negatively.

• You could play the recording again and drill the sentences chorally and individually.

Exploitation

1 • Students hear ten incomplete sentences and write the missing question tags.
  a **11.5** Play the recording, pausing after each sentence to give students enough time to write down the missing question tags. Allow time for students to compare answers. Play again if necessary.

11.5

1	Don't tell Jessica.	6	Nothing's broken.
2	You will remember.	7	You've got my number.
3	Matt looks happy.	8	Nobody else knows.
4	You didn't remember my birthday.	9	Let's decide tomorrow.
5	You don't smoke.	10	Someone's told you.

  b **11.6** Play the recording, so that students can check their answers and correct any mistakes.

11.6

1 Don't tell Jessica, will you?
2 You will remember, won't you?
3 Matt looks happy, doesn't he?
4 You didn't remember my birthday, did you?
5 You don't smoke, do you?
6 Nothing's broken, is it?
7 You've got my number, haven't you?
8 Nobody else knows, do they?
9 Let's decide tomorrow, shall we?
10 Someone's told you, haven't they?

Answers

1 b See tapescript **11.6** .

• Play the recording again and drill. Make sure that students are using the correct intonation on the tags.

2 a Do the first sentence as an example to check that students understand the task.
  • Students can write the informal requests or do them orally. They could compare ideas before they listen.
  b **11.7** Students listen and check their answers.
  • You could play the recording again.

11.7

1 You can't come back tomorrow, can you?
2 You couldn't help me with my homework, could you?
3 You wouldn't be able to come a bit later, would you?
4 It wouldn't be possible for you to work late tomorrow, would it?
5 You don't mind if I invite Tom, do you ?

3 This is a freer practice exercise in which students start conversations with statements ending with a question tag.
  • Ask students to look at the cartoon to check they have understood the task.
  • Students think of five statements, then take turns with their partner to start conversations. Encourage them to continue discussing each statement for a few minutes.
  • Monitor conversations, but do not interrupt.

4 This exercise practises informal requests (e.g. *You couldn't help me with my homework, could you?*).
  • Do an example with the class, then students work in pairs.
  • Give students time to prepare two or three requests.
  • Encourage them to go on talking beyond the immediate request and the response. If students refuse requests initially, make sure they give reasons.
  • Monitor conversations. Only interrupt if students do not remember to use the appropriate question form.
  • If students have difficulty in thinking of requests you could prompt them: *borrow car, do the washing-up, borrow a dress / suit for a party, show you a recent work report*, etc.

Word-building: prefixes

Prefixes and opposite meanings ▪▪▪▪▪ p. 110 ▪

1 • Students will already know the correct prefixes to add to some of these words, so don't spend long on this exercise.
  • You could start by smiling and eliciting the word *happy* from the class. Then look sad to elicit *unhappy*.
  • Students work individually, making the words negative.
  • Check answers.

Answers

trained	*untrained*	*literate*	*illiterate*
mature	*immature*	*efficiency*	*inefficiency*
approve	*disapprove*	*legally*	*illegally*
dress	*undress*	*responsible*	*irresponsible*
agree	*disagree*	*relevant*	*irrelevant*
practical	*impractical*	*experienced*	*inexperienced*

2 • Students now think of definitions for five of the negative words and test their partner.

• Elicit another example definition from the class, then let students work in pairs.

• Monitor the pairwork, helping where necessary. (There is no need for a rounding off exercise here.)

3 • Read this rule-completion exercise with the whole class. Get students to think of more words for each prefix.

Answers

a legible / *illegible*   logical / *illogical*   legitimate / *illegitimate*
b rational / *irrational*   regular / *irregular*   resistible / *irresistible*
c polite / *impolite*   perfect / *imperfect*   mobile / *immobile*

Note You may want to point out to students that:
1 there are no simple rules for words that take the prefixes un-, in,- or dis-.
2 not all words which start with l, r, p, or m have negative forms starting with il, i, ir / im. (Examples: *unlawful* / *unreasonable* / *unpopular*.)
3 not all words which start with il, ir, and im mean the opposite of the word without the prefix. (Examples: *illustrated* / *irritable* / *important*.)

4 • In pairs, students mark the stress on the words and then say them with and without the prefixes to decide whether there is any difference in pronunciation.
• **11.8** Students listen and check their answers.

11.8

trained / untrained
literate / illiterate
mature / immature
efficiency / inefficiency
approve / disapprove
legally / illegally

dress / undress
responsible / irresponsible
agree / disagree
relevant / irrelevant
practical / impractical
experienced / inexperienced

Note The addition of the prefix does not change the stress.

5 • Students fill the gaps in the sentences with a negative form of the word in brackets. All the words they fill in will have one of the negative prefixes, but point out they may also have to change the word in other ways. For example, in their books, *agree* changes into *disagreeable*.
• Students work through the exercise. They may need to check their answers in a dictionary.
• As students give their answers, check that they are stressing the correct part of the word.

Answers

a unexpected
b inappropriately
c disappearance

d improbability
e illegibly

■ **Prefixes and other meanings**

1 • Students match the prefixes with their meanings. They should use the example sentences (1–7) to help them.
• Students work through the exercise individually then compare answers with a partner.
• Check answers.

• You could ask students to think up other words beginning with the prefixes.

Answers

	Prefix		Meaning	Examples
1	over	f	too much	*oversleep / overuse*
2	anti	d	against	*antisocial / antiseptic*
3	multi	a	many	*multipurpose / multilingual*
4	auto	b	of / by oneself	*autograph / automatic*
5	re	d	again / back	*reapply / reappear*
6	mis	g	badly/ wrongly	*mislead / misinform*
7	under	e	not enough	*underachieve / underdone*

Note You may want to point out to students that prefixes are not an infallible guide to meaning. Sometimes these groups of letters at the beginnings of words are not actually prefixes at all. Examples: *overcoat / antique / realize / miserable / understand.*

2 • Students should complete the sentences and compare their answers before they discuss the questions with a partner.
• Check answers.

Answers

	Word with prefix	Possible answers to questions
a	*multi*	*Multi-storey car parks save valuable space.*
b	*auto*	*The plane is on auto pilot when cruising, not when taking off and landing.*
c	*anti*	*Antibiotics.*
d	*under*	*Students will answer this in a personal way.*
e	*over*	*In a restaurant, at a theatre. Bad planning, human error, computer problems, to ensure that all the seats are full.*
f	*re*	*There might be too many mistakes. / The person who wrote the letters might change what they wrote.*
g	*mis*	*Careless, absent-minded, untidy.*

▶ **Photocopiable activity 15 p.174**

Language in action

■ **Eavesdrop!** p. 111 ■

The questions could be done as a class activity or as pairwork.

• Direct attention to the picture and the three questions.
• Remind students that they are speculating about what they see and should try to come up with a variety of answers.
• You could elicit possible answers now, or move on to *Listening 1*.

■ **Listening 1**

1 • Draw attention to the extra question b.
• **11.9** Students listen to the recording to check their *Eavesdrop!* ideas and to think of an answer for b.

11.9

A Let's have a look at the programme, then. Oh, no. I don't believe it! He's playing Stevenson again!
B He's not, is he? After last week?
A Couldn't score if his life depended on it.

C   No, I've never liked him. I can't understand why we bought him.
B   How much did we pay for him?
A   Three million or something like that.
B   Three million!
A   And Davidson! How many goals has he scored this season?
C   Two. And they were before Christmas!
A   I don't know what Kennedy's thinking of. If it was up to me I'd have Thompson and Sanchez play. Wouldn't you?
B   I'm not that keen on Thompson. Take last week for instance when he came on as substitute.
C   Be fair! He was only on for ten minutes.
B   No, I'd rather have Jackson.
C   You're joking, aren't you?
B   No, I'm being perfectly serious. The thing I like about Jackson is that he gives 100 per cent.
C   He's useless.
B   And what I particularly like about him is that even when he's not playing all that well he still causes the opposition problems.
C   He's useless.
B   All right, who would you play then?
C   Well, Somerville, for example.
B   Somerville isn't fit yet. You could bring him on as a sub but you couldn't play him for a whole game, not yet.

- Check answers.

Possible answers
Eavesdrop!
- Football supporters / fans
- They are in a bar or cafe, possibly at the football club.
- They are discussing the selection of players in the football team they support.

Listening 1
b   They're going to watch the football match.

2 - Students listen again and note down the functional language used by the speakers.
   - Allocate tasks and play the recording a second and third time if necessary.
   - Students note down the expressions and then compile lists. They help and correct each other at this stage.

Note Students add to these lists during the next listening task.

Answers
See full list of expressions after *Listening 2*, question 2.

Listening 2

1 - **11.10** Play the recording.

11.10 including **11.11**
Conversation 1
J   **11.11** Well, I must say I prefer this, something a bit sort of gentle, classical. Puts you in the right mood, doesn't it?
S   This is sort of, a bit lift music, isn't it? Don't you prefer something a bit more …
J   It is a bit muzak, isn't it? Yes, yes. Oh no, I can't stand that either. That's awful …
S   Anonymous …
Ju Mmm, yeah, a bit bland …
J   You're right, you're right. No, no, no, I like jazz, actually. I'm really fond of jazz.
R   Yes, I rather like that. It's good. I particularly like flamenco, though. That's what I like.
J   Oh, do you?

R   Yeah, yeah.
J   Oh, that's exciting.
R   Your Paco de Lucias and all that sort of business, screaming and wailing. It's a bit like heavy metal, I suppose … without the amplifiers.
S   I'm afraid I really like folk music, I'm afraid.
R   Oh!
S   Do you?
Ju Yeah, yeah, folk's pretty good.
S   Is it?
Ju Yeah.
J   Oh, no, no …
R   I've never liked that …
J   I never listen to that, no.
S   I mean, not, not sort of not, not, not boring traditional …
Ju Not traditional folk …
S   Not traditional …
Ju … but, yeah, trendy folk …
S   Right, yeah, yeah …
J   No, that's not my thing at all. Oh, gosh, no, no. I think jazz, really. And I hate pop.
Ju Yes …
S   What? Ordinary pop?
J   Oh, ordinary pop. I think Radio …
S   Radio …
J   One …
S   …that sort of…
Ju Oh, no. Well, Radio One doesn't play pop.
J   Doesn't it?
Ju No.
J   You see, I don't even listen. I only listen to Radio …
S   So what sort of thing's pop?
Ju Well, sort of a bit sort of bland and sort of, oh I can't think of anybody in particular.
R   Bland?
Ju Yes. I can't think of anything worse than just some sort of little pop tune … like Boyzone and that sort of thing, that sort of pop.
J   Oh, I don't even know the names of them. Oh, it's awful, isn't it?
Ju Oh, yes. They're all a bit young.
R   Not my cup of tea.
J   No, no. Don't like that at all.

Conversation 2
B   So who's this person here?
S   Oh, him? Erm, that's Jonathan.
B   Jonathan? That …
S   Yeah, I've known him for years. He's a … he's been he's a very good friend … yes.
B   **11.11** Have I met him?
S   I don't think so, no. Erm, you might have seen him once when you came round to our house. No, he's a really great bloke, he's … what I particularly like about him is that he's, that he's always in a good mood, he's, he's quite difficult to sort of, to, to ruffle, he never gets bad-tempered, the sort of person you know that you can ring up, erm, late at night and is, and just sort of, you know, pour your heart out to him, he's, he's a great bloke.
B   So, is he your best friend, then?
S   Yeah, I suppose so. He's certainly one of my oldest friends and I suppose if I … it's not quite the same when … you're older to talk about best friends, but he is a very good friend, yeah, yeah.
B   Mmm.
S   I mean, just another example. He's, erm, the sort of person, you know, if you, if you break down in your car and you're miles from anywhere and … you can always ring him up and say, you know, 'I'm stuck. Can you help me out?' and if he can, you know, if he can he will …
B   That's really important, yeah.
S   Yeah, yeah.

B Yeah, it's funny, isn't it, how, you know, some friends are better friends than others. But you know we all look for different … qualities. You know, I mean my best friend, I mean, I don't particularly like sometimes, but she's got lots of things about her that I really admire.

S Mmm. What don't you like about her?

B Well, she's a bit bossy, she's a bit pushy, but then on the other hand that can be quite positive, erm, you know, she's very encouraging and, er, and she'll always stick by you so, you know. if you've got a problem, just like your friend you were saying …

S Yeah …

B … you know you can rely on them …

S Yeah.

B … and I think that's probably one of the most important qualities for a best friend or a …

S Yeah.

B … friend to have really …

• Check answers.

Possible answers
Conversation 1
a *music / different musical styles and tastes*
b *classical, lift music (muzak), jazz, flamenco, heavy metal, folk, traditional folk, pop*
c *Jill likes classical and jazz / Roger likes jazz and flamenco / Simon likes folk*

Conversation 2
d *best friends*
e *always in a good mood / never bad-tempered / will always help you if you're in any kind of trouble*
f *she's bossy and pushy* (always trying to attract attention or do better than other people)

2 • **11.11** Play the recording, while students follow the extracts on p.112 in their books, and mark the functional language used by the speakers.
• Students add the expressions to their lists.
• Check through the lists.

Answers
(This includes expressions from *Listening 1* and *2*.)
Expressing likes
11.9
The thing I like …   What I particularly like …
11.11 Extract 1
I like jazz, actually.   I'm really fond of jazz.   I rather like that.
I particularly like …   That's what I like.   I really like …
11.11 Extract 2
(What) I particularly like about him is that …
Expressing dislikes
11.9
I've never liked him.   I'm not that keen on …   He's useless.
11.11 Extract 1
I can't stand that …   That's awful …   I've never liked that …
No, that's not my thing at all.   I hate pop.
11.11 Extract 2
None
(From full conversation
I don't particularly like …)

Expressing preferences
11.9
If it was up to me, I'd have …   I'd rather have …
11.11 Extract 1
I prefer this …
Don't you prefer something a bit more …? (Question about preferences.)
11.11 Extract 2
None
Giving examples
11.9
Take last week for instance …   …, for example.
11.11 Extract 1
None
11.11 Extract 2
I mean, just another example. He's the sort …

Note Point out the difference between these two similar expressions: *I rather like jazz. I like jazz. / I'd rather have jazz. I prefer jazz.*

■ **Features of natural conversation** ▬▬▬▬ p. 112 ■

This focuses on the different meanings of the pronoun *you*.
• Give students a few minutes to find examples of the use of *you* in Extract 2 and discuss their meanings.
• Elicit their ideas.

Answers

Note There are other examples in the extract but the three different uses are:
1 *… you might have seen him once …* here *you* refers to the person the speaker is talking to.
2 *… he's the sort of person, you know …* here *you* is part of the conversation filler phrase *you know*.
3 *… that you can ring up late at night …* here *you* means people in general / one / anyone.

■ **Practice** ▬▬▬▬▬▬▬▬▬▬▬▬▬▬▬▬

1 • **11.12** Play the recording and drill chorally and individually.
• You could ask students to identify the syllables which they think are likely to be stressed before playing the tape.

11.12
a I hate pop. It's awful.
b I can't stand heavy metal.
c I've never liked opera.
d Folk? That's not my thing at all.
e I'm not that keen on classical music.
f I'd rather listen to jazz than folk.
g I prefer folk to jazz.
h I really like reggae.
i I'm really fond of salsa.
j I particularly like flamenco.

Answers
1 See tapescript **11.12** for stress.

2 • **11.13** Play the recording, pausing after each sentence for students to respond with an expression from **a–j**.

- Students could work in pairs or you could ask individual students to respond.

11.13
1 What do you think of modern pop music?
2 What about classical music?
3 Are you keen on jazz?
4 Do you like traditional folk?
5 What's your favourite kind of music?
6 Is there any kind of music you don't like?

3 • In pairs or groups, students ask and answer questions about their musical likes and dislikes.
   • Monitor their conversations, listening out for appropriate expressions and correct pronunciation.

■ Exploitation

- Students form groups and work through the two situations.

Note If time is short, suggest that students choose only one situation.

- Stress that students should express their real likes and dislikes and should use expressions from their lists.
- Monitor their conversations, listening for use of the functional language. Do not interrupt conversations unless the language is completely incorrect or inappropriate.

■ Writing   p. 113 ■

1 a Allow students time to read the two examples, and think about and discuss the differences between the expression of preferences in conversation and in a written review.
   • Elicit their ideas.

Suggested answers
- Style: a written review is obviously more formal.
- The main purpose of a written review is to make a recommendation to the reader.
- In a written review, opinions are normally supported by evidence or examples of some kind.
- Written reviews are usually factual and descriptive rather than just a list of personal likes and dislikes.

Note These features are in the written review in the Student's Book.

b Students underline the opinion and preference language in the written review and compare it with the language they listed from the conversations on p.111.
   • Elicit the opinion and preference language.

Answers
Opinion and preference language
- *In my opinion ,...*
- *... is not as good as his classic ...*
- *It is (certainly) worth a listen ...*
- *... for me de Lucias' music is completely original.*
- *I would say (it is) brilliant in its own way.*
- *I suggest you go out and buy it.*

c Elicit students' suggestions for alternatives to *good* and *boring*.

Answers

	from the written review	other alternatives
good	*superb / amazing / original / brilliant*	*excellent / clever / intelligent / perfect / imaginative / superb / entertaining / interesting / lively / amusing*
boring	*repetitive / unimaginative*	*unoriginal / tedious / monotonous / dull / uninteresting / lifeless / ordinary / everyday / pointless*

2 • Ask students to read both suggestions and choose one.
   • Remind students to refer to the **Writing guidelines** on p.158 of their books.
   • Suggest they write their review of something they have heard or seen recently while ideas are still fresh in their minds. (They could write about a new TV programme.)
   • Give students a few minutes to read through the suggested paragraph plans and ask any questions they may have.
   • The final reviews should be about 120 words long. If there is not enough time for students to do the writing in class, suggest that they write notes under the paragraph headings and write the review for homework.

3 • Students exchange writing with a partner who has written the same type of review.
   a They then read each other's reviews and suggest improvements based on the three questions.
   b–c Students discuss their reviews, then rewrite them incorporating improvements discussed.

■ Summary

- Encourage students to use the tick boxes to help them keep a record of their learning.

Theme

The theme of this unit is types of communication.

Preview Gossip, voice-sensitive machines, a marriage proposal
Listening The role of the interpreter
Reading The social purpose of gossip

Grammar

- Reported speech (LC p.137)
- Reported speech: reporting verbs (LC p.138)
- Infinitives or gerunds after verbs (LC p.139)

Vocabulary

- Compound nouns

Functional language

- Expressions for answering and making telephone calls

Conversation strategies

- Playing for time
- Expressions to use when you can't think of what to say

Features of natural conversation

- *I'm sorry / I'm afraid*
- *I see*
- Instructions using *if*

Pronunciation

- Stress on compound nouns
- Sounding polite

Writing

- Telephone messages (WG p.158)

Workbook

- A magazine article about body language
- Topic vocabulary: the body; Collocations; three-part verbs; Word-building
- Reported speech review; Reporting verbs; Infinitives or gerunds after verbs; Infinitives and gerunds with a change of meaning
- Register; Writing a short report and an informal letter

Preview

The theme of communication is illustrated by very different topics: gossip, voice-sensitive machines, and a marriage proposal.

■ Your thoughts ■■■■■■■■■■■■■■■■■■■■■■■ p. 114 ■

- Working in pairs or as a whole class, students suggest connections between the illustrations and the unit title.
- Elicit ideas.
- You could ask students to think of as many different types of communication as they can. This might work best as a brainstorming activity.
- **Possible ideas** mobile phones / e-mail / love letters / television and radio/ songs and music / sign language / reading / Morse code / newspapers / body language: gestures, facial expressions, etc.

Answers

- A man is asking a woman to marry him: an intimate yet formal type of communication.
- The woman is being bombarded by spoken messages from equipment in her home, an example of communication between humans and machines.
- The couple in the photograph are not talking. Silence is a powerful way of communicating.
- The cartoon figures are *gossiping* – passing on information, rumours, etc. to each other and about each other.

■ Reading ■■■■■■■■■■■■■■■■■■■■■■■■■■■■■ p. 115 ■

This introduces some of the key words from the reading texts that follow.

1 • Elicit the meanings of the words and their connection with the theme of *communication*.

Answers

All the words refer to types of communication.

a marriage proposal	A traditional and formal offer of marriage. Old-fashioned, now an unusual formality.
voice-sensitive (machine)	A machine which can 'talk' and 'reply' to human speech.
chatter	Talk quickly and in a friendly way about unimportant things.
gossip	Talk without a serious purpose, usually about other people's lives and often things that don't concern you.
silence	Silence can sometimes communicate ideas more powerfully than speech. Alternatives to speech include body language and facial expressions. Some people find silences in conversations

embarrassing and feel they have to fill them by saying something.

conversation   The spoken exchange of ideas and information between two or more people.

2 • Students read the texts and match them with the illustrations on p.114.
  • As they read Text 3, ask students to think about who *Harry*, *Sally*, and *Susan* are.
  • Check answers.

Answers

Text 1   Proposal scene (top left)
Text 2   Voice-sensitive machines (top right)
Text 3   Gossip (bottom)

Note In Text 3 *Harry* and *Sally* represent a typical man and woman. *Susan* is a friend, neighbour, colleague, etc. of Sally's. This sentence means that men like to talk about themselves, whereas women like to talk about each other (or other people).

■ Person to person ■

1–3 Students could discuss these questions in pairs, groups, or as a whole class.
  • Is there general agreement that men's and women's conversations are different?

Additional activity

Person to person focuses only on **Text 3**, so if time allows, students could discuss some of the ideas in the other texts.
Text 1
  • Do people still propose to each other in this way?
  • In your country is it always men who propose to women or is it sometimes the other way round?
  • If this formal kind of proposal has disappeared from your country, how do couples decide to get married?
Text 2
  • Do you ever talk to machines?
  • What do you think of the idea of machines talking to their owners?
  • How far do you expect this development to go?

Grammar – Reported speech review

This grammar reviews the basic rules of reported speech. If students know the basic rules, let them work through 1–3 independently. If they need more time, work through the points one at a time, checking the answers at the end of each question.
  • Remind students that they can refer to the **Language Commentary** on p.137.

1 a Give students a few minutes to work out the direct speech versions of the reported speech sentences **1–4**.
  • Students compare their answers in pairs.
  • Check answers.

Answers

1   *'I missed / I've missed you over the summer, Polly.'*

2   *'Being Edward's wife won't be an easy option. / (It won't be an easy option, being Edward's wife.)'*
3   *'I spend a couple of hours every day talking to the neighbours.'*
4   *'I'm going to buy a voice-sensitive fridge next week.'*

b • Students now work out the rules of reported speech from the sentences.
  • Elicit their ideas.

Answers

• **tense changes**
  If the reporting verb is in the past, the direct speech verb is often moved back a step in time. Example
  *I **have missed** you* becomes *he **had missed** her*. (Sentence 1)
• **pronouns**
  Some personal pronouns change depending on who is reporting. Example
  I spend becomes *she said **she** spent*. (Sentence 3)
• **time references**
  Some time references change. Example
  next week becomes *the following week*. (Sentence 4)

2 • Students could discuss this question in pairs.
  • Check answers.

Answers

a   He said (in the past) that he had missed her at a time further in the past.
b   He said (in the past) that he missed her at that time – as he said it.
c   He said (in the past) that he missed her then and still misses her now.
d   He says (now) that he misses her now (in the present).
e   He says (now) that he missed her then – in the past.

Note These sentences illustrate that you need not always move back a tense when reporting speech; it depends on meaning.

3 • Give students a few minutes to work out the direct speech versions of the reported questions 1–4 and to think about the word order differences.
  • Students compare their answers in pairs.
  • Check answers.

Answers

a 1   *Will you marry me?*
  2   *Where do you want to go for the honeymoon?*
  3   *Why do you want to marry me?*
  4   *Have you been married before?*
b In direct speech the order is:
  Verb + Subject: *Will you marry me?*
  In reported speech the subject and verb are in the 'normal' order:
  Subject + Verb: *He asked her if **she would** marry him.*

Note Remind students that when changing *Yes / No* questions into reported speech we add *if* or *whether*. (Example sentences 1 and 4).

  • Before students do the check question you could ask them to identify the four reporting verbs in question 3 (1–4).

Answers

asked, inquired, wondered, wanted to know

Check

4 • Students work through the exercise individually, then compare answers with a partner.
  • Check answers.

Answers

a *Chris asked Paul if / whether he had seen Laura recently.*
b *Paul said ('Yes') he had.*
c *(He said) he had spoken to her on the phone the day before / the previous day.*
d *He said he was meeting her in town that afternoon.*
e *Chris asked him / wondered if he could tell her to give him a ring.*
f *Paul said he would tell her if he remembered.*

— p. 116 —

Listening

Listening

The recording is of two people discussing a programme about the work of an American interpreter.

1 a The pre-listening questions introduce the topic: the role of the interpreter in international affairs.
  • Spend a few minutes eliciting what students know about Reagan and Gorbachev.

   Information about Gorbachev and Reagan
   — **Mikhail Sergeyevich Gorbachev** was born Mar. 2, 1931.
   — General Secretary of the Soviet Communist party (1985–91) and President of the USSR (1988–91).
   — By his reform programs of *GLASNOST* and *PERESTROIKA*, Gorbachev hoped to breathe new life into the Soviet system.
   — He played a key role in ending the Cold War between East and West.
   — He was awarded the Nobel Peace Prize in 1990.
   — Then he was challenged by Boris Yelstin, President of the Russian republic.
   — After resigning on Dec. 25, 1991, he no longer played an active role in public affairs, but spent his time writing and lecturing, in Russia and abroad.
   — **Ronald Wilson Reagan** was born on Feb. 6, 1911.
   — He appeared in feature films (about 53) and later on TV.
   — In 1966 he became Governor of California.
   — He was the 40th president of the United States. At 69, he was the oldest man and the first film actor to be president.
   — In December 1987, he signed an arms-control agreement which helped to bring about the historic truce in the Cold War with the Soviet Union.
   — His second term as President ended in 1988.

b–c Elicit ideas about who the third man is and why meetings between Reagan and Gorbachev were so important. Students may not know this man's name, but they might be able to guess his job.
  • Don't confirm students' ideas yet.

2 • Ask students to read the short text to find more information related to questions a–c.
  • Check answers.

Answers

b He is Pavel Paleshenko, the interpreter for Mikhail Gorbachev at summit meetings with Ronald Reagan.
c Meetings between the two men helped bring about an end to the Cold War.

3 • Check that students understand the words and phrases and then give them a few minutes to predict how they will be used in the recording.
  • Elicit students' ideas but do not say whether they are correct or not.

4 • **12.1** Play the recording. As they listen, students make notes about the use of the words and phrases listed.

12.1

J   So, what are you going to do after university?
Jen Well, I'd love to work as an interpreter for the United Nations or that kind of organization.
J   That's funny — there was a programme about international relations on TV last night. They interviewed an interpreter. You didn't see it, did you?
Jen No. Who was it?
J   He was American — I can't remember his name.
Jen Was it interesting?
J   Yeah, fascinating. They asked him how he'd become an interpreter in the first place.
Jen What did he say?
J   He said he'd started work at the United Nations.
Jen I wonder how he got into that.
J   He didn't say. Anyway he worked there for five years.
Jen Did he work with anyone famous?
J   Oh yeah, after the UN he worked for the American government – apparently his first job was an official visit to Moscow with – wait for it – the President himself!
Jen Wow! The top job! What did he say about the President?
J   Well, he said he was just a normal person – he claimed they were good friends.
Jen Did he say what it was like in Moscow?
J   Well, he confirmed what everybody thought at the time – you know – the atmosphere at that first meeting had been pretty cool.
Jen Did he say how he felt?
J   Yeah, that was really interesting. He said he was really nervous to start with, but he admitted he felt quite proud of the part he'd played.
Jen I bet he did.
J   Yeah, but he also said it was really hard work – he did concede that interpreting at that level takes incredible concentration.
Jen I can imagine. It's such an enormous responsibility. If you don't get it quite right, you could mess everything up – possibly even cause an international crisis. What else did he say?
J   Oh, it was funny, they asked him if he tried to copy the President's manner when he interpreted – you know all the gestures and things.
Jen What did he say?
J   Well, he said his interpretation was usually neutral. He explained that the speakers themselves can use body language and facial expressions to get their message over – so, he just provides the words.
Jen Hmm — I'd never thought of that. What else did he say?
J   Erm, oh yeah, at one point he implied that the President really loved the show-biz side of the job.

Jen That was pretty obvious, though, wasn't it?

J True, but he also thought that the President had made a real contribution to world peace – and he felt he'd been really lucky to be part of that process.

Jen Great job!

J Right, but I just can't imagine the sort of brain you've got to have to be an interpreter. Just imagine it, you're there between two of the most powerful men in the world. They don't speak each other's language. They're completely dependent on you. So what happens? The American president starts talking — you can tell it's going to be a long sentence — the Russian president looks puzzled. The trouble is you probably can't start interpreting until you've heard the whole sentence — and then you haven't really got time to think about the best word to use — you've just got to make an instant decision. Sounds like a nightmare to me!

- Play the recording again, if necessary.
- Check answers.

Answers

the United Nations	The woman wants to work for the United Nations. The American interpreter started working for the UN.
nervous	The interpreter felt very nervous to start with.
proud	He felt proud of the part he played in American-Russian meetings.
concentration	Interpreting requires incredible concentration.
responsibility	Interpreters have an enormous responsibility.
international crisis	Mistakes of interpretation could cause an international crisis.
body language *facial expressions*	Speakers use body language and facial expressions to help convey their message.
world peace	The interpreter thinks the president he worked for contributed to world peace.
brain	You need a special sort of brain to be an interpreter.
instant decision	Interpreters have to make instant decisions about the correct words to use.

5 • Give students time to read through questions a–c. Point out that they should make notes about the speakers' answers to these questions (i.e. not their own).

- Play the recording again, then let students compare answers in pairs.
- Check answers.

Answers

a Interpreters are an integral part of international politics.

b An interpreter does not have to act the part of the person they are speaking for. Interpreters can give a neutral translation and let the person they work for convey emotions and attitudes for themselves.

c Being an interpreter is an incredible responsibility. If you don't get the translation correct you could cause an international crisis. Pride at helping to shape world events. Lucky to be involved.

■ Interpretation

1–3 Ask students to read questions 1–3, then give them time to discuss their ideas in pairs or groups.

- Elicit their ideas.

Possible answers

1 *a normal person* here is probably someone who is not constantly asserting his authority or superiority over others, and who is used to doing all the everyday things that everyone else does.

2 Misunderstandings based on translation mistakes would tend to make already bad situations worse. Trade links might be broken off. / One side might think that the other was threatening military action and attack first.

3 Body language such as: standing up and walking out, banging fist on table, stamping feet to express anger, shaking hands, hugging to convey pleasure or satisfaction. Facial expressions are international: frowning to convey anger, smiling to convey pleasure, etc.

■ Vocabulary

- Allow students time to discuss the meanings of the words in bold. You could suggest students look at the tapescript on p.153 of their books to see the full context of the four extracts if necessary.
- Check answers.

Answers

a strange, odd, or coincidental

b Both suggest that the speaker has doubts about the truth of the information he is passing on. (Expressions like these were highlighted in Unit 10 – Passive constructions – p.97.)

c unfriendly (the opposite of *warm*)

d *show-business* – the glamorous side of being president.

■ Speaking personally

1–3 Students discuss these questions in pairs or groups.

- Monitor but do not interrupt.
- Elicit their ideas, then finish with a class discussion.

—Grammar— Reported speech: reporting verbs

■ Exploring concepts ■■■■■■■■■■■■ p. 117 ■

- Elicit examples of common reporting verbs from the class: for example, *said, reported, announced*, etc. Students might remember the other reporting verbs from p.115, (*asked, inquired, wondered, wanted to know*).
- Remind students that they can refer to the **Language Commentary** on p.138.

1 • Students work individually or in pairs through parts **a** and **b**.

Note It is not always possible to include the exact meaning of the different reporting verbs in direct speech. It is often the reporter who decides on the speaker's purpose and chooses an appropriate verb.

- Monitor and help.
- Check answers.

Answers

1 a 1 *said / claimed*   5 *explained*
      2 *confirmed*   6 *implied*
      3 *admitted*   7 *thought*
      4 *conceded*

b The interpreter's actual words — possible direct speech.

1 *He's just a normal person.*
   (The reporter chooses the verb *claim* — it is not an idea that was in the speaker's mind.)
2 *Yes, their first meeting was pretty cool. / It's quite true that their first meeting was pretty cool.*
3 *I must admit / say I am quite proud of the part I played.*
4 *It's true / I have to say / I must admit that interpreting at this level does take an incredible amount of concentration.*
5 *You see, the speakers themselves can use body language.*
   (The reporter interprets the speaker's words as an explanation.)
6 *The president enjoyed the glamour that went with the job.*
   (The verb *imply* means that something was suggested rather than stated. It is the reporter who decodes the implication and chooses his own words.)
7 *I think that the president made a real contribution to world peace.*

2 This section introduces more alternative ways of reporting speech.

a Ask students to look carefully at the sentences and say how 5 and 7 are grammatically different.
• Allow them a few minutes to discuss ideas in pairs, then elicit their answers.

Answers
Sentences 5 and 7 follow this pattern:
   verb + clause
   She insisted she had paid.
Sentences 1–4 and 6 all follow this pattern:
   verb + person (object) + *to do something*
   She **advised her to study** languages.

Note The use of *that* in 7 is not essential. It could also be added to 5: *She insisted **that** she had paid.*

b Students now transform sentences 2–7 into direct speech. Work through the example given in the book to demonstrate how there are several possible alternatives.
• Students can work individually or in pairs through the exercise.
• Check answers.

Suggested answers
2 *You (really) must work harder.*
3 *Don't tell anyone what you've seen.*
   Whatever you do, don't tell anyone what you've seen, or else.
4 *Please stay (with me). / Please don't leave me.*
5 *I'm telling you, I've paid for everything.*
   I've paid for everything – really / honestly.
6 *You must repay the money you stole / have stolen.*
   It is my obligation / duty to order you to repay the money you have stolen.
7 *I haven't stolen any money.*
   I haven't stolen any money, honestly.

■ Exploitation

• Students are going to listen to a woman talking about her experiences of learning languages.

1 a Ask students to read questions 1 and 2 before they listen.
• **12.2** Play the recording.

12.2

Part 1
I Jo, can you speak a foreign language?
J No.
I Why not?
J I don't know. I tried at school. I was taught French. When I was older, I did Spanish for a year and later on, years later when I had left school, uhm, I tried German … Now I start off fine, everything is OK, then I get to a stage when I realize that everyone around me is talking in a language, understanding one another, and I don't know what they're talking about. I can't tell you what stage it is, because I think I'm getting along fine but then suddenly … I don't know, a blank wall seems to set in. I just can't seem to learn a language. I can remember odd phrases, I can speak the odd few sentences in German if I need to, like 'Have a seat' and, you know, 'Would you like a cup of tea?' but that's about as far as it goes and if anyone actually answered me which is what happened to me at work the other week, ooh, I said to this German lady to have a seat and I would bring her a cup of tea and she turned round and said 'Ah', and I got this stream of German and I couldn't understand a word … ooh … I don't know, I haven't got an ear for languages at all.

• Check answers.

Answers
1 She mentions *French*, *Spanish*, and *German*.
2 She can say two phrases in German: *Have a seat* and *Would you like a cup of tea?*

b Students now read the interview with Jo, and transform the questions and answers into reported speech, using the reporting verbs in brackets.
• Check answers.

Suggested answers
1 *The interviewer asked Jo if / whether she could speak a foreign language.*
2 *Jo replied that she couldn't.*
3 *The interviewer wanted to know why not / why she couldn't.*
4 *Jo said she didn't know. She claimed she had tried at school.*
5 *She explained (that) she starts off fine and that everything is OK but then she gets to the stage when she realizes that everyone around her is talking in a language and …*
6 *… and she admitted that she doesn't know what they are talking about.*

Note The present tense is more likely in 5 and 6 because it is clear that what Jo says is a generalization which is still true now.

2 a Explain the task to students: they are transforming reported speech back into direct speech.
• Student A should work on the interviewer's questions and Student B should work on Jo's replies.
• Monitor the activity, helping and correcting.

b Students now read their questions and answers together to 'recreate' the interview.

c Play the second part of the recording and let students check their answers, pausing to allow them to make corrections. You may need to play the recording again.

Part 2

I Do you blame the fact that you haven't got an ear for languages, or is it just because you simply don't have the motivation because you don't have to speak it very often?

J No, I would like very much to learn another language. I love listening to Italian spoken. I think it's an absolutely beautiful language and I would love to be able to speak it.

I Do you like any other languages?

J Yes, I like German, too. When I tried to learn it I really enjoyed it but I just couldn't make progress.

I Why do you think that was?

J I just seem to have a total blank when it comes to learning languages, but I really have tried.

Note It is quite likely that students will have correct, but different, direct speech from the recording. Spend a few minutes checking any alternatives suggested by students.

3 This exercise provides practice of reporting verbs in a more personalized context.

a–b Elicit one or two examples for **a** and **b** to check that students understand. Example

My parents used to warn me not to mix with certain kinds of people.

· Monitor the writing, correcting where necessary.

c Students compare sentences with a partner. Encourage them to tell each other more about the situations or occasions referred to in their sentences.

■ Free speech ■■■■■■■■■■■■■■■■■■■■■■■■■■■■■■■

4 · You could start by giving an example of a conversation you remember. Emphasize the fluency aspect of the activity. Students then work in pairs on two of the situations. They should describe the situation in which the conversations took place and report what was said.

· Monitor conversations but do not interrupt or correct.

▶ **Photocopiable activity 16 p.175**

— p. 118 —

Reading

1 · Students discuss possible connections between the two photographs.

· Elicit their ideas but do not say if they are correct or not.

2 · You may wish to teach these words and phrases before students read the article: *to evolve* (to develop naturally and gradually), *primate* (class of animals that includes humans, monkeys, apes, etc.), *to be descended from* (to have as an ancestor), *in close proximity to* (very near to), *to bond* (to establish a trusting affectionate relationship).

Note Don't pre-teach *to groom* or *to gossip* as these are the verbs students are looking out for in question **2b**.

a–b Ask students to read the questions.

· Students read the text, then compare their answers to the questions with a partner.

Answers

1 The monkeys are *grooming* each other; the women are *gossiping*. The author of the book being reviewed says that human gossip has a similar social function to monkeys grooming each other.

2 a The text is a book review.
b The two verbs are *groom* and *gossip*.

■ Close up ■■■■■■■■■■■■■■■■■■■■■■■■■■■■■■■

· Allow students time to work through the questions individually or in pairs.

· Check answers.

Close up

· l.4 *nitty-gritty* the most important part of something. Here it is used as an adjective, but normally it is a noun. Example *Let's get down to the nitty-gritty.*
argy-bargy noisy quarrelling or arguing
hurly-burly energetic, noisy activity
willy-nilly whether one wants something or not.
wishy-washy weak (in colour, character, or quality)

· l.6 The *ci* in both words is pronounced /ʃ/, so the
+ l.14 pronunciation of the words is: *species* /spiːʃiːz/ and *crucial* /kruːʃl/.

· l.8 *in* and *out* in this context mean popular / unpopular or fashionable / unfashionable.

· l.13 *witter* speak in a long, boring way, usually about something unimportant. The particle *on* adds the idea of this continuing.

· l.28 a *coalition* coming together or joining of different groups or people for a particular purpose, usually for a limited time. The pronunciation is /kəʊəlɪʃn/.

■ Comprehension ■■■■■■■■■■■■■■■■■■■■■■ p. 119 ■

1–3 Students read the text again and make notes.

· Check answers.

Answers

1 Language was developed to co-ordinate men's hunting activities in primitive societies, and to facilitate the exchange of stories about tribal origins and the supernatural.

2 Professor Dunbar says that language developed to allow people to gossip. Gossip is the human equivalent of grooming in animals and enables people to form supportive groups.

3 Language is more efficient than grooming because it allows humans to bond in larger groups.

■ Speaking personally ■■■■■■■■■■■■■■■■■■■■■■■

1–2 Students exchange ideas and experiences in pairs or groups.

· Monitor but do not interrupt.

· Finish with a brief feedback of ideas from the class.

Grammar — Infinitives or gerunds after verbs

Exploring concepts

- You could introduce this grammar by writing two incomplete sentences on the board and eliciting endings from students.
  On holiday this year I really want …
  When I was younger I used to enjoy …
- Use students' suggestions to establish the idea that some verbs are followed by the infinitive and others by the gerund (or *-ing* form). They can also read the two examples in their books. Once the idea is established, let students work independently through questions 1–3.
- Remind students that they can refer to the **Language Commentary** on p.139.

1–3 Students work through the questions individually or in pairs. Monitor, correcting and helping.

Answers

1 Verbs followed by the infinitive
agree, attempt, choose, decide, expect, fail, hope, learn, offer, pretend, refuse, threaten
Verbs followed by the gerund
can't help, consider, deny, dislike, imagine, miss, postpone, prevent, put off, resist, risk

2 In sentences **a**, **b**, **d**, and **e** there is no difference in meaning between the infinitive and the gerund. In sentence **c** the choice of the infinitive or gerund affects the meaning.
*He went on **to represent** his country.* He represented his country after he had done something else (e.g. represented his school).
*He went on **representing** his country.* He had already represented his country and he continued to represent it.

3 Students now have to work out the different meanings of verbs which can be followed by the infinitive or the gerund.
  a 1 I didn't forget to book.
     2 I recall the occasion when I booked.
  b 1 We stopped the car in order to give our friends a lift.
     2 Drivers no longer give lifts to hitch-hikers. It's something they used to do, but do not do now.
  c 1 Unfortunately we have to announce… (It's not something we want to do.)
     2 I travelled by plane and now wish I hadn't travelled by plane.
  d 1 I have made several attempts to phone you.
     2 You should have telephoned my mobile number to see / find out if I was available.
  e 1 Offending you was not my intention.
     2 I won't do it if it involves offending them.

Exploitation

1 • Elicit a few different completions of the first question to check students understand.
- Students work individually, completing the remaining sentences in at least two different ways
- Students compare and discuss their answers with a partner.
- Monitor this final stage, helping and correcting where necessary.
- Elicit some answers.

Sample answers

1 When I'm older I hope … (+ inf)
   … **to live** in a house in the country.
2 I'm the sort of person who can't resist … (+ gerund)
   … **buying** things on impulse.
3 I've never denied … (+ gerund)
   … **being** impatient and quick-tempered.
4 Within the next five years I'm going to learn… (+ inf) …
   to ski.
5 I'd always refuse … (+ inf)
   … **to get** in a car with someone who had been drinking.
6 When I'm away from home I miss … (+ gerund)
   … **going out** with my friends.

Free speech

2 • Suggest that students spend a few minutes on each topic. Don't insist on the repeated use of the verbs followed by the infinitive or gerund, but stress interest in the topics.
- Monitor conversations but do not interrupt or correct.
- Finish by eliciting a few reactions to each of the topics.

— p. 120 —

Compound nouns

- Read through the introductory definition of compound nouns with students, but don't give any more examples than *football* and *goalkeeper*.

1 • Students underline the ten compound nouns in **a–g**.
- Check answers.

Answers

a *drug-smuggling / university students*	**d** *job application form*
b *church leader / airport*	**e** *garage receptionist*
c *postman / post office*	**f** *summit meetings*
	g *food poisoning*

2 • Students could work in pairs to correct the three statements about compound nouns.
- Check answers.

Answers

a Compound nouns can be formed from two or more words:
job application form is three words
drug-smuggling is made up of a noun and an *-ing* form.

Note There are other kinds of compound nouns:
Adjective + noun   *little finger / big toe*
Verb + preposition   *breakdown / printout.*

b An *-s* is only added to the last word to form the plural of compound nouns: *university students / summit meetings*.

c Compound nouns can be written as one word, as separate words, or they can be joined with a hyphen:
postman / drug-smuggling / food poisoning.

3 This exercise shows students how they can use compound nouns instead of longer phrases.
- Work through the examples.
a Students work through sentences 1–5, forming compound nouns.

b **12.3** Students listen to check their answers.

12.3

1 I've always wanted to be **a newspaper reporter**.
2 On several occasions I've spent the night in **a prison cell**.
3 As soon as I saw **the newspaper advertisement**, I wrote off for further information and a job description.
4 **Car drivers** should take a test every ten years.
5 **Drug addiction** is a problem in most countries of the world.

Answers

3a / 4a See tapescript **12.3** for compound nouns (bold) and stress.

4 a Students listen again, repeating the compound nouns and noting them down with the correct stress.
   • Check answers.
   b Students look at the illustrations and answer questions 1–6 with a compound noun.

Answers

4b See tapescript **12.4** for compound nouns (bold) and stress.

   c **12.4** Students listen and check their answers.

12.4

1 He's a **window cleaner**.   4 It's a **television screen** or a **TV screen**.
2 It's a **teapot**.   5 It's their **wedding day**.
3 It's an **apple tree**.   6 It's a **fax machine**.

   • Play the recording a second time and get them to repeat the words with the correct stress.

5 • Ask students to read the introduction to check they understand the idea of different meanings.
   • Read the example aloud to demonstrate that the stress pattern reveals the meaning of the compound noun. Example *blue bottle* (a type of fly) and *blue bottle* (a bottle which is blue).
   a Students work through the five pairs of words, marking the stress.
   • Check their ideas.

Answers

The first pair of words in each set is an adjective and a noun. Both words are stressed but the noun has the main stress. The second set are compound nouns. In compound nouns the stress is on the first part of the compound.

1 a black bird / a blackbird (a particular type of bird)
2 a green house / a greenhouse (a glass house where flowers and vegetables are grown)
3 a long jump / the longjump (an event in athletics – athletes compete to see who can jump the furthest)
4 a heavy weight / a heavyweight (a boxer in the heaviest group / an important person in any field)
5 a short list / a short-list (a group of people selected for interview for a job)

   b Students are going to listen to a recording and decide, from the stress patterns, which words from **1–5** are being used, the adjective + noun or the compound noun.

• **12.5** Play the recording.

12.5

1 Did you see that strange **black bird** in the garden last night?
2 My father grows tomatoes in his **greenhouse**.
3 I've always been athletic. At school I always won the **long jump**.
4 Your case is a really **heavy weight**. What have you got in it?
5 I know what to get. I've made a **short list**.

• Check answers.

Answers

5 See tapescript **12.5**.

▶ **Photocopiable activity 17 p.176**

Language in action

The language focus in this unit is useful expressions for making and answering telephone calls.

■ Eavesdrop! ■■■■■■■■■■■■■■■■■■■■■■ p. 121 ■

The questions could be done as a class activity or as pairwork.

• Direct attention to the picture and the three questions.
• Remind students that they are speculating and should try to come up with a variety of different answers.
• You could elicit possible answers now, or move on to *Listening 1*.

■ Listening 1 ■■■■■■■■■■■■■■■■■■■■■■■■■■■

1a–b Draw attention to the extra question.

• **12.6** Students listen to the recording to check their *Eavesdrop!* ideas and listen for the exact purpose of each call.

12.6

Call 1
R Hello, Fringe Benefits. Mandi speaking. How may I help you?
C Good morning. My name's Mrs Davidson. Is Wayne there, please?
R I'm afraid he's not in today. Can I help?
C No, not really, I need to speak to Wayne. It's rather urgent. When will he be in?
R Well, erm, I'm afraid he's on holiday now for two weeks. I could put you through to the manager.
C Yes, please, if you would.
R Sorry to keep you waiting.
M Patrick here. Can I help you?
C Hello. This is Mrs Davidson. I had an appointment with Wayne yesterday afternoon and …
M Oh, hello, Mrs Davidson, yes I remember seeing you in the salon. I'm afraid Wayne's on holiday …
C I know. The thing is I came in yesterday to have highlights put in. And I, well, I washed my hair this morning and, the thing is, it's gone a funny shade of green. I have to have it put right immediately – I've got an important business meeting this afternoon. When can you fit me in?
M Well …
C I won't take no for an answer. I hold your salon to blame for this.

M Let me see. How about midday?
C Not soon enough I'm afraid. My meeting starts at one o'clock.
M Erm. Eleven-thirty?
C I have contacted my solicitor.
M Come in straight away, Mrs Davidson. We'll see what we can do.

Call 2
W Hello.
C Oh, hello. I'm ringing about the advert in the paper.
W Oh, yes. You need to talk to my son. I'm afraid he's out at the moment.
C Erm. Do you know when he'll be back?
W Well, he usually gets home about six o'clock.
C Can I leave a message?
W Yes, of course, hang on a minute, I'll just get a pen. OK.
C My name's Ed North and I'm interested in the motorbike. My number's 986402.
W OK, dear. I'll get him to ring you when he comes in.
C Thanks a lot. Bye bye.

Call 3
R Hello. The surgery. How can I help you?
C Oh, good morning. Yes. I'd like to make an appointment with Mr Barbury.
R Certainly, sir. Can I take your name, please?
C Yes, it's Paul Collins.
R Let me see. The first appointment I've got with Mr Barbury is September the twenty-third.
C What? That's six weeks away. I need to see him before that. I'm not sleeping and eating is very painful.
R I see, well, if you need an emergency appointment, Mr Collins, I could fit you in at half-past three tomorrow afternoon.
C That's better.
R But I'm afraid you'll have to pay an emergency supplement.
C That's OK.

• Check answers.

Possible answers
Eavesdrop!

Call 1	Call 2	Call 3
• The hairdresser	Someone whose phone number he has found in the newspaper.	The dentist
• Getting something done about her hair	Enquiring about an advertisement in the paper.	Making an appointment
• Annoyed, angry, humiliated	Interested / curious	In pain – he has toothache

Listening 1

b	To make an emergency hair appointment – her hair has turned green.	To enquire about a motorbike which is advertised in the paper.	To make an emergency dental appointment for bad toothache.

Additional activity

Conduct a brief class survey to find out if and how many students have made phone calls similar to the ones they have just heard:

• in answer to a newspaper advertisement
• to make an emergency appointment
• to express dissatisfaction or make a complaint.

2 • Students work in pairs, listen again, and note down the telephone language used by the speakers. They compile lists of the expressions. (They help and correct each other at this stage.)
   • If you think students can cope, ask them to look at question 3 and also listen for expressions the speakers use when they can't think of what to say next.

Note Students add to these lists during the next listening task.

3 • Play the recording a final time. Students now listen out for and note down expressions speakers use when they are playing for time or can't think of what to say next.

Answers
See full list of expressions after *Listening 2*, question 2.

▮ Listening 2 ▮

1 • **12.7** Ask students to read the questions and then play the recording.

12.7
Conversation 1
J … rather ill, erm, and I'd like to make a personal complaint to him.
H I see. If you'd like to hold on just one moment, I'll put you through to his secretary.
J Thank you.
Ju Hello. Can I help you?
J Yes, as I've just explained to your colleague, I'd like to speak to Mr James, please, urgently.
Ju Oh, I'm afraid he's not in today. Can I help you?
J No, you can't. I want to speak to Mr James, the Chairman of the company, please. It's rather urgent. I've been taken ill on one of your airlines and I believe I've had food poisoning. Now, can I speak to Mr James in person, please?
Ju Well, I'm very sorry, he's not in today. Maybe someone else can help you if I can't, but I'm sure if you give me all the details, I'll be able to help you.
J Well, there's nothing more that I can say, other than I've been to my doctor and the tests have shown that I have had food poisoning on your airline. I'd like to speak to Mr James in person and nobody else. Thank you.
Ju Oh, well, I see. I'm very sorry, but erm, I'm afraid you just can't. I can put you through to his Personal Assistant if you really insist.
J Yes, I do. Thank you.
Ju OK, well, if you'd like to hold on.

Conversation 2
K … and I really want to talk to somebody about it.
H I see. Can you tell me when you wrote to us?
K Er, it was, er, it was two weeks ago. And the bill came yesterday, so really you should have, er, you know, sorted it out by now. Er, is it possible to talk to somebody?
H No, I'm afraid not at the moment. Erm, can you tell me how much the bill was for?
K Well, er, er, well it was for twenty-eight pounds thirty, but I, I really need to speak to somebody, erm, who can do something about this, erm. I'm going to be going away for a week, erm, and I don't want you to invoice me again.
H I see. And you say that you've paid this twice?
K No, I've paid it once but you're, you're invoicing me twice and I can't afford to pay it twice.
H Well, what I can do for you is I can leave a message with the person concerned and make sure that they don't invoice you again. And that the money isn't taken from your account.
K Well …

H Would that be all right?
K Well, that, that seems fine, but I mean, will somebody get back to me and let me know that,... will confirm that with me?
H Yes, certainly, but it won't be today.
K When will it be?

• Check answers.

Possible answers

Conversation 1	**Conversation 2**
a Someone who had been a passenger on a plane.	Someone who had been sent two invoices for the same thing.
b To complain about food poisoning she got on the plane	To complain about being sent two invoices and to make sure that she is not invoiced again.
c Annoyed, angry, dissatisfied persistent (in no mood to be pacified).	Anxious and worried, rather than angry or annoyed.

2 • Play the recording again, while the class follow the conversations on p.122 in their books, marking the telephone expressions used by the speakers.
   • Because there are a lot of expressions for students to write down, you may need to pause the recording or play it several times. Students add the expressions to their lists.
   • Check through the lists.

Answers
(This includes expressions from *Listening 1* and *2*.)
Answering a call
12.6 (1)
Hello. (Mandi) speaking. How may I help you?   I'm afraid he's not in today.   Can I help?   I could put you through to the manager.   Sorry to keep you waiting.
12.6 (2)
I'm afraid he's out at the moment.   ... hang on a minute, (I'll just get a pen).   I'll get him to ring you (when he comes in).
12.6 (3)
Hello. How can I help you?   Can I take your name, please?
12.7 Extract 1
... if you'd like to hold on just one moment ...   I'll put you through to his secretary.   Can I help you?   I'm afraid he's not in today.   I can put you through to (his Personal Assistant) ... if you'd like to hold on ...
12.7 Extract 2
I can leave a message for the person concerned.
Making a call
12.6 (1)
Is Wayne there, please?   When will he be in?
12.6 (2)
I'm ringing about (the advert in the paper).   Do you know when he'll be back?   Can I leave a message?
12.6 (3)
I'd like to make an appointment with ...
12.7 Extract 1
I'd like to speak to (Mr James), please ...   I want to speak to (Mr James) in person.   Can I speak to ...?
12.7 Extract 2
I really want to talk to someone about it.   Is it possible to talk to ...?   Will somebody get back to me ...?   Playing for time

12.6 (1)
Well, erm ...   Well ...   Let me see ...
12.6 (2)
Erm ...
12.6 (3)
*Let me see ...
Well ...*
12.7 Extract 1
erm ...   Well ...   Oh, well, I see ...
12.7 Extract 2
I see ...   Er ...   Erm ...   Well, er, er ...

© Oxford University Press **PHOTOCOPIABLE**

■ **Features of natural conversation** ▬▬▬▬ p. 122 ■

1 • Students find the examples of *I'm very sorry* (x2) and *I'm afraid* (x3) in the extracts and decide why they are used.
   • They then discuss in pairs why the expressions are used and what they mean.
   • Elicit their ideas.

Answers
a Extract 1
I'm afraid *he's not in today.   Well,* ***I'm very sorry****, he's not in today.* ***I'm very sorry****, but* ***I'm afraid*** *you just can't.*
Extract 2
No, ***I'm afraid*** *not at the moment.*
b *I'm afraid* and *I'm sorry* are commonly used to introduce bad news. The functional or communicative meaning is *unfortunately* or *It's bad luck, but... I'm very sorry* in the first extract is more of a genuine apology.

2 • Elicit students' ideas about the meaning of *I see.*

Answers
I see is used in response to what another person has said and means *I understand what you are saying.*

3 • Ask students to read the example and explain that unfinished *If* sentences like this are frequently used to ask or tell someone to do something. It is an indirect and therefore polite command.
   • Elicit their ideas about ways of finishing the *If* sentence, and alternatives.

Answers
a *Well, if you'd like to hold on, ...
... I'll put you through to Mr James' Personal Assistant.
... I'll see if Mr James' Personal Assistant is available.
... I'll try to get in touch with Mr James' Personal Assistant.*
b *Could you hold on (a minute), please?
Hold on (a minute), please.*

■ **Practice** ▬▬▬▬▬▬▬▬▬▬▬▬▬▬▬

1 **a** **12.8** Students listen and decide which speaker sounds polite, and how the other speaker sounds.

12.8

1 Can I help you? (polite)
  Can I help you? (insincere)
2 Could you hold the line a minute, please? (insincere)
  Could you hold the line a minute, please? (polite)
3 I'm afraid he's not here at the moment. (polite)
  I'm afraid he's not here at the moment. (insincere)
4 I'll put you through to his secretary. (polite)
  I'll put you through to his secretary. (insincere)
5 Sorry to keep you waiting. (insincere)
  Sorry to keep you waiting. (polite)

- Elicit students' ideas.

Answers

1 a See tapescript **12.8**.

b **12.9** Play the recording which has the polite version of the sentences from **12.8** and drill them with students.

12.9

1 Can I help you?
2 Could you hold the line a minute, please?
3 I'm afraid he's not here at the moment.
4 I'll put you through to his secretary.
5 Sorry to keep you waiting.

2 a **12.10** Students listen and decide which of the two speakers sounds determined and polite, and how the other speaker sounds.

12.10

1 Can I speak to Mr Gray, please? (polite)
  Can I speak to Mr Gray, please? (angry)
2 I'd like to speak to Mr Gray. (angry)
  I'd like to speak to Mr Gray. (polite)
3 Is it possible to talk to somebody about my holiday? (polite)
  Is it possible to talk to somebody about my holiday? (angry)
4 I need to talk to someone about my holiday. (angry)
  I need to talk to someone about my holiday. (polite)

- You could pause after each pair of sentences and elicit ideas. Alternatively, play the whole recording and get students to note down their ideas and compare with a partner.
- Check answers.

Answers

2 a See tapescript **12.10**.

b Play the recording again and drill chorally and individually.

■ Exploitation Role play ■

- Allow time for students to read through and ask questions about the three situations.
- Students form pairs and choose roles.

- Remind the class to use some of the telephone language from their lists and allow them time to prepare (but not script) what they are going to say.
- Monitor their conversations, listening for use of the telephone language. Do not interrupt conversations unless the language is completely incorrect or inappropriate.

■ Writing ■━━━━━━━━━━━━ p. 123 ■

1a–d Allow students time to read through the spoken language, the writing, and questions **a–d**.

- They could discuss their ideas in pairs for a few minutes.
- Check answers.

Suggested answers

a The conversation, though quite formal, is nevertheless spontaneous. The caller is responding directly to the person she is speaking to. Her feelings are expressed by her tone of voice and choice of assertive language. The written message is made up mainly of factual information fitted into an existing format (a phone message note-pad). The message itself is written in clear, objective reported speech.

b The word *Urgent* at the beginning of the message and the choice of the word *demanded* both help to convey impatience.

c By using *claims*, the person who took the message makes it clear that she is allowing for the possibility that Mrs Radley's story is inaccurate.

d The use of *claims* and *was taken ill* make it very clear that this incident is still an issue for the caller. It is something which still affects her.

2 • Explain the task. Students could write their messages in a similar format to the example on the page.
- Remind students to refer to the **Writing guidelines** on p.158 of their books.

Note Times are not mentioned in the recordings.

- Remind them to use reported speech in their messages, and to find a way to convey the speaker's attitudes. (Sometimes the reporting verb can achieve this.)
- **12.11** Play the recording, one message at a time, and play again if necessary.

12.11

Call 1
A Good morning, Hopkins Engineering.
B Oh, good morning, could I speak to Mr North, please?
A I'm afraid he's not here at the moment. Can I take a message?
B Yes, thank you. Could you tell Mr North that Jenny phoned and …
A Jenny?
B Yes, that's right, Jenny Staples. And could you say I'm really sorry but I can't make our meeting this evening. Problems at home, I'm afraid. I'll ring him tomorrow. OK?
A You can't make this evening's meeting.
B That's right. Thanks, and don't forget to say how sorry I am.

Call 2
A Hello. TVs Direct. Sarah speaking.
B Hello. I'd like to speak to Mr Flag, please.
A I'm sorry, but he's out of the office at the moment. Can I help?
B No, I don't think so, but I would like to leave a message for Mr Flag.
A Yes, certainly.
B Right. My name's Boycott, Tim Boycott, and I'm calling about the TV I ordered from your shop three weeks ago.

A Did you say Boycott?

B Yes, that's right. That's B–O–Y–C–O double T. It's about the TV I ordered three weeks ago. I'd like you to let Jerry Flag know that I am cancelling my order because I am fed up with waiting.

A I see. You wish to cancel.

B That's right. Oh, and incidentally, tell Mr Flag that Price-Savers have the same TV in stock at a lower price. Goodbye.

Call 3

A Hello, City Bank. How can I help?

B Hello, this is Elaine Barker. I really wanted to speak to my sister, Helena, but she's probably out at the moment.

A Erm, yes, I'm afraid she is.

B OK. Could you to ask her to ring me back as soon as she gets in, please? Just say that Elaine rang. It's about our party on Saturday.

A The party?

B Yes, I'm going to get the food and drink this afternoon and I really need to know how many people have told her they're coming.

Call 4

A Hello.

B Oh, good morning. I'd like to speak to Mr Collins, please.

A I'm sorry, but he's at work today. Can I take a message?

B Yes, if you wouldn't mind. This is the Wheels Insurance Company claims department. My name's Paul Baker.

A Wheels Insurance, yes, and what was your name again?

B Paul Baker.

A Paul Baker.

B Yes, could you let Mr Collins know that we have still not received his completed claims form and that until we do we cannot deal with his claim.

A Oh, yes, I'll tell him as soon as he gets in. Has he got your number?

B I don't know, but tell him he can phone me on 327859 or simply post or fax us his form in the next day or two.

Sample messages

1 Phone message
For: Mr North
From: Jenny Staples
Contact: /
Subject: This evening's meeting
Message: She says she is sorry but she can't make the meeting, due to problems at home. She will ring you tonight. She is very sorry.

2 Phone message
For: Mr Flag
From: Tim Boycott
Contact: /
Subject: TV ordered three weeks ago
Message: Mr Boycott says he wishes to cancel his order because he is fed up with waiting. He also claims that Price-Savers are selling the same TV at a lower price.

3 Phone message
For: Helena
From: Your sister Elaine
Contact: /
Subject: Party on Saturday
Message: Elaine needs to know many people have told you they are coming to the party on Saturday. Can you to ring her back as soon as you get in.

4 Phone message
For: Mr Collins
From: Wheels Insurance Company Claims Department – Paul Baker
Contact: 327859
Subject: Insurance claim
Message: Paul Baker says that the company has not received your completed claim form. He insists that they cannot deal with your claim until they receive the form. You can phone him at the above number or post or fax the form in the next day or two.

3 • Students compare their completed forms, paying particular attention to the use of reported speech and the ways in which the callers' attitudes have been conveyed.

▓ Summary

• Encourage students to use the tick boxes to help them keep a record of their learning.

Formal letters

Features – with examples

1 Full, uncontracted verb forms.
   You are / we are

2 Link clause.
   *Please complete the reply slip and return it to us no later than 14th April, **so that** staff can arrange the timetable of appointments.*
   *Every effort will be made to see you on the day you would prefer, **but** we are sure you will understand that it may not be possible for everyone to have the time of their choice.*

3 Formal words and phrases.
   to discuss (NOT *talk about*) / staff (NOT *teachers*)

4 Single-word verbs.
   complete (NOT *fill in*) / *return* (NOT *send back*)

5 Alternatives to the personal pronouns *I* and *we*.
   *so that **staff** can ...* (NOT *we*) / *it may not be possible* (NOT *we may not be able to ...*)

6 Passive verbs can make your writing more formal or less personal.
   *Every effort **will be made** to see you* (NOT *We will make every effort to see you*)

Making notes

Features – with examples

1 The example notes are brief and to the point.

2 There are no unnecessary words.
   STAFF comfort – city / stress. (NOT *The comfort of the staff is an important reason to move. Working in the city can cause stress.*)

3 Numbers –*1, 2, 3, 4.*

4 Capital letters, underlining and highlighting.
   MONEY / Next year / May -> July

Informal letters

Features – with examples

1 Contracted verb forms.
   it's (NOT *it is*) / *you're* (NOT *You are*) / *I'd* (NOT *I would*) / *there'd* (NOT *there had*) / *I'd* (NOT *I would*) / *You've* (NOT *You have*) / *I'm* (NOT *I am*)

2 Certain words left out.
   Sorry (NOT *I'm sorry*) / *Tried to…* (NOT *I tried to…*) / *Due in April* (NOT *It's due in April.*)

3 Short sentences.
   Thanks for phoning this morning. / Where were you? / Anyway, I thought I'd write instead.

4 Slang or colloquial words and phrases.
   Thanks (NOT *Thank you*)

5 Phrasal verbs.
   to get back to you (NOT *to return your call*)

6 Active verbs.
   I'd have told you the great news. (NOT *You'd have been told the great news.*)

7 Conversational questions.
   Where were you?

8 Dashes [–]and exclamation marks [!!].
   Sorry I was in such a hurry – but you know what it's like.
   Where were you ? – Anyway, I thought I'd write.
   You've probably guessed already – I'm expecting a baby! Due in April!

9 This letter is in a personal tone, showing the two people are friends.

Narratives

Features – with examples

1 First paragraphs
   a The background to the main event.
      It was late by the time we left the house-warming party. Frost sparkled on the grass ... ... but it had been a great evening and we were feeling very relaxed.
   b The main 'characters'.
      ... Mary and I slowly strolled towards the front gate.
   c The beginning of the sequence of events of the story. End the paragraph at an exciting point in the story.
      Suddenly, we heard a loud crack and, when we turned round, we saw smoke pouring from the upstairs window of the house we'd just left.
      'Oh no!' I screamed. 'My letters!'

2 General features
   a The model only includes the first paragraph.
   b Mood or atmosphere phrases.
      Frost sparkled on the grass ... / It was nearly a quarter past twelve ... / We were tired but it had been a great evening and we were feeling very relaxed.
   c Adjectives, adverbs and verbs.
      sparkled / slowly / strolled / chatted / loud / pouring / screamed
   d Appropriate narrative tenses.
      Past simple   *was / left / sparkled / strolled / was / was / chatted / were / heard / turned / saw / screamed*

Past continuous   *were feeling*
Past perfect   *had booked / we'd talked to / we'd met /*
had been we'd just left

e Direct speech.
'Oh no!' I screamed. 'My letters!'

Instructions

Features – with examples

1 Direct, recognizable language structures e.g. imperatives.
Check …
Choose … / … press …
Don't press …

2 The models do not contain indirect forms.

3 Separate staged instructions.
***Check** the battery …*
***Make** sure you use the right kind of film …*
***Choose** the shape of picture you want …*

4 Sequenced instructions.
1 *Click the Reply button.*
2 *Type the text of your message in the box …*
3 *To send the message click the Send icon.*

A radio script

Features – with examples

1 This applies to the performance aspect of the commercial.

2 The commercials all use simple, repetitive language.

3 Repetition of important points.
Star TV and Audio / Deals on Wheels are both repeated twice
in their adverts.

4 Alliteration.
*a **Star store** near you* [1]
Rhyme.
*At **Deals** on **Wheels**, we'll give you a good **deal** on your*
***wheels**.* [2]
Onomatopoeia.
None used in the models.

5 A range of tones and style.
serious and informative: e.g. model 3
light or humorous: e.g. model 2

6 Clear context or situation.
You could be paying too much for your TV and video [1]
Thinking of selling or trading in your car? [2]
In model 3 sound effects establish the context:
Noise of car / music in background / mobile phone numbers
being dialled / Music is turned down.

Reviews

Features – with examples

1 Factual information.
***Nell**, starring Jodie Foster and Liam Neeson, …*

2 Subject matter and background information.
It's the fascinating story of … … she needs to be looked after.

3 Opinions and the reasons or explanations for these
opinions.
… a wonderful film. / the fascinating story …
… Nell is sympathetically portrayed by Neeson and Foster. For
me this was the most interesting aspect of this film which
gripped me from beginning to end.

4 The style of the model is neutral – neither formal nor
informal – for general readers.

5 A Recommendation to the reader.
Don't miss Nell if it comes to a cinema or video shop near you.

Phone messages

Features – with examples

1 The models are clear, simple, and easy to understand.

2 The models contains only the most important information.

3 Abbreviations.
C. [1]
Ext. / a.s.a.p. / Jan. [2]

4 Details from message 2.
a Who the message is for.
Penny Holton
b Who the call is from.
Jeremy Gratton
c Who has taken the message.
Paul Nixon
d The subject or purpose of the call.
Today's meeting cancelled. Next Monday okay instead –
8.30 in morning?
e Any specific instructions from the caller.
Ring to confirm a.s.a.p.
f The time of the call.
17 Jan / 10.05 am

5 Attitude of the speaker or personal opinion.
Really sorry – don't think it was an excuse.

Test 1 (Units 1–2)

Grammar

Present tenses, action verbs and state verbs, aspect

1 Choose the correct form of the verb.

1 She .... for her father this summer.
   a works
   b working
   c is working

2 Good – at last I can go out. I .... my homework.
   a have finished
   b finished
   c am finishing

3 He first .... to Russia ten years ago.
   a has gone
   b went
   c has been

4 We always .... people to bring extra money.
   a are advising
   b advise
   c have advised

5 .... dinner yet?
   a Have you been making
   b Are you making
   c Have you made

6 Things are looking bad but .... for a miracle.
   a I'm hoping
   b I hope
   c I've hoped

7 He's never come before so .... he'll turn up.
   a I'm doubting
   b I've always been doubting
   c I doubt

8 Since January 1st .... for six jobs.
   a I've applied
   b I applied
   c I've been applying

`8`

Present and perfect tenses

2 Choose the correct answer.

So far this year everything *has been / is being* [1] different from last. At the moment I *have been trying / am trying* [2] to change jobs but without much luck. That's why I *learn / have been learning* [3] to speak two new languages in the last six months and hope to be fluent soon. The problem is, if I *haven't been having / don't have* [4] a job interview to go to I *have spent / spend* [5] the whole day at home just staring out of the window. My friends all *have been agreeing / agree* [6] that being unemployed *has changed / has been changing* [7] me; I always *get / have got* [8] annoyed with little things and this is affecting my friendships. Something *has had / has* [9] to be done about this soon or things will get even worse.

`9`

Past simple, Past perfect, Past continuous, *used to*, *would*

3 Correct the sentences.

1 When I was a child I would know the capital city of virtually every country in the world.

   ....

2 He was going to school by bike every day when he was living in the old house down the road.

   ....

3 After she has finished her homework she went out for a walk.

   ....

4 The people leaving the party said goodbye and told me they were having a really good time.

   ....

5 I would believe in ghosts when I was younger, but not now.

   ....

6 By the time she was twenty she was bored; she did everything she ever wanted to do.

   ....

7 When I was a child our New Year's parties were always the same; the entire family had got together to sing songs.

   ....

8 I used to cook the dinner when the phone rang.

   ....

9 You're soaking wet! What had happened?

....

10 But officer – I worked in Rome at the time of the murder!

....

10

Vocabulary

do and make

4 Rewrite these sentences, using using the words in brackets and expressions with *do* or *make*.

Example
We've got a lot of dirty plates and bowls to wash. (washing up)
We've got to do a lot of washing up.
We've got a lot of washing up to do.

1 She earns a lot. (money)

....

....

2 He explained why he was late. (excuse)

....

....

3 I studied the background to the subject. (research)

....

....

4 His business is doing very well. (living)

....

....

5 I think you're doing something wrong. (mistake)

....

....

6 Could you help me please? (favour)

....

....

7 We need to buy some things. (shopping)

....

....

8 She told the manager she wasn't happy with the service. (complaint)

....

....

9 The detective wrote down a few words while the victim talked to him. (notes)

....

....

9

Language in action

Agreeing, disagreeing, trying to get into a conversation

5 Complete the sentences using the words listed.

about	along	but	idea	like	opinion	right
rubbish	see	so	sure	think	with	word

Agreeing

1 I agree .... you.

2 Yes, you're ....

3 I'd go .... with that.

4 I'm not so ....

5 That's a good ....

6 I .... your point.

Disagreeing

7 I don't know .... that.

8 Yes, ... don't you think ...

9 No, I don't think ....

10 That's complete ....

Trying to get into a conversation

11 Excuse me, could I just say what I ....

12 Can I just say what my .... is?

13 I'd just .... to say ...

14 Can I just get a .... in?

14

TOTAL **50**

Test 2 (Units 3–4)

Grammar

Language of contrast

1 Which sentences **a–f** can follow words and phrases **1–10**? Tick the boxes.

a	... waiting here let's go and do something exciting.
b	... dogs are much better company than cats.
c	... eat chocolate, eat fruit, it's much healthier.
d	... only meeting him once, I don't trust him.
e	... she came to meet me every day, I never got used to it.
f	... I play the guitar, my brother plays the saxophone.

Sentence	a	b	c	d	e	f
1 Instead of						
2 However,						
3 Despite						
4 Rather than						
5 In fact,						
6 Whereas						
7 On the other hand,						
8 Even though						
9 While						
10 Although						

10

2 Choose the correct word to fill the gap.

1 .... running, let's walk just for once.
  a Whereas
  b Instead of
  c Although

2 I know that's usually what happens .... , I don't think it's always true.
  a Even though
  b However
  c On the other hand

3 .... the bad weather, we all had a marvellous time.
  a Despite
  b In fact
  c While

4 .... apologize directly, she decided to write a letter.
  a Instead of
  b On the other hand
  c Rather than

5 .... many people would say you're talking rubbish I think you are completely right.
  a In fact
  b However
  c Although

6 Trains are faster, ... buses are cheaper.
  a instead of
  b although
  c despite

7 .... , the truth is she spent every penny on presents for her children.
  a Despite
  b In fact
  c On the other hand

8 .... the northern hemisphere is quite cold in December, the southern hemisphere is very hot.
  a Whereas
  b Rather than
  c In fact

9 .... that would be one way of doing it, I think we'll go for the first idea.
  a Rather than
  b Despite
  c Although

10 .... , we mustn't forget that he can also be serious when he wants to.
  a Whereas
  b Even though
  c However

10

Modal verbs

3 Choose the most appropriate answer in the following sentences.

1 You're terribly sunburnt! You *must* / *ought to* / *can* be English!

2 With her exams coming up she *can* / *needn't* / *has to* do a lot of homework.

3 He's very late today. He *should have* / *might have* / *can't have* had an accident.

4 Of course it's up to you, but if you *mustn't* / *could* / *ought to* tell her before tomorrow, I'd be glad.

5 I can't believe my luck – this *must* / *mustn't* / *needn't* be the happiest day of my life.

6 Are you sure about that? You *should* / *must* / *needn't* have made a mistake.

7 I'm not sure but this *can* / *needs to* / *might* be the tallest building in the world.

8 I'm always broke and my boss couldn't care less; he *should / might / may* pay me more.

9 Where is she? I suppose she *should have / could have / needn't have* already gone, but I can't be sure.

10 They've been here all night. They *ought to / should / can't* work any harder.

11 You can go if you want, you know. You really *shouldn't / needn't / can't* stay.

12 I begin work at 7, so I *have to / may / might* get up at 6 every morning.

> **12**

Vocabulary

Confused words

4 Choose the correct version.

1 I was *grown up / brought up* by foster parents.

2 She *reminded / remembered* me of my first girlfriend.

3 The detective secretly *watched / stared at* the house all day.

4 What's your *special / favourite* pop group?

5 He's always so *grumpy / angry*, especially first thing in the morning.

6 You'll have to be *easygoing / patient* with my grandmother, she's quite deaf.

7 You've *given / put* yourself away – now we know you were lying.

8 The princess politely *sipped / knocked back* her drink.

9 He *gazed / peered* lovingly at her favourite film star for the whole film.

10 He *gobbled down / nibbled* his food for a few moments, then pushed the plate away and said he didn't like it.

11 They *threw / put* away two bags of rubbish.

12 When she went to live in Australia she *gave / took* away everything she had to her friends and relatives.

13 A soldier has to keep a *cold / cool* head at all times.

> **13**

Language in action

Asking for and giving explanations

5 Re-order the words to make sentences.

1 is what on earth this?

....

....

2 don't simple late I have late always reason watch that for I'm the a.

....

....

3 cancelled was bad the because was main weather the it reason of.

....

....

4 exactly me can you tell were where you?

....

....

5 it only slipped that is the mind reason my.

....

....

> **5**

> **TOTAL** **50**

Test 3 (Units 5–6)

Grammar

Conditionals, *wish*

1 Rewrite these sentences, starting with the word or phrase in brackets.

Example
You didn't tell me earlier, so I didn't go to the party.
(If) *If you'd told me earlier I would have gone to the party.*

1 I don't know the facts so I can't answer the question.

   (If) ....

   ....

2 I don't like your habit of whistling early in the morning.

   (I wish) ....

   ....

3 I'm not happy with my flat. It's too small.

   (I wish) ....

   ....

4 She didn't work hard at school so now she's got a badly paid job.

   (If) ....

   ....

5 Dave really wants to go on holiday. It depends on whether he's got enough money.

   (If) ....

   ....

6 Everything started to go wrong the day I met Tom.

   (I wish / meet) ....

   ....

7 You seem to know the answer, so you should write it down.

   (If) ....

   ....

8 I'm not very fit.

   (I wish) ....

   ....

9 The postman always leaves my gate open. I'm really annoyed.

   (I wish) ....

   ....

10 Jane only needs one more point to win the match.

   (If) ....

   ....

   ☐ **10**

Past tense with future meaning

2 Match the two parts of the sentences.

1	It's about time we	a could afford a new car – what kind would you choose? ......
2	If only I	b spoke to her yourself – I wouldn't know what to say. ......
3	Imagine you	c could remember her number I'd phone her right now. ......
4	Suppose a robber	d got down to some work, isn't it? ......
5	I'd rather you	e walked in now – what security arrangements have you got? ......

   ☐ **5**

3 Answer these questions related to sentences in **2** above. Which sentence/s …

1 expresses a preference? ......

2 refer to probable results of an imaginary situation? ...... / ......

3 expresses dissatisfaction with a present situation? ......

4 suggests that something is almost too late? ......

   ☐ **4**

4 Match the two parts of the sentences.

1 I'd rather   a someone offered you the boss's job – would you take it? ......

2 If only   b you got a job if you ask me. ......

3 It's about time   c you weren't already married; we're made for each other. ......

4 Imagine   d you didn't do that; it's getting on my nerves. ......

☐ 4

Present perfect simple, Present perfect continuous

5 Fill in the gaps.

I .... (learn) **1** French for the last two years and now I'm quite fluent. I .... (finish) **2** two coursebooks and now I'm on the third level. This is the third foreign language I .... (try) **3** to learn. I just couldn't pick up Italian and Spanish, so I thought I'd try another one. Recently the classes .... (become) **4** more interesting; the teacher .... (get) **5** us to practise our speaking at every opportunity and it's surprising how much most of us .... (improve) **6** since he started doing this. I've .... (read) **7** the first book on our booklist and I'm looking forward to finishing it. It's amazing how much I .... (learn) **8** just from the first 30 pages.

☐ 8

Vocabulary

Homonyms

6 Complete these sentences. Choose from the list.

banned	lead	trunk	forth	roar	saw	raw
fourth	band	sore

1 The lion started to .... when the hunters approached.

2 All political opposition has been ....

3 .... – free petrol is used in more cars nowadays.

4 Mary bought a new .... to cut down the old tree.

5 The elephant used its .... to give itself a shower.

6 On Saturday we went back and .... to the supermarket all afternoon.

☐ 6

Euphemisms

7 Choose the correct word or phrase.

1 Old Mr Davis *passed away* / *passed up* last year.

2 She's not exactly *bright* / *shiny*; she thought Paris was the capital of Mexico.

3 She's becoming a little *plump* / *skinny*; do you think she's getting enough exercise?

4 He used to have such wonderful hair but now he's going *thin on top* / *over the top*.

5 Speak up, she can't hear you, she's *hard of hearing* / *hard up*.

6 I think all his terrible experiences have made him a bit soft *in the head* / *in the brain*.

☐ 6

Language in action

Language of anger

8 Choose the correct word.

A I'm so angry – my brother's just told me he's not coming with his family for Christmas after all.

1 B You're *joking* / *lying*!

2 A No, it's true. With only two days' warning. It's absolutely *infuriating* / *horrific*.

3 B But that's *nonsense* / *outrageous*. He can't expect to do that at such short notice.

A I know. He claims his boss told him he has to work late over the next few days.

4 B And whose brilliant *wish* / *idea* was that?

A Head office. New working hours.

5 B Well, I suppose there are *worse* / *terrible* things. I expect he'll get paid extra for it.

6 A But it's *making* / *caused* me so angry! I couldn't even get to sleep last night!

7 B I'm not surprised. It's really *getting me down* / *getting me over* just hearing about it.

☐ 7

TOTAL ☐ 50

Test 4 (Units 7–8)

Grammar

Can and *be able to*

1 **Choose the correct form.**

1 *Am I able to / Can I* use your phone, please?

2 After two attempts I *could / was able to* start my car.

3 By the time he's finished his course he*'ll be able to / can* speak fluently.

4 If you hadn't shown me how, I *wouldn't have been able to / couldn't* do it.

5 That book *can / is able to* be either for self-study or classroom use.

6 Do you think I *could / am able to* finish it later?

[6]

A / an / the / zero article

2 **Fill in the gaps with *a, an, the* or (–) no article.**

.... **1** forest outside our village is full of .... **2** wildlife, some of it dangerous. .... **3** hunter who was shooting there last year was badly injured; a bear and its family were surprised by .... **4** hunter and attacked him. As everybody knows, ... **5** bear is always dangerous when protecting its young. Even .... **6** rifle wouldn't always be useful in such a situation. .... **7** most frightening things about .... **8** bears are their strength, size and speed, all combined in .... **9** aggressive animal.

[9]

Relative pronouns

3 **Complete these sentences. Choose from the list of words and phrases. (One possible answer is to miss out the relative pronoun.)**

from which	why	whose	with whom	which	that
in which	(–)				

1 This is the woman .... car was stolen last night.

2 Her more famous sister, ... she is always compared, is four years older.

3 The last time .... I saw her she was very unhappy.

4 New York, ... can get very hot in summer, is often freezing in winter.

5 The thing .... annoys me is everybody seems to like him.

6 The state .... she was found led the doctors to keep her in hospital for a week.

7 This is the prison .... he escaped twenty years ago.

8 No-one really knows the reason .... she acted like that.

[8]

Emphasis

4 **Complete the sentences using the words from the box.**

indeed	on earth	herself	does	did	am	really

1 What .... are you talking about?

2 Thank you very much ....

3 But I really .... sorry, honestly.

4 She said it was .... well decorated.

5 Although everybody says it wasn't her fault. She .... insists that she caused the accident.

6 I suppose she .... make the effort to get here last year.

7 She doesn't do much to help but she .... wash the car every Sunday.

[7]

Vocabulary

Connotation

5 Match these words into pairs with similar meanings. The first word in each pair should be positive, the second negative.

Example
confident .....*big-headed*.....

---

arrogant   skinny   cheap   ~~big-headed~~   stuffy   macho
obsessed with   pushy   fat   mad   stubborn

---

1 keen on   ....

2 chubby   ....

3 determined   ....

4 serious   ....

5 ambitious   ....

6 inexpensive   ....

7 slim   ....

8 eccentric   ....

9 masculine   ....

10 proud   ....

> | 10 |

Language in action

Giving advice

6 Choose the best phrase.

1 If *I were you / only I knew / you asked* I wouldn't have anything to do with him.

2 Have you really *thought / worked / considered* your decision through?

3 Surely *it could be / it would be / it's a possibility to be* more sensible to wait till next year.

4 What *can you do / would I say / can I say* to persuade you to change your mind?

5 But *have you got to be / shouldn't you be / needn't you be* thinking about the possible consequences?

> | 5 |

Requests

7 Choose the correct phrase to complete the sentences.

1 Do .... borrow your bike?
  a you think I could
  b you think there is a chance I

2 .... possibly lend me some money?
  a Could you
  b Can I

3 Is .... my using your phone?
  a it possible
  b there any chance of

4 .... that's just not possible.
  a I'm afraid
  b I can but

5 .... if I could but I can't.
  a I'm afraid
  b I would

> | 5 |

> | TOTAL | 50 |

Test 5 (Units 9–10)

Grammar

Time and reason clauses

1 Write these sentences out in full.

Example
please wash dog after take walk
Please wash the dog after you have taken him for a walk.

1 She go out later on after clean kitchen.

....

2 As soon as you arrive go bus station.

....

3 When I know answer I ring you.

....

4 Nobody talk him because think strange.

....

5 She try phone you before leave work.

....

6 The moment I get home I phone you I promise.

....

           6

Cause and effect

2 Fill each gap with the correct form of one of these verbs.

bring	cause	lead	make	result

1 The pollution in the capital .... people's hair fall out.

2 Inflation can .... in greater unemployment.

3 Bad parenting can .... to problems for children later in life.

4 Losing her job .... her to start committing crimes.

5 The government's policy will probably .... many social changes.

           5

Participle clauses

3 Combine the two sentences into one sentence using participle clauses.

1 The streets were full of people. They were shouting and screaming.

The streets ....

2 The government introduced wage limits. This provoked civil unrest.

....

3 The wind howled and whistled all night. This disturbed our sleep.

....

4 He wandered around the town. He didn't know where to go.

....

5 She phoned her best friend. She did this because she had finished her homework.

....

           5

Passives

4 Rewrite the sentences in a more natural style, using passives when appropriate.

Example
Some people believe that Leonard Uglow was the inventor of plastic.
Leonard Uglow is believed to be the inventor of plastic.

People said that he was already the richest man in Boreville when he announced his invention.

1 *He* ....

His staff marketed the new product all over the southern states.

2 *The new product* ....

When Uglow died in 1925 an unknown businessman took over the company.

3 *The company* ....

At this point someone decided to use its original name again.

4 *It* ....

By 1952 some people claimed that Uglow Plastics was the fifth biggest company in the United States.

5 *Uglow* ....

But by the 1960s someone had separated it into three companies.

6 *It* ....

And in 1984 someone else closed it down.

7 *It* ....

           7

Vocabulary

Synonyms

5 Choose the best words in these sentences.

1 After midnight the town centre is *lonely / deserted*.

2 Can't you understand? It's so *definite / obvious*.

3 Yesterday I *learned / picked up* that a work colleague has been stealing from the company for the last two years.

4 What *leisure / spare* activities do you do at the weekends?

5 As soon as he got to the party he *took to / made for* the best-looking person in the room.

6 I'm *wealthy / rich*! I've won first prize!

7 Buses that *give out / distribute* dirty fumes should be banned from roads.

8 The plan fell through because the team members were *uncooperative / complicated*.

9 She's very active and *appreciates / takes part in* all sports.

10 This new machine is a really *stylish / clever* idea; it does the job better than any other.

☐ 10

Metaphorical language

6 Answer the questions True or False.

1 She lost her temper and stormed out, slamming the door behind her.

She went out slowly but noisily. True or false? ....

2 The basketball player towers over all his classmates.

He is taller. True or false? ....

3 You like him so much personally that it clouds your professional judgement of him.

You think he is better than he really is. True or false?

....

4 I've been beavering away for weeks trying to finish the book on time.

I haven't been working as hard as I should have. True or false? ....

5 Her table manners are terrible – she wolfs down all her food as if each meal is her last.

She eats slowly but makes a lot of noise. True or false?

....

☐ 5

Language in action

Suggestions

7 Re-order the words to make sentences.

1 be idea it a early would good go to?

....

2 you be to don't it'd think better wait?

....

3 could place always another we try

....

4 don't just and see why wait we?

....

5 about him now what up ringing?

....

6 thought harder of have working you?

....

☐ 6

Responding to suggestions and ideas

8 Write out a full acceptance or rejection of someone's ideas, using the words in brackets.

Example
Let's go out to eat.
(idea) .....*That's a good idea!*.....

1 Do you fancy seeing the new film at the ABC cinema? I've heard it's full of exciting action.

(not keen) ....

2 I think we should go and tell him exactly what we think of him.

(not sure) ....

3 That's the best concert we've been to this year.

(wouldn't) ....

4 I think he's really a great player.

(agree) ....

5 What about all of us going to France for Christmas this year?

(go along) ....

6 I think our best bet would be to catch the earlier flight.

(exactly / think) ....

☐ 6

TOTAL ☐ 50

Test 6 (Units 11–12)

Grammar

Have something done

1 Mark the sentences which refer to a service (S) and those which emphasize the dramatic nature of an action (D).

1 She had her nose completely transformed by a plastic surgeon. ......

2 He actually has his meals cooked for him by the next door neighbour! ......

3 I had my bag stolen in London. ......

4 Could you possibly get that rubbish cleared away before next weekend? ......

5 I've had all my hopes destroyed. ......

☐ 5

2 Change these sentences, using *have something done*.

Example
He can't afford to pay someone else to paint his house; he has to do it himself.
He can't afford to have his house painted. ....

1 After the car accident a surgeon reconstructed the bones in her foot.

....

2 The dictator ordered his political rivals to be killed.

....

3 This virus has ruined the holidays of thousands of people.

....

4 The authorities say they will confiscate her passport if she causes any more trouble.

....

5 She pays someone to tidy up her garden once a year.

....

☐ 5

Question tags

3 Complete the sentences.

1 You couldn't wait a minute, ... ?

2 Oh, I see – so he's won the competition,
.... ?

3 Let's do it, ... ?

4 You're not Russian, ... ?

5 She really lost her temper, ... ?

6 He doesn't act like a student, ... ?

7 You speak Urdu, ... ?

8 For the last time – wash the car, ... ?

☐ 8

Reporting verbs

4 Use the words in brackets to complete the dialogue.

A Why did you choose to go to university in the end?

1 B (My friend / suggest) ....

....

A But didn't anybody else tell you it was a terrible place?

2 B (my father / warn / place) ....

....

A What happened when your father found out you'd failed your first term exams?

3 B (He / order / come home) ....

....

A And did you come home immediately?

4 B (I / tell / impossible) ....

....

A I bet he was annoyed by that.

5 B (I / explain / work / waiter / pay back / debts) ....

....

A Did that seem to satisfy him?

6 B (I / imply / no other choice) ....

....

A So what happened then?

7 B (I / beg / give me one last chance) ....

....

A And did he let you go back to complete the year?

8 B (Yes / but / advise / me / try / harder) ....

....

☐ 8

150   Test 6   Landmark Upper Intermediate © Oxford University Press   PHOTOCOPIABLE

Vocabulary

Prefixes

5 Add one of the prefixes from the box to complete the words in these sentences.

anti	multi	over	re	under

1 I think I've ....-done it this time – I'm exhausted.

2 She's really ....-talented – she can sing, dance, play the piano and juggle.

3 This steak is really ....-done – it's practically raw.

4 His work is such a mess I always end up ....-doing most of it myself.

5 This new ....-theft device should stop my car being stolen.

5

Compound nouns

6 Match the two parts to make compound nouns.

1	wedding	a	centre
2	food	b	anniversary
3	school	c	description
4	town	d	addiction
5	application	e	brush
6	job	f	meeting
7	tooth	g	form
8	summit	h	principal
9	drug	i	poisoning

9

Language in action

Likes, dislikes, preferences

7 Rewrite the sentences using the word in brackets.

1 I prefer beach holidays to mountain holidays.

   (rather) ....

2 I'm not really into classical literature.

   (thing) ....

3 I don't like learning languages.

   (keen) ....

4 I like going for long walks in the winter.

   (fond) ....

5 I really dislike our new neighbours.

   (stand) ....

5

Telephoning

8 Re-order the words to form sentences.

1 if to just moment hang like you'd one on ...

   ....
   ....

2 put to just I'll her through secretary you

   ....
   ....

3 to to is talk it the manager possible?

   ....
   ....

4 concerned for a can I message leave person the?

   ....
   ....

5 get possible soon will back somebody you to as as

   ....
   ....

5

TOTAL **50**

Test 1 key

1 1 c   3 b   5 c   7 c
   2 a   4 b   6 a   8 a

2 1 has been   6 agree
   2 am trying   7 has changed
   3 have been learning 8 get
   4 don't have   9 has
   5 spend

3 1 When I was a child I **used to** / (**knew**) know the capital city of virtually every country in the world.
   2 He **went** to school by bike every day when he **lived** in the old house down the road.
   3 After she **had** finished her homework she went out for a walk.
   4 The people leaving the party said goodbye and told me they **had had** a really good time.
   5 I **used** to believe in ghosts when I was younger, but not now.
   6 By the time she was twenty she was bored; she **had done** everything she ever wanted to do.
   7 When I was a child our New Year's parties were always the same; the entire family **got** together to sing songs.
   8 I **was cooking** the dinner when the phone rang.
   9 You're soaking wet! What **has** happened?
   10 But officer – I **was working** in Rome at the time of the murder!

4 1 She makes a lot of money.
   2 He made an excuse.
   3 I did some research into the background of the subject.
   4 He makes a good living from his business.
   5 I think you're making a mistake.
   6 Could you please do me a favour?
   7 We need to do some shopping.
   8 She made a complaint to the manager.
   9 The detective made notes while the victim talked to him.

5 1 with   6 see   11 think
   2 right   7 about   12 opinion
   3 along   8 but   13 like
   4 sure   9 so   14 word
   5 idea   10 rubbish

Test 2 key

1
	Can be followed by sentences
1 Instead of	a
2 However,	b
3 Despite	d
4 Rather than	a / c
5 In fact,	b
6 Whereas	f
7 On the other hand	b
8 Even though	e
9 While	f
10 Athough	e

2 1 b   3 a   5 c   7 b   9 c
   2 b   4 c   6 b   8 a   10 c

3 1 must   7 might
   2 has to   8 should
   3 might have   9 could have
   4 could   10 can't
   5 must   11 needn't
   6 must   12 have to

4 1 brought up   8 sipped
   2 reminded   9 gazed
   3 watched   10 nibbled
   4 favourite   11 threw
   5 grumpy   12 gave
   6 patient   13 cool
   7 given

5 1 What on earth is this?
   2 I'm always late for the simple reason that I don't have a watch.
   3 The main reason it was cancelled was because of the bad weather.
   4 Can you tell me exactly where you were?
   5 The only reason is, that it slipped my mind.

Test 3 key

1 1 If I knew the facts I could answer the question.
   2 I wish you wouldn't whistle early in the morning.
   3 I wish my flat wasn't so small.
   4 If she had worked harder at school she would have got a better paid job.
   5 If Dave has enough money he will go on holiday.
   6 I wish I hadn't met Tom.
   7 If you know the answer you should write it down.
   8 I wish I was fit.
   9 I wish the postman wouldn't leave my gate open.
   10 If Jane wins / gets one more point, she'll win the match.

2 1 d   2 c   3 a   4 e   5 b

3 1 5   2 2, 3   3 2   4 1

4 1 d   2 c   3 b   4 a

5 1 have been learning
   2 have finished
   3 have tried to learn
   4 have become
   5 is getting / gets
   6 have improved
   7 been reading
   8 have learned / learnt

6 1 roar   3 lead   5 trunk
   2 banned   4 saw   6 forth

7 1 passed away   4 thin on top
   2 bright   5 hard of hearing
   3 plump   6 in the head

8 1 joking   5 worse
   2 infuriating   6 making
   3 outrageous   7 getting me down
   4 idea

Test 4 key

1 1 Can I
2 was able to
3 'll be able to
4 wouldn't have been able to
5 can
6 could

2 1 The   4 the   7 The
2 (–)   5 a   8 (–)
3 A   6 a   9 an

3 1 whose   5 that / which
2 with whom   6 in which
3 (–) / that   7 from which
4 which   8 why

4 1 on earth   5 herself
2 indeed   6 did
3 am   7 does
4 really

5 1 obsessed with
2 fat
3 stubborn
4 stuffy
5 pushy
6 cheap
7 skinny
8 mad
9 macho
10 arrogant

6 1 I were you
2 thought
3 it would be
4 can I say
5 shouldn't you be

7 1 a   2 a   3 b   4 a   5 b

Test 5 key

1 1 She'll go out later on after she has cleaned the kitchen.
2 As soon as you arrive go to the bus station.
3 When I know the answer I'll ring you.
4 Nobody talks to him because they think he's strange.
5 She'll try and phone you before you leave work.
6 The moment I get home I will / I'll phone you I promise.

2 1 makes   3 lead   5 bring
2 result   4 caused

3 1 The streets were full of people shouting and screaming.
2 The government introduced wage limits provoking civil unrest.
3 The wind howled and whistled all night disturbing our sleep.
4 He wandered around the town not knowing where to go.
5 After finishing her homework she phoned her best friend.

4 1 He was said to be the richest man in Boreville when he announced his invention.
2 The new product was marketed all over the southern states.
3 The company was taken over in 1925.
4 It was decided to use its original name again.
5 Uglow was claimed to be the fifth biggest company in the United States.
6 It was separated into three companies.
7 It was closed down in 1984.

5 1 deserted   6 rich
2 obvious   7 give out
3 learned   8 uncooperative
4 leisure   9 takes part in
5 made for   10 clever

6 1 False   3 True   5 False
2 True   4 False

7 1 Would it be a good idea to go early?
2 Don't you think it'd be better to wait?
3 We could always try another place.
4 Why don't we just wait and see?
5 What about ringing him up now?
6 Have you thought of working harder?

8 1 I'm not keen on that idea / the ABC / action films.
2 I'm not sure we should do that / we should tell him / I agree / about that.
3 I wouldn't say that.
4 I agree with you.
5 I'd go along with that.
6 That's exactly what I think.

Test 6 key

1 1 S   2 D   3 D   4 S   5 D

2 1 After the car accident she had the bones in her foot reconstructed.
2 The dictator had his political rivals killed.
3 Thousands of people have had their holidays ruined.
4 She will have her passport confiscated if she causes any more trouble.
5 She has her garden tidied up once a year.

3 1 could you   5 didn't she
2 has he   6 does he
3 shall we   7 don't you
4 are you   8 will you

4 1 My friend suggested that it was a good place to go.
2 My father did warn / had warned me about the place.
3 He ordered me to come home immediately.
4 I told him it was impossible.
5 I explained that I was working as a waiter to pay back my debts.
6 I implied that I had no other choice.
7 I begged him to give me one more chance.
8 Yes, but he advised me to try harder.

5 1 over-done   4 re-doing
2 multi-talented   5 anti-theft
3 under-done

6 1 b   3 h   5 g   7 e   9 d
2 i   4 a   6 c   8 f

7 1 I'd rather go on a beach holiday than a mountain holiday.
2 Classical literature is not my thing (at all).
3 I'm not keen on learning languages.
4 I'm really fond of going for long walks in the winter.
5 I can't stand our new neighbours.

8 1 If you'd just like to hang on one moment …
2 I'll just put you through to her secretary.
3 Is it possible to talk to the manager?
4 Can I leave a message for the person concerned?
5 Somebody will get back to you as soon as possible.

Photocopiable materials

Teacher's notes

1 Taking risks maze   p.157
- Divide students into groups of three or four. Copy as many sets of cards as there are groups.
- Hand out Card 1 to each group. Students discuss the problem, decide which route they want to follow, and ask you for the appropriate card.
- Continue until all groups have reached a conclusion. There is one satisfactory outcome (Card 20), and other conclusions which ask students to re-think their decisions.

2 Past tenses practice   p.159
- Copy and cut the sheets in half.
- Hand out sheets to Students A and B. They answer their questions individually.
- Students work in pairs, and tell each other their answers. The other in the pair has to guess what the question was, and write it down.
- They check their guesses, then get further information about each other.

3 Feelings adjectives   p.160
- Copy a sheet for each student. Cut Part One from Part Two.
- Hand out Part One. Students complete the questionnaire, first for themselves, then by asking their partner, then by asking another student in the class. They can ask one student all the questions, or walk round the class asking a different student each question.
- Divide students into groups of three or four. Hand out Part Two.
- Students use the information they got in their questionnaire to answer the questions.
- Have brief whole class feedback on any interesting findings, if appropriate.

4 Link words   p.161
- Divide students into groups of four. Copy as many sets of cards as there are groups. Cut up the 'Say something about …' cards and keep in one set, and the 'Link words' cards and keep in another set.
- Hand out both sets to each group. They put them on the table, face down.
- The first student picks up a card from each pile, and tries to produce a sentence on the topic using the link word. The other students in the group decide if the sentence is grammatically acceptable. If it is, the student stays 'in'; if not, they are 'out'. If the student can't make a sentence, they drop out.
- Play continues round the group until only one player remains.

5 Suffix card game   p.162
- Divide students into groups of four. Copy as many sets of cards as there are groups. Cut up the 'stem' cards and keep in one set, and the 'suffix' cards and keep in another set.
- Hand out a set of stem cards to each group. They each take four, and do not show them to the others in the group. They leave the rest face down.
- Give each group a set of suffix cards, and put them face down.
- Students take it in turns to take a card from the suffix pile and read it out, then return it to the bottom of the pile. The others call out as fast as possible any possible words from one of their stem words and the suffix. (The student who reads the suffix cannot take part in that round.) The first student to get a correct answer discards the stem card, and picks up another from the pile.
- The next student takes a card and reads out the suffix. The winner of each round picks up another stem card until there are no stem cards left. They then simply discard a card each time they win.
- The winner is the first student to lose all their stem cards.

6 Personality questionnaire   p.163
- Copy a sheet for each student in the class.
- Hand out a sheet to each student. They work individually to complete Part One about their partner.
- Students compare their guesses in pairs, writing in the correct answers.
- Students mingle to find another person in the class who their partner has most in common with. (They have to ask about each other's partners, not about the person they talk to.)
- Open class feedback.

7 Third conditional story   p.164
- Divide students into pairs. Copy one sheet for each pair, and cut up the pictures.
- Hand out one set of pictures to each pair.
- Students put the sequence in order.
- When they have decided on a sequence, elicit the narrative from the whole class.
- Students then work in pairs to make as many third conditional sentences as they can, linking the pictures in the story, for example *If he hadn't gone to the party, he wouldn't have got home late.*
- Whole class feedback.

8 Phrasal verbs card game   p.165
- Divide students into groups of four. Copy as many sets of cards as there are groups. Cut up the 'verb' cards and keep in one set, and the 'particle' cards and keep in another set.
- Hand out a set of verb cards to each group. They each take four. They leave the rest face down.
- Give each group a set of particle cards, and put them face down.
- Students take it in turns to pick up a particle card and try

to form a phrasal verb using one of their verb cards. If they can form a verb, they discard their verb card.

- The other students in the group may challenge the student to explain the meaning of the phrasal verb they have formed. If they can explain it correctly, they get another turn. If they can't, they pick up another verb card.
- The winner is the first student to lose all their verb cards.

9 Find someone who …   p.166
- Copy a sheet for each student.
- Give each student a sheet, and follow one of these three procedures.
- Either allocate one question to each student. They ask a number of other students in the class, taking notes as necessary.
- Feedback, whole class.
- Or each student asks all ten questions to one other student.
- Feedback, whole class.
- Or each student asks all ten questions, but to a different student each time.
- Feedback, whole class.

10 Board game   p.167
- Divide students into groups of four or five. Copy one board, one set of instructions, and a set of cards for each group. Cut up the cards and divide them into four sets.
- Hand out a board, a dice, and a set of cards to each group. Give each person in the group a counter (or they could use a coin).
- Students take it in turns to throw the dice, move the appropriate number of squares and follow the instructions. The winner is the first player to reach FINISH.

11 Travel brochures   p.169
- Divide students into groups of three. Copy one sheet for each student.
- Hand out sheets. Students work together to guess where each place is, then decide between themselves which place they would like to visit.
- Check answers.

Answers

1	Nepal	7	Ibiza
2	Uzbekistan	8	Mediterranean cruise
3	Tanzania	9	Hong Kong
4	Morocco	10	Australia
5	New Mexico, USA	11	South Pacific – Fiji or Tahiti
6	Peru		

- Form new groups of three. Students now work through question 3 together.
- Feedback, whole class.

12 Cut-up story   p.170
- Make one copy of the page and cut it into 15 strips.
- Hand out one strip per student. (If the class has fewer than 15 students, give some students more than one strip. If the class has more than 15 and does not comfortably divide into two smaller groups, then appoint the remaining students as monitors for this activity.)
- Students memorize the sentence on their strip. When they are sure they can remember it, they give it back to you. Keep a note of who had which sentence as you may need to help or prompt.
- When they have all memorized their sentence, students work together to put the story in order. If there are monitors in the group, they should help and make suggestions as necessary.
- When they have decided the sequence, students form a line in chronological order. Everyone says their sentence aloud in turn.

13 Famous frauds   p.171
- Make one copy of both sheets for each student.
- Hand out Part One. Students work in pairs and decide which stories interest them.
- Hand out Part Two. In pairs, students match the quotes with the extracts.
- Check answers.

Answers

1	d	3	e	5	j	7	f	9	c	11	l	13	g
2	k	4	n	6	l	8	m	10	h	12	b	14	a

- Students form new groups or pairs and discuss the stories they found interesting.
- Whole class feedback, if appropriate.

14 Hobbies questionnaire   p.173
- Make one copy of the sheet for each student. Cut Part One and Two.
- Hand out Part One. Students work in pairs, and complete the questionnaire for each other. They then guess the hobby described.
- They check their guesses with their partner. You could display the questionnaires on the wall at this stage and get students to guess who each one refers to.
- Divide students into groups of up to eight students. Hand out Part Two. Students take it in turns to lead a discussion on each question.
- Whole class feedback if appropriate.

15 Prefix card game   p.174
- Divide students into groups of three, four or five. Copy as many sets of cards as there are groups. Cut up the 'word' cards and keep in one set, and the 'prefix' cards and keep in another set.
- Hand out a set of prefix cards to each group. They each take four.
- Give each group a set of word cards, and put them face down.

- Students take it in turns to turn over a word card. The first student to call out a word using the word on the card and one of their prefixes gets a point. If they can use the word correctly in a sentence they get another point. If someone calls a wrong answer they lose a point. The word card is put aside.
- When all the word cards have been used, the winner is the student with the most points.

16 Reporting verbs   p.175

- Divide students into pairs. Copy as many sheets as there are pairs, and cut them in half.
- Hand out one part to Student A, the other to Student B. Individually, they complete as much of the story as they can.
- They then work in pairs to complete the story.
- Check answers.

Answers

When she got home late Nicola explained to the surprised Robert that she had been delayed by the roadworks in Mill Road. But Robert was still suspicious. 'I wouldn't lie if I were you,' he advised her. 'But it's the truth!' Nicola insisted. 'You've been out with your friends again,' Robert said accusingly. 'I haven't!' denied Nicola. 'If I find out you've been lying again there'll be trouble,' warned Robert. he immediately rang Nicola's best friend Hannah and she confirmed that Nicola hadn't been with her that night. But Robert was still angry. 'Get out of here!' he ordered. He made another phone call, this time to his own best friend Sam. Sam claimed to have seen her with a group of friends in a restaurant near her work place. 'OK, I did go there,' she admitted, 'but only for a few minutes.' She acknowledged that perhaps it hadn't been the best thing to do in the circumstances, but that she was free to do whatever she wanted. An hour later Robert realized his mistake. 'Please, please stay,' he begged. Nicola continued packing her suitcase. She told him to stop making a fool of himself. 'I think this relationship is over,' she said as she closed the door behind her.

- Students work in pairs to change direct speech into reported speech, and reported speech into direct speech.
- Check answers.

Possible answers

When she got home late Nicola explained to the surprised Robert, 'I was delayed by the roadworks in Mill Road'. But Robert was still suspicious. He advised her not to lie to him. Nicola insisted it was the truth Robert accused her of going out with her friends again. Nicola denied that she had. Robert warned her that if he found out she was lying again, there would be trouble. He immediately rang Nicola's best friend Hannah and she said, 'Nicola hasn't been with me tonight.' But Robert was still angry. He ordered her to get out of there. He made another phone call, this time to his own best friend Sam. Sam said 'I saw her with a group of friends in a restaurant near her work place.' She admitted she had been there, but only for a few minutes. She said 'Perhaps it wasn't the best thing to do in the circumstances, but I am free to do whatever I want.' An hour later Robert realized his mistake. He begged her to stay. Nicola continued packing her suitcase. She said 'Stop making a fool of yourself.' She said she thought the relationship was over as she closed the door behind her.

- Students turn over their sheets and act out the conversation from memory.

17 Compounds crosswords   p.176

- Divide students into pairs. Copy as many sheets as there are pairs, and cut them in half.
- Hand out a different crossword to each student in the pair. Explain that the clues for each crossword are different parts of the same compound words.
- They work individually to see how many of the compounds they can guess, and fill in the answers on their crossword.
- When they have done as much as they can individually, they should ask each other questions to find any words they can't guess.

1 Taking risks maze

You and a group of your closest friends – Amanda, Jerry and Chris – are all trying to decide on what kind of holiday to go on together. Amanda suggests an activity holiday. What do you say?

A You're not sure. You want to get more information.
▶ **Go to 16**

B Absolutely not. Activity is work, not a holiday.
▶ **Go to 8**

1

You tell the others you've had enough of all this. You just want to find a solution or compromise to the original idea. What happens next?

A Jerry and Chris tell you that you're shouting more than anyone. They decide to go off on a nice, quiet, safe holiday together.
▶ **Go to 17**

B Everyone calms down but asks you what you suggest as an alternative.
▶ **Go to 18**

2

You think it might be better for you to go on holiday with different combinations of people, rather than all together. Who will it be?

A You with Amanda.
▶ **Go to 14**

B You with Jerry and Chris, with Amanda there just for part of it.
▶ **Go to 9**

3

Jerry announces that he has a bad back.

A You think it's just an excuse – he's always been scared of taking any physical risks.
▶ **Go to 10**

B You try to persuade him that he needn't do the most physically difficult things.
▶ **Go to 15**

4

Jerry and Chris whisper together for a while and finally decide that the whole thing is just too dangerous. You go on holiday with Amanda and have a good time, though Amanda breaks her leg on the last day trying to do a parachute jump off a cliff. Jerry and Chris visit her in hospital but keep saying 'We told you it was risky,' until she asks them to leave. The whole group sees less and less of each other. This is a possible conclusion to the maze but not a very good one. Go back to number **1** and see if you can find a better one.

5

Chris calms down and listens to what you have to say. She decides that maybe she could manage a 15-minute slow walk in the forest every day but nothing more dangerous than that.

A Amanda gets angry and tells Chris that she's useless.
▶ **Go to 19**

B Jerry says he'd like to do only one short walk a day as well.
▶ **Go to 10**

6

Jerry and Chris get annoyed and complain that you don't seem to care about what they want to do.

A You tell them they're adults and can make up their own minds. You don't all have to go together anyway.
▶ **Go to 5**

B You ignore them and just keep repeating, 'I'm going.'
▶ **Go to 12**

7

Amanda admits that it would be a very active two weeks, with at least one compulsory activity every day.

A You tell Amanda that she's trying to force you all to do something you might hate.
▶ **Go to 19**

B You decide that just one compulsory activity wouldn't be too bad. It's the others' problem if they don't all want to go.
▶ **Go to 7**

8

Jerry smiles and says, 'Great idea. Let's start packing our suitcases now.' You say, 'Don't forget to pack your cold weather clothes. The mountains are very high.'
▶ **Go to 15**

9

You keep calm and explain that the whole idea of an activity holiday is to be active and to try different activities. Jerry then asks if there could possibly be a compromise.

A You decide to change the original idea and consider some non-active things.
▶ **Go to 18**

B You lose your temper. 'Don't you want to try something interesting and new for once in your life!' you shout at Jerry and Chris.
▶ **Go to 2**

10

Amanda says it will cost quite a lot but there are qualified instructors, a good variety of exciting activities and no chance to get bored – every day is full of things that people have always wanted to learn how to do but never had the chance.

A You think it might not be a very relaxing way to spend a holiday.
▶ **Go to 8**

B You realize Jerry and Chris are much less active than Amanda. This could cause major problems on holiday.
▶ **Go to 3**

11

Jerry says, 'Well if you won't even discuss it let's cancel the whole idea.' You go on holiday with Amanda but feel bad about the way it was eventually decided. You never see Jerry and Chris again. This is a possible end to the maze, but not a very good one. Go back to number **1** and see if you can reach a better conclusion.

12

Chris angrily gets up to leave. 'I've had enough of this,' she says.

A You apologize. You explain that you're trying to sort things out.
▶ **Go to 6**

B You explain calmly that you just think it wouldn't work if all of you went together.
▶ **Go to 14**

C You say, 'Well, leave then,' and she starts shouting at you.
▶ **Go to 2**

13

You tell Amanda that you think it might be better for you and her to go on the holiday alone. Jerry and Chris would just complain all the time that it was all too tiring, dangerous, cold and new.

A You suggest that Jerry and Chris might go for the first two days to try it, then if they don't like it they can leave.
▶ **Go to 15**

B Jerry gets upset and says he thinks it's all too risky. You remind him that he's 28 years old and he can decide for himself.
▶ **Go to 2**

14

Jerry seems quite happy with this. But Chris starts crying and says she'd prefer a nice warm beach holiday.

A You tell her then she should just go on one alone.
▶ **Go to 13**

B You try to persuade her to change her mind.
▶ **Go to 6**

15

Amanda says it's an all-action holiday in a mountainous area 500 miles away. The holiday includes rock-climbing, parachuting, hunting, white-water rafting, etc.

A You want to know if all these activities are compulsory.
▶ **Go to 8**

B You jump at the chance. An active two weeks is just what you need to liven up your life.
▶ **Go to 4**

C You would like more information about all this.
▶ **Go to 11**

16

Jerry and Chris go off together for a camping holiday in a nice safe place ten miles from your town. You go on the holiday with Amanda but decide the holiday is too active for you, and you leave after one week, exhausted. You and Amanda never see Jerry and Chris again and the group of friends breaks up. You lose touch with everyone. Not a very satisfactory conclusion. Go back to number **1** and see if you can reach a better end to the maze.

17

You suggest that the first week could be mainly adventure or activity-based, with the second week being more restful, possibly by the sea near the mountains. Everybody agrees.
▶ **Go to 20**

18

Everyone starts shouting at everyone else angrily. You realize that this is all pointless.

A You start to think it might be better just to give up the whole idea.
▶ **Go to 2**

B You try to calm everyone down.
▶ **Go to 3**

19

Amanda especially enjoys the first week, but is so exhausted that she's quite ready for a week of relaxation afterwards. Jerry's back improves fast with his daily walk, Chris learns not to be frightened of rabbits and nature in general and you have a great couple of weeks. Your group of friends comes back feeling more positive about each other. A good end to the maze!

20

2 Past tenses practice

Student A

1 **Answer the questions for yourself.**
2 **Tell your partner your answers. They have to guess the question.**
3 **Find out some more information about your partner.**

1 What were you doing between 7 and 8 p.m. yesterday?

2 What two things did you do regularly when you were ten years old that you don't do now?

3 What did you do after you'd finished your dinner last night?

4 Where did you go for your last holiday?

5 When was the last time you were exhausted? Why?

6 When you entered the classroom today, what were two of the other people doing?

Student B

1 **Answer the questions for yourself.**
2 **Tell your partner your answers. They have to guess the question.**
3 **Find out some more information about your partner.**

1 How was your life different when you were five years old? Think about things you used to do regularly.

2 What two things did you do last weekend?

3 What did you do on your last birthday?

4 When did you last get annoyed about something? What was it about?

5 When was the last time you laughed a lot, and what you caused you to?

6 What exactly were you doing at 6 p.m. yesterday?

3 Feelings adjectives

Part One

Answer these questions.

	You	Your partner	Another student
1 What's the most terrifying experience you've ever had?			
2 What's the most incredible thing you've heard recently?			
3 Do you find it scary walking home alone late at night?			
4 What's the most embarrassing thing that's happened to you (or to someone you know) in the last year?			
5 Where is the most awe-inspiring scenery that you've ever seen?			
6 What's the most thrilling film you've ever seen?			
7 What sounds horrendous to you about the future?			
8 Do you know any horrifying statistics?			
9 Have you ever had an exciting holiday? Where?			
10 Name three things that you find frightening.			
11 Name one appalling book, film or piece of music.			
12 What's the most brilliant work of art you've ever seen/read/heard?			

Part Two

Now work in groups. Use your answers from the questionnaire to find out how many people in the class:

1 don't like the dark.
2 have been more impressed by scenery in other countries than in their own.
3 have answered a question with the name of the same film, book, piece of music, or work of art.
4 don't mind being out late at night.
5 agree on the worst prospect about the future.
6 can't think of a surprising statistic.
7 have been embarrassed when with friends.
8 have answered a question with the name of the same place.

4 Link words

Say something about ... cards

your daily routine	a member of your family	the future of television	your home
the future of your town/city/country	your last holiday	your feelings about pets	computers
modern life	the weather today	your best friend	someone you really dislike
your appearance	relaxation	fast food	cars and transport

Link cards

although	even though	however	in fact
in spite of	despite	instead of	rather than
whereas	but	not	on the other hand

5 Suffix card game

Stem cards

associate	invent	explode	include
communicate	infect	react	regulate
modern	hospital	private	industry
popular	fame	adventure	humour
mystery	nerve	religion	compete
teach	nature	profession	person

Suffix cards

+ ion	+ ize	+ ous	+ ly
+ er	+ al	+ ive	

6 Personality questionnaire

Part One

How much do you know about your partner? Guess the answers to these questions about them.

1 Their perfect weekend would be _____

_____

2 If they inherited a lot of money they'd _____

_____

3 They worry about _____

_____

4 They like _____

_____

5 They dislike _____

_____

6 They think children _____

_____

7 Their favourite kind of pet would be _____

_____

8 Their favourite type of holiday is _____

_____

9 At the weekend they _____

_____

10 At parties they _____

_____

Part Two

1 When you have written your guesses, check your answers with your partner. If you got an answer wrong, write in the correct one.
2 Now go around the class and find out about other people's partners. Find out who your partner has most in common with.

Landmark Upper Intermediate © Oxford University Press PHOTOCOPIABLE

8 Phrasal verbs card game

Verb cards

bring	make	take	break	go
come	bring	make	take	go
come	break	bring	make	take
go	come	break		

Particle cards

up	down	in	out	off
away	round	up	down	away
off	in	out	round	up

9 Find someone who . . .

1 could ride a bike when they were five years old.

2 has never been able to understand how some people can lie on a beach for a two-week holiday.

3 thinks they'll probably learn to drive some time during the next two years.

4 has never managed to go out every night for a week.

5 can speak more than three languages well.

6 thinks they could possibly be a millionaire one day.

7 can't stay out at night as late as they'd like to.

8 can be moody at times.

9 would like to be able to travel more.

10 has never succeeded in using a computer successfully.

10 Board game

START	**1** Say a true sentence about your father. Include the word *what*.	**2** What's another word for …?	**3** Do you have more than two brothers? Yes/No	**4** Say a true sentence about a female relative. Include the word *whose*.	**5** What's another word for …?
11 What's another word for …?	**10** **True or False?** Your aunt	**9** Do you see any members of your family more than once a week? Yes/No	**8** What's another word for …?	**7** Say a true sentence about your aunt. Include the word *where*.	**6** **True or False?** Your mother
12 Do any members of your family live in another country? Yes/No	**13** Say a true sentence about your grandparents. Include the word *why*.	**14** **True or False?** Your youngest relative	**15** What's another word for …?	**16** Say a true sentence about your uncle. Include the word *what*.	**17** Have you ever spent longer than one year without seeing a brother or sister? Yes/No
23 Do you have any living relative older than 80 years of age? Yes/No	**22** **True or False?** Your furthest relative (geographically)	**21** Say a true sentence about your family. Include the word *that*.	**20** Do you think a big family is nicer than a small one? Yes/No	**19** What's another word for …?	**18** **True or False?** Your oldest relative
24 What's another word for …?	**25** Say a true sentence about a brother-in-law. Include the word *whose*.	**26** Have you ever lied to your parents? Yes/No	**27** **True or False?** Your grandmother	**28** What's another word for …?	**29** Would you prefer to have a daughter to a son? Yes/No
FINISH	**34** Say a true sentence about a cousin. Include the word *who*.	**33** **True or False?** Your favourite relative	**32** What's another word for …?	**31** **True or False?** Your nearest relative (geographically)	**30** Say a true sentence about your family. Include the word *which*.

Instructions. If you land on a . . .

Word prompt square - make a true sentence using the word prompts. If the other players agree it is grammatically correct, move **forward two** spaces.

True/False square - make a true or false sentence about the person on the square. If a majority of the other players guess correctly whether your sentence is True or False, move **back one** space. If they don't guess correctly, move **forward one** space. Be honest!

Yes/No square - answer the question **Yes** or **No**, then take a **Yes** or **No** card and follow the instructions.

What's another word for . . . square - pick up a **What's another word for . . .** card. If you can give another word for the word on the card, move **forward one** space.

Yes Move back two spaces	**Yes** Throw a six to continue	**Yes** Miss a turn	**Yes** Go back to the start
Yes Go forward to the next Yes/No square and answer the question	**Yes** Move back to the last True/False space and answer the question	**Yes** Move forward to the next What's another word for . . . square and answer the question	**Yes** Throw the dice again and move back the number of squares you throw
No Move forward two spaces	**No** Throw a one to continue	**No** Take another turn	**No** Go back to the start
No Go forward to the next What's another word for ... square and answer the question	**No** Move forward to the next Word Prompt square and answer the question	**No** Move back to the last True/False square and answer the question	**No** Throw the dice again and move forward that number of squares
your brother's wife **another word**	your sister's daughter **another word**	your mother's aunt **another word**	your brother's son **another word**
your uncle's children **another word**	your grandmother's father **another word**	your son's daughter **another word**	the second of three children **another word**
your aunt's sister **another word**	the first of four children **another word**	your husband's parents **another word**	a child with no brothers or sisters **another word**

11 Travel brochures

Work in groups of three.

1 Read these extracts. Where do you think these places are?
2 Choose ONE place which all three of you would like to visit.

a This country contains the highest point on earth - Mount Everest. Our holiday combines amazing mountain walks with trips to jungles where tigers still live - only a day's journey away. The variety of the wildlife and the friendliness of the villagers will make this a holiday to remember forever. But remember - you need to be fit and healthy for this trip.

b This is a scenic trek, visiting the valleys of the Pamirs. The holiday includes an excursion to ancient Samarkand and a visit to Tashkent. This is one of the wildest inhabited places on earth, with ancient cultures that connect back to the Persian emperors. A mixture of history and challenging valley walks is available in this wonderful country.

c Climb Africa's highest mountain, then go on safari to see a rich variety of wildlife. The Serengeti Plains are a relaxing break after the mountain climb, and you can take close-up photos of lions, cheetahs, rhinos and giraffes.

d A place on the edge of the biggest desert in the world, this country is a contrast of rocky mountains, forests and oases of palm trees. Nomadic shepherds, camels, exotic markets where you can haggle for a cheaper price, and a final day in Marrakech.

e The first half of this trip is to the greatest and most famous canyon in the world. You can visit ancient Navajo and Hopi Indian cliff dwellings, ride horses in the National Parks, then contrast it all with a visit to the gambling capital of the world.

f This is the most beautiful trek in the Andes. It takes you along the Inca Trail from Cuzco through mountains and jungle to the lost city of Machu Picchu. White-water rafting, horse-riding and mountain walks are all available in this wonderful country.

g The best place in the world if you're young and love going to clubs and dancing all night to loud music. Not only the best island in the Mediterranean but one of the most beautiful in the world, it's perfect for partying all night then hiring a car and getting away from it all to quiet beaches on the other side of the island. Big-name DJs work here all summer.

h For the young at heart but also for those who want to save their energy. A quiet cruise round the ancient cities of this most varied and ancient of seas. Ancient Rome, Ancient Greece, Byzantine castles - all are here for you to enjoy at your leisure, carried from one to the next in absolute luxury.

i After 150 years of British rule, this unique part of Asia has returned to Chinese rule. It is an exciting, dynamic place where tradition and modernity co-exist. Skyscrapers, crowds, and noise on one side, with temples, floating restaurants and markets on the other. Something for everyone who loves life and colour.

j From the Great Barrier Reef and its excellent diving opportunities to journeys across empty desert by 4-wheel drive vehicle, this huge country has everything. The coast has some of the best beaches in the world (and the most sharks!) while inland there are sometimes hundred of kilometres between tiny towns. More kangaroos in one day than you would see in a thousand zoos.

k The warm waters of the biggest ocean in the world offer the holiday of a lifetime in these islands of white beaches and secret, unspoilt corners. A tropical paradise with thousands of kilometres in any direction before you reach the nearest land in Australia or New Zealand.

3 Work in a different group. Choose the best holiday for these people, then tell the rest of your class what you have decided.
  a Two 20-year-old friends. They love the outdoor life, sports, wildlife. They like to keep moving and are easily bored.
  b A 73-year old couple who enjoy spending all their savings.
  c Three 18-year-old girls whose parents are happy for them to have holidays where there are other young people. They find home boring, and go out as often as possible. Love parties, crowds.
  d A fluent Arabic-speaker (as a foreign language) with a husband who loves shopping - any kind of shopping. She prefers exploring the countryside and meeting the locals.
  e A history teacher and his son. They have a particular interest in ancient civilizations and want to practise their Spanish.

12 Cut-up story

Alex Burton first became interested in the Loch Ness monster at the age of 16.

He was on holiday with his family in Scotland at the time.

Halfway through the holiday they were having a picnic on the shores of Loch Ness.

He had just finished eating when he saw a huge creature swim across the water.

He immediately told his parents but they had seen nothing.

He stayed alone, watching the lake, for two more hours but he didn't see it again.

After the holiday he rang his local newspaper.

A journalist came to his house and asked him lots of questions.

Alex described everything he had seen and a story appeared in the paper a week later.

As a result, a news editor from the national TV station invited him to appear on television.

Alex was nervous but he tried to ignore the cameras and described the monster again.

As a result of his TV appearance a Professor of Zoology wrote and told him he had described exactly a prehistoric creature known as a *Trefaksemon*.

Alex was very excited and told his parents about the Professor's letter.

His father pointed out that *Trefaksemon* was 'monster fake' with the letters rearranged.

Alex was so disappointed that he never talked to anyone about it again, nor about the UFOs that landed in his garden every night.

13 Famous frauds

Part 1

Work in pairs. Read these extracts. Which stories do you know something about? Which would you like to know more about?

1 The Roswell Alien
Fifty years ago an alien being was captured in the deserts of New Mexico in the United States. Scientists examined it and took photographs. This is the incredible story of the discovery of the century.

2 Tom Keating - painter extraordinary
He was the greatest forger of them all. He painted perfect versions of famous paintings and made a fortune from them. But in the end he was discovered …

3 Elvis lives
Since his death in 1977, Elvis Presley has been sighted hundreds of times in hundreds of places world-wide, from supermarkets to football crowds. Here is proof that he still lives today.

4 War of the Worlds
People all over America started to panic - an alien invasion force was on its way to destroy Earth! They hadn't realized it was only Orson Welles' masterly and realistic radio play …

5 The Loch Ness Monster
Countless people have personally witnessed an enormous creature in this Scottish lake. Is it a prehistoric monster? A dinosaur? A submarine? This book gives the real answer.

6 The Cottingley Fairies
A 1917 photograph clearly shows a girl looking at fairies dancing in her garden. It was the first photo ever taken of these strange beings. But fifty years later, two old ladies revealed the truth …

7 Anthony Moreno
Mr Moreno, from Spain, had 197 families and 3000 children to claim social security benefits for - all of them invented. He eventually retired to Spain, having obtained more than $5 million from the French social security system. This is his true story.

8 Computer Fraud
Stanley Rifkin was arrested in California in 1978 and charged with defrauding a Los Angeles bank of $10.2 million. He was a computer expert who …

9 Life and Death
In 1916 a soldier died in the First World War. This account by his father shows how humans can survive after death and communicate with the living. A moving and amazing story.

10 Ossian's Fingal
In 1760 a Scottish writer published poems which he claimed were by the third century poet Ossian. He was never able to produce the originals, but for more than thirty years many people believed an incredible discovery had been made …

11 Round the World?
Nearly thirty years ago Donald Crowhurst was in a round-the-world yacht race when he decided to lie about his real position. He managed to convince everyone that he'd sailed around the world and was about to win the greatest yacht race in history. Then disaster and madness struck …

12 The Zinoviev Letter
A prominent influence in the 1917 Russian revolution, Zinoviev was accused of writing a letter encouraging British communists to rise against their government. But did he really write the letter or was it forged by his enemies?

13 The Turin Shroud
Does the famous cloth show the face of Jesus Christ? Is it old enough to be the original? Or is it just a fake only a few hundred years old? Find out the truth.

14 UFOs
Governments all around the world have kept secret thousands of sightings of lights and spacecraft in the sky which have no explanation. This book investigates many of these secret files and comes to some alarming conclusions.

Famous frauds

Part Two

Match each of these quotes to the right extract in Part One. Then find someone else in the class who is interested in the same stories as you and tell each other what you think.

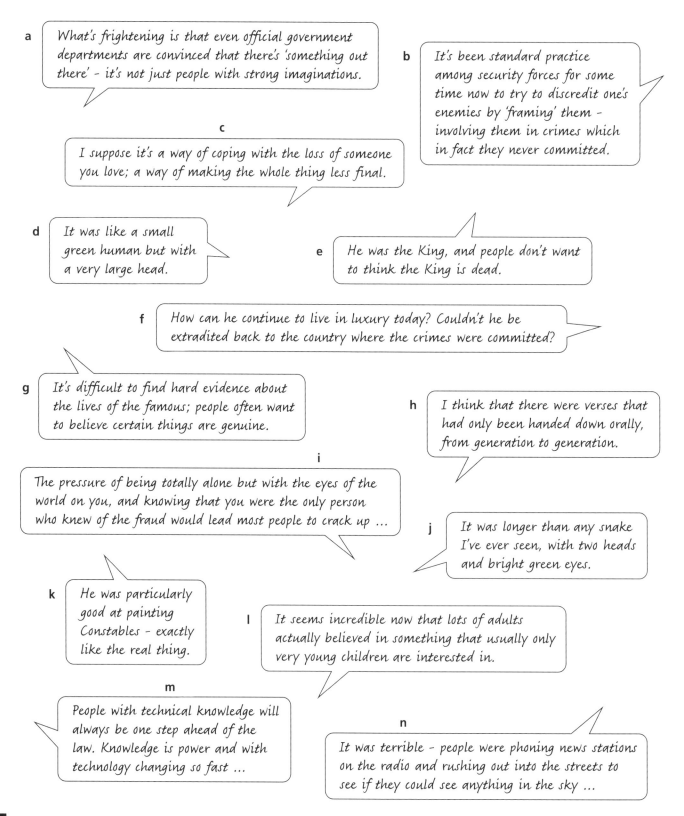

a What's frightening is that even official government departments are convinced that there's 'something out there' – it's not just people with strong imaginations.

b It's been standard practice among security forces for some time now to try to discredit one's enemies by 'framing' them – involving them in crimes which in fact they never committed.

c I suppose it's a way of coping with the loss of someone you love; a way of making the whole thing less final.

d It was like a small green human but with a very large head.

e He was the King, and people don't want to think the King is dead.

f How can he continue to live in luxury today? Couldn't he be extradited back to the country where the crimes were committed?

g It's difficult to find hard evidence about the lives of the famous; people often want to believe certain things are genuine.

h I think that there were verses that had only been handed down orally, from generation to generation.

i The pressure of being totally alone but with the eyes of the world on you, and knowing that you were the only person who knew of the fraud would lead most people to crack up …

j It was longer than any snake I've ever seen, with two heads and bright green eyes.

k He was particularly good at painting Constables – exactly like the real thing.

l It seems incredible now that lots of adults actually believed in something that usually only very young children are interested in.

m People with technical knowledge will always be one step ahead of the law. Knowledge is power and with technology changing so fast …

n It was terrible – people were phoning news stations on the radio and rushing out into the streets to see if they could see anything in the sky …

14 Hobbies Questionnaire

Part One

Ask your partner questions to find out the answers to these questions, then guess the hobby.

1 Do you think people who spend a lot of time and money on their hobbies or particular interests are

- [ ] **a** strange?
- [ ] **b** understandable?
- [ ] **c** probably normal people?

2 Do you have a hobby or particular interest yourself?

- [ ] **a** No, but I used to.
- [ ] **b** Yes.

3 Do / did you ever feel this interest or hobby is / was taking up too much of your time, and could be unhealthy for you socially?

- [ ] **a** Yes.
- [ ] **b** No.

4 How much time do / did you usually spend on this?

- [ ] **a** Less than 1 hour per week.
- [ ] **b** A few hours a week.
- [ ] **c** A few hours a day.

5 Is / was it an expensive hobby?

- [ ] **a** No - almost free.
- [ ] **b** I can/could afford it quite easily.
- [ ] **c** It uses/used up most of my spare money.

6 Does / did this interest involve other people?

- [ ] **a** Yes.
- [ ] **b** No.
- [ ] **c** Sometimes.

7 Is / was it an indoor or outdoor hobby?

- [ ] **a** Indoor.
- [ ] **b** Outdoor.
- [ ] **c** Both.

8 Is / was it dangerous?

- [ ] **a** Yes.
- [ ] **b** No.
- [ ] **c** Sometimes.

9 Does / did it involve collecting something?

- [ ] **a** Yes.
- [ ] **b** No.

10 Do / did other people think it is / was a strange or unusual thing to do?

- [ ] **a** Yes.
- [ ] **b** No.

Now try to guess your partner's hobby or interest and write it down here. _____

Part Two

Take turns to lead discussions on these topics.

1 Would you ever consider doing a hobby that was dangerous?
2 Would you ever consider doing a hobby that took up more than two hours a day?
3 What different categories could you divide hobbies and interests into?
4 What sort of hobby could you never imagine getting yourself into?
5 Do men and women tend to have different hobbies? Do more men than women have serious hobbies?
6 How would you decide that your or someone else's hobby had 'gone too far'?
7 What's the strangest hobby or interest you've ever heard of?
8 If a hobby or interest causes no harm to anyone else, should people be allowed to do anything?

15 Prefix card game

Word cards

efficiency	experienced	appropriate	approve
agree	agreeable	appear	cooked
charged	paid	booked	dressed
wind	do	type	take
understand	placed	decisive	management

Prefix cards

in-	dis-	over-	re-
mis-	un-	dis-	over-
re-	mis-	in-	un-
over-	re-	mis-	dis-
un-	in-	re-	in-

16 Reporting verbs

Student A

You and Student B have slightly different versions of a story.

1 Complete the story with single words or whole phrases.
2 Ask your partner for help. Where you both have the same gaps, work together to find the answer.
3 When you have a complete version of the story, change any direct speech into reported speech, and change any reported speech into direct speech.
4 Finally, turn over your sheets and try to recreate the dialogue from memory.

When she got home late Nicola _____ to the surprised Robert that she _____ by the roadworks in Mill Road. But Robert was still suspicious. 'I wouldn't lie _____ ,' he advised her. 'But it's the truth!' Nicola _____. 'You _____ out with your friends again,' Robert said accusingly. 'I haven't!' _____ Nicola. 'If I find out you've been lying again _____ trouble,' warned Robert. He immediately rang Nicola's best friend Hannah and she _____ that Nicola _____ (not) with her that night. But Robert was still angry. 'Get out of here!' he ordered. He made another phone call, this time to his own best friend Sam. Sam _____ _____ Nicola with a group of friends in a restaurant near her work place. 'OK, I _____ go there,' she admitted, 'but only for a few minutes.' She _____ that perhaps it _____ (not) the best thing to do in the circumstances, but that she _____ free to do whatever she wanted. An hour later Robert realized his mistake. 'Please, please stay,' he begged. Nicola continued packing her suitcase. She _____ him to stop making a fool of himself. 'I think this relationship is over,' she said as she closed the door behind her.

✂ -

Student B

You and Student A have slightly different versions of a story.

1 Complete the story with single words or whole phrases.
2 Ask your partner for help. Where you both have the same gaps, work together to find the answer.
3 When you have a complete version of the story, change any direct speech into reported speech, and change any reported speech into direct speech.
4 Finally, turn over your sheets and try to recreate the dialogue from memory.

When she got home late Nicola explained to the surprised Robert that she _____ by the roadworks in Mill Road. But Robert was still suspicious. 'I wouldn't lie _____ ,' he _____ her. 'But it's the truth!' Nicola insisted. 'You _____ out with your friends again,' Robert said _____ly. 'I haven't!' denied Nicola. 'If I find out you've been lying again _____ trouble,' _____ Robert. He immediately rang Nicola's best friend Hannah and she confirmed that Nicola _____ (not) with her that night. But Robert was still angry. 'Get out of here!' he _____. He made another phone call, this time to his own best friend Sam. Sam claimed _____ Nicola with a group of friends in a restaurant near her work place. 'OK, I _____ go there,' she _____, 'but only for a few minutes.' She acknowledged that perhaps it _____ (not) the best thing to do in the circumstances, but that she _____ free to do whatever she wanted. An hour later Robert realized his mistake . 'Please, please stay,' he _____. Nicola continued packing her suitcase. She told him _____ making a fool of himself. 'I _____ this relationship is over,' she said as she closed the door behind her.

17 Compounds crossword

Crossword 1

Clues

Across
1. _____ meeting (6 letters)
2. long ____ (4 letters)
3. food _____ (9 letters)
6. _____ web (7 letters)
9. ____ office (4 letters)
10. newspaper _____ (13 letters)
12. short ____ (4 letters)
13. wedding ___ (3 letters)
14. ___ driver (3 letters)
15. _____ brush (5 letters)

Down
1. drug _____ (8 letters)
4. town _____ (6 letters)
5. _____ form (11 letters)
7. _____ weight (5 letters)
8. goal _____ (6 letters)
11. national ____ (4 letters)
16. green _____ (5 letters)

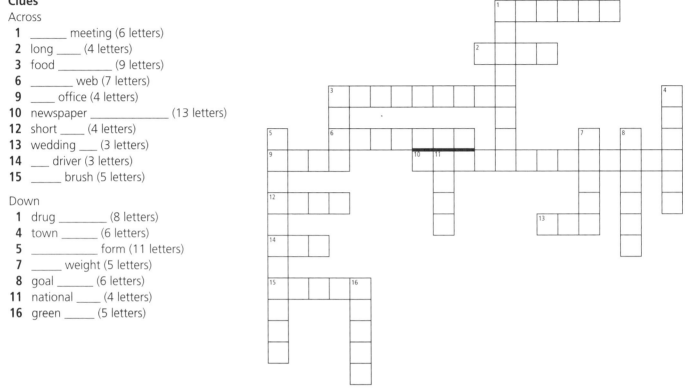

Crossword 2

Clues

Across
2. post _____ (6 letters)
4. application ____ (4 letters)
6. _____ house (5 letters)
7. _____ day (7 letters)
9. tooth _____ (5 letters)
11. ____ jump (4 letters)
13. heavy _____ (6 letters)
14. _____ debt (8 letters)
15. car _____ (6 letters)

Down
1. ____ centre (4 letters)
3. ____ poisoning (4 letters)
5. summit _____ (7 letters)
6. ____ keeper (4 letters)
7. spider's ___ (3 letters)
8. ____ list (5 letters)
10. ____ smuggler (4 letters)
12. _____ advertisement (9 letters)

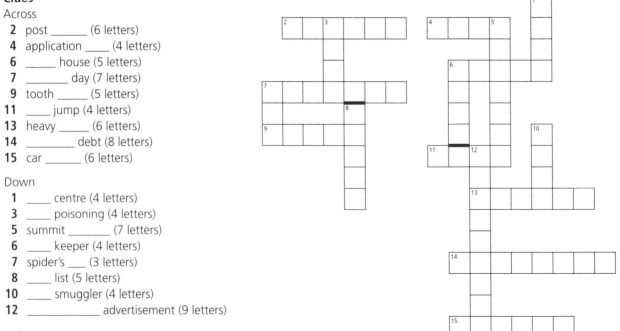